D1545936

WEALTH AND BENEFICENCE
IN THE PASTORAL EPISTLES

SOCIETY OF BIBLICAL LITERATURE

DISSERTATION SERIES
David L. Petersen, Old Testament Editor
Charles Talbert, New Testament Editor

Number 122

WEALTH AND BENEFICENCE
IN THE PASTORAL EPISTLES

by
Reggie M. Kidd

Reggie M. Kidd

WEALTH AND BENEFICENCE IN THE PASTORAL EPISTLES
A "Bourgeois" Form of Early Christianity?

Scholars Press
Atlanta, Georgia

WEALTH AND BENEFICENCE
IN THE PASTORAL EPISTLES

Reggie M. Kidd

Ph.D., 1989
Duke University

BS
2735.6
.S55
K53
1990

Advisor:
Franklin W. Young

© 1990
The Society of Biblical Literature

Library of Congress Cataloging in Publication Data

Kidd, Reggie M.
    Wealth and beneficence in the Pastoral Epistles: a "bourgeois"
form of early Christianity? / Reggie M. Kidd.

        p. cm. -- (Dissertation series / Society of Biblical Literature ;
    no. 122)
    Thesis (Ph.D.) --Duke University, 1989.
    Includes bibliographical references.
    ISBN 1-55540-445-6 (alk. paper). -- ISBN 1-55540-446-4
    1. Bible. N.T. Pastoral Epistles--Criticism, interpretation,
etc. 2. Sociology, Biblical. 3. Charity--Biblical teaching. 4.
Wealth--Biblical teaching. 5. Church history--Primitive and early
church, ca. 30-600. I. Title. II. Series: Dissertation series (Society of
Biblical Literature) ; no. 122.
BS2735.6.S55K53   1990
227' . 83067--dc20   90-44981
                                                                   CIP

Printed in the United States of America
on acid-free paper

ACKNOWLEDGEMENTS

Franklin W. Young has an infectious love for the later New Testament epistles, for their cousins the early Apostolic Fathers, and for the Greek in which these writers thought and made their thoughts known. I have been grateful for his willingness to work with me throughout my program at Duke, but especially for the generous way he has shared with me part of what should have been—and hopefully now will become—a quieter retirement.

Before enduring a debilitating bicycle accident, John H. Schütz introduced me to the social history of early Christianity. I doubt anyone ever had an abler, wittier, and more gracious tour guide through the worlds of the likes of Dio Chrysostom, on the one hand, and M.I. Rostovtzeff, on the other. At so many turns in this dissertation I found myself asking: "Which way would Schütz go from here?" I have sorely missed his input, and know the project has suffered without it (just before his accident he was able to offer important feedback on the draft of the first chapter). Though I know he would challenge some of my conclusions, I hope my questions and tack honor him. The many of us who love him and have learned from his love of learning wish him well in his continuing recovery.

My parents, Rex and Linnie Kidd, are both dedicated (now retired) educators. I am grateful for the desire to know and understand which they nurtured in me (even though it has kept me in school for much too long). As the classical texts recognize, parental beneficence is unique, inexhaustible, and forever asymmetrical. Even so, "Thanks, Mom and Dad."

Bob and Roberta Slater are friends who exemplify the Pastorals' ideal of Christian beneficence—they have been generous in their material, personal, and spiritual support.

The Chapel Hill Bible Church, a special community of faith, has been patient with a distracted pastor. Emily Williams, a treasured co-laborer in the worship ministry of the church, has been an invaluable help in this dissertation—from her thoughtful interaction over the material, to her copying articles and out-of-print books, to her proofreading the manuscript and inserting Greek accent marks, to her making the manuscript camera-ready for publication. Also deserving of specific thanks are Clint Shaffer for his help with the translation of several German passages and Margie Burd for giving the camera-ready version a good going over with her typesetter's eye. I alone am responsible for whatever mistakes are left, as well as for places I may have failed to follow good advice.

But no one deserves thanks more than Shari, my wife and my teacher in what it means to live a life of self-abandonment in the service of others. It is her life that has for me utterly put the lie to the notion that attention to life's "little" duties and to "average morality" cannot be an expression of heroic faith and radical hope. How I thank her for her *imitatio Christi*—for the countless sacrifices that have simultaneously made our heavenly Benefactor's love visible and my work possible.

TABLE OF CONTENTS

CHAPTER I: The Pastoral Epistles and "Bourgeois"
   Christianity 1
 A. Introduction: Celsus versus Origen 1
 B. Historical-Critical Issues 4
  1. External Attestation 4
  2. Historical Situation 5
  3. Language and Style 6
  4. Theology, Ethics, and Ecclesiology 7
 C. The "Bourgeois" Pastorals: Two Views 9
  1. Martin Dibelius 9
   a. Socially Ascendant 12
   b. Culturally Accommodative 16
   c. Unheroically Conservative 20
  2. Ceslas Spicq 25
 D. Points of Comparison and Issues to Pursue 29
  1. A Christian Bourgeoisie? 30
  2. Cultural Accommodation? 32
  3. An Unheroic Ethic? 33

CHAPTER II: The Social Provenance of the Pastoral Epistles:
   A Christian Middle Class? 35
 A. Aristotle and the Perils of Common Sense 35
 B. *Ordo*, Class, and Status 38
  1. *Ordo* 38
  2. Class 40
   a. Gradational Approaches to Class 41
   b. Relational Approaches to Class 46
  3. Status 50
  4. Summary 55
 C. E.A. Judge and Early Christianity's Social World 56
  1. Institutional Differentiation and Client
   Relationships 57
  2. The Social Provenance of Early Christianity 61

    3. Reaction to and Use of Judge 66
        a. Use of Acts.. 66
        b. Corinth as Paradigm... 67
        c. A New Consensus?.. 69
        d. The Church and Analogous Institutions 73
        e. Conclusions 74
    D. Pastoral Christianity: The Presence of the Rich and
    the Shape of the Community 75
        1. L. William Countryman...................................... 75
            a. The Danger of the Rich to the Church.............. 75
            b. The Church as Association (κοινωνία) 76
            c. Buttressing the Leadership, Co-opting
                the Rich 77
        2. David C. Verner 78
            a. The Church as Household (οἰκονομία)............. 78
                1) Development of the *Haustafeln*................. 78
                2) Verner's Reconstruction for the
                    Pastorals... 80
                3) The Role of the Household
                    Management Motifs, and the
                    Primacy of γαμική..................................... 81
            b. Other Indices of Stratification............................ 82
                1) Household Heads as Officers................... 83
                2) Church Office as Parallel with Civic
                    Office 84
                3) Wealthy Women 85
                4) Attitude Toward Slave Owners and
                    the Rich 86
                5) Function of the Letters:
                    To Conserve an Aristocratic Order
                    in the Name of Aristocratic Values........ 87
        3. Evaluation of the Data................................... 87
            a. Linguistic Milieu: The Eulogistic
                Tradition 87
            b. Use of the Household Topos 91
                1) The *Haustafeln* and the Rich..................... 93
                2) The Unity of 1 Timothy 6:3-21:
                    On Godliness and Gain 93
            c. The Economic Dimension of the Gender
                Conflicts 100
            d. Honoring Elders................................... 106
            e. Conclusions 108

CHAPTER III: Beneficence in the Pastoral Epistles:
A Culturally Accommodative Ethic?...................... 111
A. Beneficence and *Bürgerlich* Life.............................. 111
   1. Aristotle on Wealth, Beneficence, and Honor 112
   2. Menander on Securing the Future through
     Friendship 115
   3. Dio Chrysostom on the Moral Worth of the
     Wealthy 118
   4. The Inscriptions and the Quest for Lasting
     Glory 120
B. *Bürgerlich* and Anti-*bürgerlich* Elements in the
  Pastorals' Instructions to the Rich 124
   1. *Bürgerlich* Elements... 126
     a. The Precariousness of Wealth............................ 126
     b. Wealth in Others... 126
     c. Liberality and Generosity 127
     d. The Good and the Noble................................... 129
   2. Anti-*bürgerlich* Elements 130
     a. Against Haughtiness... 130
     b. Epiphany and Resurrection 131
     c. Not Earthly Friends, but Heavenly
       Rewards 134
     d. The Apostle as Model of Christian
       Beneficence 136
     e. Honor and Status in the Church......................... 137
   3. A Special Case: Christian Benefactors and
     their Slaves... 140
     a. ἡ εὐεργεσία: Beneficence Up? or Down? 142
     b. ἀντιλαμβάνεσθαι: Giving? or Getting?............. 144
       1) Receive a return on a benefit..................... 145
       2) Receive a benefit..................................... 148
       3) Give a return on a benefit 149
       4) Give a benefit... 150
     c. Contextual Considerations................................. 155
C. Summary 157

CHAPTER IV: Ethics and Eschatology in the Pastoral Epistles:
              An Unheroically Conservative Ethic? 159
   A. Framing the Question... 159
   B. Social Ethics and Eschatology in the Acknowledged
       Pauline Letters 160
       1. Paradigms in Paul's Social Ethics................................. 160
           a. Jew and Gentile.. 162
           b. Slave and Free.. 164
           c. Male and Female... 164
           d. Rich and Poor.. 166
       2. The Eschatological Dimension 169
       3. "Love-Patriarchalism" in Paul and the
           Pastorals 177
   C. The Eschatological Base for the Pastorals' Social
       Ethical Posture 181
       1. The Critical Consensus 181
       2. Points of Demurral 185
           a. Spirit and Office.. 185
           b. Provision for the Future 188
           c. The Presence of Salvation 189
           d. Apocalyptic Hope 190
           e. Eschatology and Ethics 191

CONCLUSIONS: Celsus Versus Origen, Revisited 195
   A. Social Provenance (Chapter II).. 195
   B. Cultural Accommodation (Chapter III)................................... 197
   C. Unheroic Conservatism (Chapter IV)..................................... 200

BIBLIOGRAPHY 205

CHAPTER I

The Pastoral Epistles and "Bourgeois" Christianity

A. INTRODUCTION: CELSUS VERSUS ORIGEN

Around A.D. 180, about the time of the persecution under Marcus Aurelius, a philosopher of middle Platonist persuasion named Celsus mounted a philosophical attack against the Christian sect. Though his argument is chiefly aimed at Christianity's ideas, or lack thereof, Celsus is also troubled by the scruffy circles within which the Christian faith travels. He characterizes Christians as "wool-workers, cobblers, laundry-workers, and the most illiterate and bucolic yokels (οἱ ἀπαιδευτότατοί τε καὶ ἀγροικότατοι), who would not dare to say anything at all in front of their elders and more intelligent masters."[1] They enjoin, he charges:

> "'Let no one educated, no one wise, no one sensible draw near. For these abilities are thought by us (Christians) to be evils. But as for anyone ignorant, anyone stupid, anyone uneducated, anyone who is a child, let him come boldly.' By the fact that they themselves admit that these people are worthy of their God, they show that they want and are able to convince only the foolish, dishonourable and stupid, and only slaves, women, and little children" (Quoted in Origen, *Contra Celsum* 3.44).

Celsus' influence can be inferred from the fact that some seventy years later (ca. A.D. 250), a Christian intellectual found it necessary to undertake an extensive point by point rebuttal of his arguments. Anxious to allay concerns among the literate about the lowly origins of Christians, Origen, himself a product of the rarefied Christian

---

[1]Quoted in Origen's *Contra Celsum* 3.55. Unless otherwise noted, the English translation is Henry Chadwick's—*Origen: Contra Celsum*, trans. with introduction and notes by Henry Chadwick (Cambridge, at the University Press, 1953; reprinted with corrections, 1965); for the Greek text: *Origene: Contre Celse*, 5 vols., trans. with introduction and notes by Marcel Borret, S.J., Sources Chretiennes, no. 132 (Paris: Les Editions du Cerf, 1967).

school at Alexandria, suggests that a passage in Paul's first letter to
the Corinthian church may be responsible in part for the impression
left with Celsus:

> "But you see your calling, brethren, how that not many wise men after
> the flesh, not many mighty, not many noble are called; but God chose
> the foolish things of the world, that he might put to shame those who
> are wise; and God chose the base things, and the things that are
> despised, and the things that are not, that he might bring to nought the
> things that are, that no flesh should glory in his presence" (1
> Corinthians 1:26-29, quoted at Origen, *Contra Celsum* 3.48).

Origen is quick to note that Paul says *not many* wise after the flesh,
not *none* wise after the flesh. And it is this *not-many-rather-than-none*
that is generally thought to be notable about Origen's response.

No less interesting, however, is what follows this caveat: an
appeal to the first letter to Timothy for evidence to the contrary:

> And clearly, when Paul describes the character of those who are called
> bishops and portrays what sort of a man a bishop ought to be, he
> appoints that he should be a teacher, saying that he must be "able also
> to refute the adversaries," that by his wisdom he may restrain those
> who speak vainly and deceive souls. Just as he prefers for the epis-
> copate a man once married rather than one twice married, and a man
> unblameable rather than blameable, and a sober man rather than one
> not of this character, and a prudent man rather than one imprudent,
> and an orderly man rather than one even slightly disorderly; so he
> wishes that the man who is to obtain preferment to the episcopate
> should be a teacher and capable of "refuting the adversaries" (Titus
> 1:9-11; cf. 1 Timothy 3:2). How, then, is it reasonable for Celsus to
> criticize us as though we asserted, "Let no one educated, no one wise,
> no one sensible draw near"? On the contrary, let the educated, wise
> and sensible man come if he wishes, and none the less let anyone
> ignorant, stupid, uneducated, and childish, come as well. For the
> word promises to heal even such people if they come, and makes all
> men worthy of God.
>
> It is a lie that those who teach the divine word want to convince only
> the foolish, dishonourable, and stupid, and only slaves, women, and
> little children. *Not only does the gospel call these that it may make them
> better, but it also calls people much superior to them.* For Christ is the
> Saviour of all men and specially of believers (1 Timothy 4:10), whether
> intelligent or simple-minded... .[2]

---

[2]Origen *Contra Celsum* 3.48-49, emphasis mine.

The quote is revealing for what it says about the common ground shared by Origen and his opponent: the easy division of people into the superior and refined and the inferior and crude. Of course, it also holds within it one of the chief arguments upon which Christians argued the worth of their particular philosophy: Christians too aim at the ennobling of the race, unencumbered, however, by the sterile elitism of the classical tradition.

Origen's attempt to offset 1 Corinthians' admitted vulgarity with 1 Timothy's urbanity also sets in relief one of the lingering points of contention in modern scholarship in the Pauline corpus. His appeal to 1 Timothy reflects the unanimous opinion of students of the New Testament from at least Irenaeus' day (fl. ca. A.D. 170)[3] to Schleiermacher's in the early nineteenth century[4] that the Pastoral epistles (including 2 Timothy and Titus as well as 1 Timothy)[5] speak for Paul. But he could not have made his argument so easily today.

For in the modern era the authenticity of the Pastoral epistles has been formidably challenged. The grounds of this challenge are several, chiefly: 1) external attestation; 2) historical situation; 3) language and style; and 4) theology, ethics, and ecclesiology. While we intend to isolate a single issue under the last of these rubrics, a brief overview of the several rubrics follows.

---

[3]Used liberally by Irenaeus in his attack on Marcion and the gnostics near the end of the second century (*Against Heresies*).

[4]See W.G. Kümmel, *The New Testament: The History of the Investigation of Its Problems*, trans. S. McLean Gilmour and Howard C. Kee (New York: Abingdon Press, 1972), pp. 84-85. Schleiermacher expressed doubts about 1 Timothy (but not 2 Timothy or Titus) in 1807 on the basis of its language, historical situation, and lack of homogeneity. By 1812, J.G. Eichhorn had raised questions about all three letters, insisting that they be treated as a unit.

[5]The term dates to the eighteenth century (D.N. Berdot in 1703 of Titus, and P. Anton of all three letters in 1753/55) and has become standard terminology. See W.G. Kümmel, *Introduction to the New Testament*, trans. Howard Clark Kee (New York: Abingdon Press, 1975), p. 367, and Donald Guthrie, *New Testament Introduction*, 3rd ed. rev. in one volume (Downers Grove, IL: Inter-Varsity Press, 1973), p. 584.

B. HISTORICAL-CRITICAL ISSUES

1. *External Attestation*

Marcion (fl. ca. A.D. 140)—the first to attempt a definition of a New Testament "canon"—either rejected the Pastorals (says Tertullian, *Contra Marcion* 5.21) or was unaware of them. It is possible that they did not appear in the earliest papyrus collection of Paul's letters yet to have surfaced (Chester Beatty Papyrus 𝔓46, ca. A.D. 200). Though the first and last seven leaves of 𝔓46 are missing, it appears as though there were too few leaves to have included the Pastorals (and Philemon).[6] Some discount has to be given to the lack of testimony in 𝔓46, for a generation earlier (ca. A.D. 170) Irenaeus does not so much argue the case for the authenticity of the Pastorals as much as presuppose it in using the letters in refuting Marcion.[7] So strong are the linguistic ties with Polycarp's letter to the Philippians[8] that for some they are decisive in proving the existence of the Pastorals by this date;[9] to a minority, these ties are hints that Polycarp himself or someone close to him wrote the Pastorals to bring the weight of apostolic authority to bear against

---

[6]Joachim Jeremias argues, however, that the evidence from 𝔓46 is inconclusive: the reduced handwriting and greater number of lines per page in the second half of the codex could indicate the scribe realized he had miscalculated the number of leaves he needed; additional leaves could have been added; alternatively, this particular collection could have confined itself to the letters addressed to communities rather than individuals. See his "Die Briefe an Timotheus und Titus" in *Das Neue Testament Deutsch*, Teilband 9, 11. Auflage, ed. Gerhard Friedrich (Göttingen: Vandenhoeck & Ruprecht, 1975), pp. 4-5. Jerome D. Quinn argues that 𝔓46 was one of a number of collections in circulation in Egypt of Pauline letters to churches rather than individuals; see his "𝔓46 —The Pauline Canon?" *Catholic Biblical Quarterly* 36 (1974): 379-385.

[7]It should also be noted that there is doubt that 𝔓46 points to the circulation in its Egyptian environs of only a ten-letter Pauline corpus inasmuch as Clement of Alexandria during the same time period treats the Pastorals as Pauline.

[8]Especially clustered in chapters 4 and 5. It should also be noted there are linguistic parallels between the Pastorals and earlier Apostolic Fathers, notably 1 Clement and Ignatius—the data are scant and can be accounted for by dependence in either direction or simply by the sharing of a common milieu.

[9]E.g., J.N.D. Kelly *A Commentary on the Pastoral Epistles* (London: A. & C. Black, Ltd., 1963; reprint ed., Grand Rapids: Baker Book House Co., 1981), p. 3.

Marcionism.[10] The external testimony for the Pastorals is not as strong as that for the main letters; nonetheless, it is clear that prior to Irenaeus' use of the Pastorals no positive challenge against the letters is mounted, and from Irenaeus on (including their inclusion in the Muratorian Canon, generally dated toward the end of the second century) the early church owns them as Paul's.

2. Historical Situation

Most modern defenders of the authenticity of the Pastorals assume that Paul wrote them after he was released from the imprisonment recorded in Acts 28 and which is in view in Philippians, Colossians, Philemon, and Ephesians. According to this scenario, 1 Timothy and Titus were written during a subsequent but otherwise unrecorded ministry in the eastern Mediterranean; 2 Timothy would have been written during a second imprisonment in Rome perhaps as late as the late 60s.[11] This so-called second imprisonment theory was first enunciated by Eusebius ca. A.D. 325 (*Ecclesiastical History* 2.22.2) and was apparently based in part on an inference from 1 Clement (5:7) and in part on an inability to square the historical references internal to the Pastorals with the data of Acts or the homologoumena. Skeptics note the softness of support outside the Pastorals themselves for such a reconstruction, and variously treat the personal notes in the Pastorals as fragments of genuine letters[12] or as attempts at verisimilitude.[13] J.A.T. Robinson argues both for

---

[10]Hans von Campenhausen, "Polykarp von Smyrna und die Pastoralbriefe," in *Aus der Frühzeit des Christentums* (Tübingen: J.C.B. Mohr, 1963), pp. 197-252; Helmut Koester (*Introduction to the New Testament*, Vol. 2: *History and Literature of Early Christianity*, trans. by the author from *Einführung in das Neue Testament*, chaps. 7-12 [Philadelphia: Fortress Press, 1982], pp. 304-305) follows von Campenhausen in identifying Polycarp as the author without specifying Marcionism as the target.

[11]For a full defense of the traditional position, see Ceslas Spicq, *Les Epitres Pastorales*, 2 vols., 4th revised ed. (Paris: J. Gabalda, 1969), pp. 121-146.

[12]E.g., P.N. Harrison, *The Problem of the Pastoral Epistles* (New York: Oxford University Press, 1921).

[13]E.g., Burton Scott Easton, *The Pastoral Epistles* (New York: Charles Scribner's Sons, 1947), p. 19, argues that it would have been a literary device recognized by the readers; Kurt Aland, "The Problem of Anonymity and Pseudonymity in Christian Literature of the First Two Centuries," *Journal of Theological Studies,* N.S. 12 (1961): 39-49, suggests that a pseudonym was appended to a letter out of a conviction that the work's primary author was the Spirit; and Lewis R. Donelson, *Pseudepigraphy and Ethical Argument in the Pastoral Epistles* (Tübingen: J.C.B. Mohr, 1986), places the Pastorals (and a number of other early Christian

Pauline authorship and for the proposition that the letters can be fit into the framework of the Acts chronology—i.e., prior to the Roman imprisonment of Acts 28. He posits an origin for 2 Timothy during Paul's Caesarean imprisonment (Acts 23:31-26:32), but admits the difficulty of taking 2 Timothy 1:17 as referring to a search for Paul on Onesiphorus' part that began in Rome and ended in Caesarea.[14]

3. *Language and Style*

Decisive for many who dispute Pauline provenance are the Pastorals' language and style. P.N. Harrison's study of the vocabulary of the Pastorals relative to the Pauline homologoumena, on the one hand, and second century writers, on the other, marks a watershed in critical opinion.[15] As much as his methods and conclusions have been challenged[16] and revised,[17] the overall impression that dominates the field is that something is quite different in the Pastorals' mode of expression. Conservative scholars note the differences but offer a host of mitigating considerations—e.g., the greater likelihood that a stylistically unself-conscious Paul would have produced the differences than his supposed imitator, the effects of his advanced age and/or exposure to the language and thought of the western Mediterranean, the possibility of the use of a

---

letters) within the stream of Greek and Roman pseudepigraphical letters which employ deliberate deception in the cause of philosophical argumentation; see also Donald M. Penny, *The Pseudo-Pauline Letters of the First Two Centuries* (Ann Arbor, MI: University Microfilms International, 1980). One could well imagine that a Guthrie, who defends the authenticity of each of the New Testament epistles, would respond that Donelson does not so much demonstrate as assume the widespread use of epistolary pseudepigraphy by early Christians—see especially the appendix, "Epistolary Pseudepigraphy," in his *Introduction*, pp. 671-684.

[14]John A.T. Robinson, *Redating the New Testament* (Philadelphia: The Westminster Press, 1976), pp. 67-85.

[15]P.N. Harrison, *Problem*.

[16]W. Michaelis, *Pastoralbriefe und Gefangenschaftsbriefe* (Gütersloh: Bertelsmann, 1930), pp. 130-132; M. Hitchcock, "Tests for the Pastorals" *JTS* 1929, pp. 276ff; J.N.D. Kelly, *Pastoral Epistles*, pp. 22-27; Guthrie, *The Pastoral Epistles* (London: The Tyndale Press, 1957; reprint ed., Grand Rapids: Eerdmans Printing Co., 1980), pp. 212-228, and *The Pastoral Epistles and the Mind of Paul* (London: The Tyndale Press, 1956).

[17]P.N. Harrison, *Paulines and Pastorals* (London: Villiers Publications Ltd., 1964).

different amanuensis.[18] A number of scholars—some of conservative and some of non-conservative bent—propose the author of Luke-Acts as the source of the differences.[19]

4. Theology, Ethics, and Ecclesiology

The discussion over theology, ethics and ecclesiastical situation has ranged over a number of issues—whether gnosticism is in the background, why the mode of theological expression is more formulaic and less creative than Paul's, why the author uses denunciation rather than argumentation against his opponents, whether the ethics are more rule-oriented than Paul, whether the process of institutionalization is more advanced.[20] It is roughly under this rubric that our interest lies, for a number of scholars characterize the general approach to the faith, especially its style of theological, ethical, and ecclesiological thinking, as being decidedly "bourgeois," and to this extent non-Pauline.

---

[18]Spicq offers a particularly full list of possibilities: *Pastorales*, pp. 179-200. F.D. Gealy outlines and rebuts Spicq's arguments in his "1 and 2 Timothy, Titus," in *The Interpreter's Bible*, (Nashville: Abingdon, 1955), 11:360-364.

[19]Some allow the possibility of Luke's (the beloved physician of Colossians 4:14 and Paul's travelling companion) considerable contribution as amanuensis—e.g., C.F.D. Moule, "The Problem of the Pastoral Epistles: A Reappraisal," *Bulletin of the John Rylands Library* 47 (1965): 430-452, and *The Birth of the New Testament*, 3rd ed. (New York: Harper and Row, 1982), pp. 281-282; Guthrie, *Introduction*, pp. 621-622; Spicq, *Pastorales*, p. 199—cf., pp. 233-238; and George W. Knight III, *The Faithful Sayings in the Pastoral Letters* (N.V. Kampen, the Netherlands: J.H. Kok, 1968; reprint ed., Grand Rapids: Baker Book House Co., 1979), pp. 150-151. Some see Luke as a second generation Christian who writes a three volume work on the life of the early church with the emphasis falling decidedly on the contribution of Paul—e.g., Jerome D. Quinn, "The Last Volume of Luke: The Relation of Luke-Acts to the Pastoral Epistles," in *Perspectives on Luke-Acts*, ed. C.H. Talbert (Danville, VA: Association of Baptist Professors of Religion, 1978), pp. 62-75; and Stephen G. Wilson, *Luke and the Pastoral Epistles* (London: SPCK, 1979). Norbert Brox argues against Luke's authorship of or influence on the Pastorals, contending that the similarities can be accounted for by the sharing of Pauline traditions in the post-Pauline era— see his "Lukas als Verfasser der Pastoralbriefe?" *JAC* 13 (1970): 62-77.

[20]The discussion is readily available in the introductions and commentaries— e.g., Kümmel, *Introduction*, pp. 378-384; Guthrie, *Introduction*, pp. 591-594, 599-606; Koester, *Introduction*, Vol. 2, pp. 302-305; Norbert Brox, *Die Pastoralbriefe*, Regensburger Neues Testament, 7. Band, Zweiter Teil. 4th ed. (Regensburg: Verlag Friedrich Pustet, 1969), pp. 31-55, and "Historische und theologische Probleme der Pastoralbriefe des Neuen Testaments," *Kairos* 11 (1969): 81-94; Spicq, *Pastorales*, pp. 65-119, 243-297.

It is, in fact, virtually a commonplace in modern New Testament scholarship to describe a critical divide between the acknowledged letters of Paul and the Pastoral epistles in terms of the latter's being "bourgeois," products of a "middle class," or transitional in a certain *Verbürgerlichung* of the faith. Helmut Koester, for instance, asserts that in dating the Pastorals one must presuppose "the strong growth of Christianity in the middle classes of the cities," a phenomenon of the second rather than the first century.[21] Likewise, A. Malherbe puts the Pastorals among those late writings of the New Testament "which have a recognized tendency to describe Christianity as 'middle class.'"[22] Howard C. Kee finds in these letters such a preoccupation with reputation, hierarchy, doctrine, and stability, he is led to conclude the community behind them "is the early-second-century equivalent of a middle-to-upper-middle-class organization."[23] Its language of preparation for persecution and for Jesus' "appearing" masks its greater concern for pious respectability, marking it a "bourgeois group."[24] R. Bultmann asserts that "the Christian faith is becoming a piety which, though it by no means surrenders its aloofness from the world, nevertheless is making a place for itself within the framework of bourgeois living."[25] Though he says that it is legitimate for the writer of the Pastorals to extend Paul's thinking to the power of God's grace to mold everyday bourgeois living, the product is nonetheless a "somewhat faded Paulinism" that has about it a "plodding one-sidedness."[26]

Thus, we could very well expect a modern Celsus to be disinclined to allow 1 Timothy to speak directly for Paul, due to the relatively soft external attestation of these letters, a historical situation that cannot easily be squared either with the acknowledged letters or the book of Acts, language and style that do not share the idiosyncrasies of the main letters of Paul, and a more formalized theology and routinized ethics and church life. We could expect our modern Celsus vigorously to challenge the propriety of appealing to a passage in the Pastorals to demonstrate for *Paul's* churches a more

---

[21]Koester, *Introduction*, 2:305 (not in German original).

[22]Abraham J. Malherbe, *Social Aspects of Early Christianity*, 2nd ed., enlarged (Philadelphia: Fortress Press, 1983), pp. 30-31.

[23]Howard Clark Kee, *Christian Origins in Sociological Perspective: Methods and Resources* (Philadelphia: The Westminster Press, 1980), p. 119.

[24]Kee, *Christian Origins*, p. 119.

[25]Rudolf Bultmann, *Theology of the New Testament*, 2 vols. trans. Kendrick Grobel (New York: Scribner's Sons, 1951, 1955), Vol. 2, p. 183.

[26]Bultmann, *Theology of the NT*, Vol. 2, p. 186.

refined pedigree and urbane lifestyle than is evident in the passage he knows from 1 Corinthians.

The question we should like to ask—bracketing other questions of continuity and discontinuity between the acknowledged Pauline letters[27] and the Pastorals—is whether the Pastorals represent so slight a move in a "bourgeois" direction that their hints at a more elevated social constituency and more sophisticated social world than is evident in 1 Corinthians 1:26-29 offer a mere corrective to the sort of impression a Celsus could have of Christianity's origins? Or is it the case that the Pastorals are so much more "bourgeois" than the acknowledged letters that these letters mark a watershed transformation in the faith and in its constituency in a generation subsequent to the apostle?

First it will be necessary to propose a working understanding of what "bourgeois" means in this context. To help define the issues we turn to the contrasting use of the concept in the work of two major commentators on the Pastorals: Martin Dibelius, in whose writings the epithet first appears, and Ceslas Spicq, who vigorously contests certain features of Dibelius' use of the term.

C. THE "BOURGEOIS" PASTORALS: TWO VIEWS

1. Martin Dibelius

As the following quotations illustrate, Martin Dibelius gets the credit for dubbing the Pastoral epistles "bourgeois." In summarizing his own introductory remarks on the Pastoral epistles, W.G. Kümmel says, "M. Dibelius has described as bourgeois this strongly Hellenistic-speaking Christianity which is establishing itself in the world...."[28] Of Luke-Acts, H. Conzelmann remarks, "The church has adjusted itself to an extended existence in the world. It is developing a 'Christian bourgeoisie' (M. Dibelius) which is related to the Pastoral letters. The world becomes a place where the church is at

---

[27]Because Colossians and Ephesians are contested on grounds so similar to those used to challenge the Pastorals, and since there is nothing in 2 Thessalonians vital to our analysis, we shall proceed with a homologoumena that includes: 1 Thessalonians, Galatians, 1 and 2 Corinthians, Romans, Philippians, and Philemon.

[28]Kümmel, *Introduction*, p. 384. Kümmel's original has *bürgerlich*.

home, a notion which Paul sharply rejected (Philippians 3:20)."[29] And from Wayne Meeks' comments on the Pastoral epistles: "We see a 'bourgeois Christianity' (Dibelius) making itself at home in the world, equating 'faith' with 'sound teaching,' which is expected to produce a rather conservative and commonplace morality as the mark of 'piety' or 'religiosity.'"[30]

Commentators who follow Dibelius in so designating Pastoral Christianity appear to mean that these members of a Christian bourgeoisie espouse a version of the faith which is establishing itself in the Hellenistic world, and which aims at a piety marked by a conservative and commonplace morality. To be sure, this summary of what is bourgeois about this brand of Christianity is more suggestive than substantive. Nonetheless, the ease with which commentators assume the self-evidence of its meaning is evidence of the epithet's remarkable hermeneutical power.

In his commentary on the Pastoral epistles,[31] Dibelius frequently characterizes the ethics of the epistles as being *bürgerlich*, in places naming this mode of existence *die christliche Bürgerlichkeit*.[32] So significant, in fact, is the concept that he attributes much of the

---

[29]Hans Conzelmann, "Luke's Place in the Development of Early Christianity," in *Studies in Luke-Acts*, eds. Leander E. Keck and J. Louis Martyn (Philadelphia: Fortress Press, 1980), pp. 302-303.

[30]Wayne A. Meeks, *The Writings of St. Paul*, A Norton Critical Edition (New York: W. W. Norton & Co., 1972), p. 134.

[31]Martin Dibelius, *Die Pastoralbriefe*, Handbuch zum Neuen Testament, no. 13, 2nd ed. (Tübingen: Verlag von J.C.B. Mohr [Paul Siebeck], 1931), and Martin Dibelius and Hans Conzelmann, *Die Pastoralbriefe*, Handbuch zum Neuen Testament, no. 13, 4th ed. (Tübingen: Verlag von J.C.B. Mohr [Paul Siebeck], 1966). Dibelius' last edition was the former—the 2nd, published in 1931—hereafter referred to as, Dibelius, *Die Pastoralbriefe* (1931). The edition commonly used is the latter—the 4th edition, revised in 1966 by Hans Conzelmann— referred to hereafter as, Dibelius/Conzelmann, *Die Pastoralbriefe* (1966). The latter is also the text translated in the Hermeneia series—Martin Dibelius and Hans Conzelmann, *The Pastoral Epistles*, trans. Philip Buttolph and Adela Yarbro, ed. Helmut Koester (Philadelphia: Fortress Press, 1972)—hereafter referred to as, Dibelius/Conzelmann, *The Pastoral Epistles*. Normally I shall refer to the 4th (1966) edition or to the Hermeneia translation; however, in a number of critical places on our topic, Conzelmann expands or contracts Dibelius' original. Therefore, where it is necessary to indicate something in Dibelius' final edition (the 2nd, 1931) but which Conzelmann elides (and which is thus missing also from the English edition), I shall do so. Similarly, where it is necessary I shall note Conzelmann's amplifications (these also appear in the English edition).

[32]Dibelius/Conzelmann, *Die Pastoralbriefe* (1966), see, e.g., the excursus *das Ideal christlicher Bürgerlichkeit*, pp. 32-33.

Pastorals' importance to "the fact that they are the only documents in the canon which enjoin a structuring of life under *einer solchen christlich-bürgerlichen Lebensgestaltung.*"[33] And yet as important as the term is to him and as provocative as it has been to others, Dibelius never exegetes his epithet. He, too, appears to assume its sense to be self-evident.

It is curious that Dibelius, whose form-critical analysis was expressive of an interest in the emergence of patterns of tradition from their social setting,[34] should have left unexplored such a sociologically pregnant expression. Especially helpful, however, in supplying a background for inferring the nuance he would give to the term is his 1928 Heidelberg lecture *Urchristentum und Kultur,*[35] addressing as it does the broader social and intellectual setting within which the church emerged in the first three centuries. Also helpful is his 1923 commentary on the Shepherd of Hermas.[36] Like the Pastorals, Hermas is supposed to be a document of second century Christianity which shows a particular concern for people of higher social standing within the church; Dibelius' commentary on Hermas is more attentive to indicators of social rank than is the commentary on the Pastorals, and thus offers suggestive points of comparison. When his commentary on the Pastorals is augmented by *Urchristentum und Kultur* and by the commentary on the Shepherd of Hermas, three layers of meaning emerge for Dibelius' understanding of *bürgerlich*: a) socially ascendant, b) culturally accommodative, and c) unheroically conservative.

---

[33]Dibelius/Conzelmann, *Die Pastoralbriefe* (1966), p. 33. The Hermeneia translation opts for "the ideal of good Christian citizenship," *The Pastoral Epistles,* p. 40. But the phrase could be rendered in various ways—e.g., "such a Christian, bourgeois mode of living," or "the mode of living of a Christian middle class." Buttolph and Yarbro consistently adopt the language of "citizenship" or of "everyday existence" for their translation of *bürgerlich* and related terms.

[34]See the comments by John Schütz on form criticism's interest in the social setting of tradition in the introduction to Gerd Theissen, *The Social Setting of Pauline Christianity: Essays on Corinth,* trans. John H. Schütz (Philadelphia: Fortress Press, 1982), pp. 7-10.

[35]Martin Dibelius, *Urchristentum und Kultur* (Heidelberg: Carl Winters Universitätsbuchhandlung, 1928).

[36]Martin Dibelius, *Der Hirt des Hermas,* vol. 4 of *Die apostolischen Väter,* Handbuch zum Neuen Testament, Ergänzungs-Band (Tübingen: Verlag von J.C.B. Mohr [Paul Siebeck], 1923).

a. Socially Ascendant

In Dibelius' view, the Christianity of Jesus and Paul begins with a distance from the world (*Weltferne*) that is sociologically grounded.

> The leading ranks (*die führenden Schichten*) of the old world are not among the hearers of the gospel. Thus no place is found in the sphere of the gospel's influence for the claim to power of the noble of birth nor for the cultural obligations felt by the noble of spirit nor for the worldly needs of those who are noble by virtue of wealth (*der Machtanspruch des Geburtsadels noch die Kulturverpflichtung des Geistesadels noch das Weltbedürfnis des Besitzadels*). This distance from all that is excellent to man as man[37] not only makes clear the distance from the noble humanity of antiquity, it also shows a characteristic feature of the history of Christianity itself: we know no other historical movement of such scale which began so exclusively as a movement of the lower ranks (*die unteren Schichten*) and became so extensively the regimen of all ranks.[38]

Indeed, a function of its lowly social origins is earliest Christianity's ability to forego judgments about matters of everyday life (*die Alltagsfragen*). As the movement grows numerically and rises socially, however, it cannot ignore certain issues:

> The greater the number of adherents becomes, the more necessary it is to establish family- and household-duties. The more the proclamation finds adherents among the well-to-do, the more pressing become questions about the use of possessions. The more Christianity penetrates the strata of officeholders and the military, the more burning becomes the problem of "Christianity and the State." In this way early Christians saw themselves being assigned the task of establishing an ethic of the family, of possessions, and of the state.[39]

If the author of the Pastorals can borrow from the honorific inscriptions the language of "piety" (εὐσέβεια) and "dignity"

---

[37]On a number of occasions when translating scholars of a previous generation—notably Dibelius and Spicq—I did not consider it apt to modernize their generic use of masculine nouns and pronouns.

[38]*Urchristentum*, pp. 5-6; and note fn. 1, p. 33, to the effect that as an apocalyptic movement Christianity's origins among the lower classes is not remarkable, as it follows "a certain law of social life." What is special about the development of Christianity is not its origins in circles alienated from the world, rather the unprecedented expansion of its social reach.

[39]*Urchristentum*, p. 18.

(σεμνότης) to encourage prayer for the civil authorities,[40] if he finds himself turning to the Greek ethicists' doctrine of "prudence" (σώφ-ρων) as a principle that ought to be applied to issues ranging from wealth to food to sex,[41] and if he betrays an advanced family ethic severed from that eschatological viewpoint which had conditioned family issues in the acknowledged Pauline letters,[42] it can only mean that the gospel's influence is being felt outside the lowest ranks of society. These ethical views—highlighted by Dibelius in his commentary's excursus, *das Ideal christlicher Bürgerlichkeit*—betray nothing less that a concern for "all that is excellent to man as man," for claims to power, cultural obligations, and for worldly needs—a concern missing when the leading ranks are unrepresented in the church. If these signs of *christliche Bürgerlichkeit* set the Pastorals apart from other canonical documents, they do so in part by pointing to a more elevated social background for these churches.

Indicative, maintains Dibelius, is the early church's stance towards wealth, an attitude which is at first dismissive and then hesitantly accepting:

---

[40]Dibelius/Conzelmann, *The Pastoral Epistles*, p. 39, *Die Pastoralbriefe* (1966), p. 31. He claims that the terms εὐσέβεια and σεμνότης are obviously intended to illustrate *das Ideal bürgerlich-ehrbaren Lebens*. And he observes that the use of εὐσέβεια is exclusive to the most Hellenistic of the New Testament writings (Acts, the Pastorals, and 2 Peter) and is nearly exclusive to the single most Hellenistic OT document, 4 Maccabees (owning 47 of the 59 occurrences of the word in the Septuagint). Further, he wants to associate the use of εὐσέβεια in the Pastorals with its use alongside terms like "virtue" (ἀρετή), "righteousness" (δικαιοσύνη), and "goodness" (καλοκάγαθία) as they occur in the honorary inscriptions.

[41]Dibelius/Conzelmann, *The Pastoral Epistles*, p. 40, *Die Pastoralbriefe* (1966), pp. 32-33. As exemplary of this moderation Dibelius offers the Pastorals' attitude towards goods and the necessities of life: asceticism is rejected with respect to food, drink, sexuality, and possessions (1 Timothy 4:3ff; 5:23; 5:14; 3:2; Titus 1:6; 1 Timothy 6:17-19; 5:16), yet so are drunkenness (1 Timothy 3:3,8; Titus 1:7; 2:3), sexual immorality (2 Timothy 2:22), and the love of money (1 Timothy 6:6-10).

[42]Dibelius/Conzelmann, *The Pastoral Epistles*, p. 40, *Die Pastoralbriefe* (1966), p. 33. Indicative of a strong family ethic are: 1) the development of a kind of religious family tradition (2 Timothy 1:3,5; 3:14f; 1:16); 2) the Christianizing of the duty to care for aged members of the family (1 Timothy 5:4,8,16); 3) the emphasis on bringing up children so that they become faithful, obedient Christians (1 Timothy 3:4,12; 5:10; Titus 1:6); and 4) the pointed reduction of a woman's Christian obedience to her domestic role; even what teaching function she is allowed is aimed at preparing other women to assume their place within a household (1 Timothy 2:15; 5:14; 2:9ff; Titus 2:4f).

In consequence of a gaze directed toward the end of the world, the question of making use of possessions for the benefit of the general public was shifted into the background as immaterial. Then, too, the problem did not even arise for the many Christians who were themselves without possessions. In addition, bad experiences of Jesus and the congregations with reluctance to sacrifice on the part of the wealthy were reflected in radical words filled with animosity toward riches, especially in the Gospel of Luke and the Epistle of James, and such words markedly influenced Christian sensibility. And this sensibility was ultimately reinforced by the poverty pathos of the Jewish scriptures, from the Psalms all the way to the admonitions of the Book of Enoch, in which poverty is not a social, but rather a socio-religious concept, and according to whose view poverty and piety coincide, as do godlessness and wealth. It is not a proletarian class consciousness which moves these people to speak so; they have not been disenfranchised through the progress of the economy, and their pride does not come from this world; rather, their bearing is better designated a pietistic pride in poverty (*Armenstolz*), for which indigence is a sign of acceptance with God.

All this makes it clear that well into the second century Christianity remained a religion of the poor. And even when the church came to include quite a number of wealthy people, it remained an embarrassment to speak of them. In Rome around 130 Hermas uses the image of the unfruitful elm which serves as a support for the fruitful vine: so should the rich in the community provide support for the poor so the latter can pray for them (Sim 2). One senses clearly that there is still a preference granted to the poor; only the further social ascent of Christianity put an end to this.[43]

Revealing is Dibelius' reference at this point in his lecture to the Shepherd of Hermas. For as attenuated as it is, the so-called early pride in poverty is still alive in Hermas. In an excursus in his commentary on James, Dibelius contrasts James, on the one hand, who writes to make sure the rich do not become a part of the Christian community, with Hermas, on the other, who must accommodate a significant number of them.[44] Indeed, in his commentary on Hermas, Dibelius acknowledges that the presence of business people in Hermas' congregation, the expressing of the ideal of a quiet *bürgerlich* life (i.e., μηδενὶ ἀντιτάσσεσθαι, ἡσύχιον εἶναι), and the taking up of social admonitions to the propertied classes—including

[43]*Urchristentum*, pp. 20-21.

[44]Martin Dibelius, *A Commentary on the Epistle of James*, rev. Heinrich Greeven, trans. Michael A. Williams, ed. Helmut Koester (Philadelphia: Fortress Press, 1975), p. 45.

the assumption that the dispensing of charity presupposes profit from labor—shows that Christianity is no longer purely a religion of the poor.[45] Nevertheless, he goes to some lengths to stress that the level of wealth in Hermas is modest. He points to the unliterary nature of the tract, to indications that the business people are (like Hermas himself) for the most part artisans and shopkeepers, and to the way the warning against preoccupation with business is clarified with the concession that the pursuit of but *one* business enterprise is not incompatible with Christianity: "A piece of the world is permitted, but not too close an entanglement in its affairs; the Christian is allowed to be a merchant, but as much as is possible a small merchant!"[46] In his judgment, Hermas "is most significant as a monument of the everyday Christianity of the poorer classes (*die kleinen Leute*) and a broad stratum whose inner needs dare not be forgotten by the experiences of the prophets and the thought-concepts of the teacher."[47]

Whether Dibelius is correct about the social description of Christians in Hermas' church,[48] his comments are suggestive as to his assumptions about the social level represented in the Pastorals. If, for instance, the lack of literary acumen in Hermas may be taken by Dibelius as an index of a lower class readership, one is probably justified in assuming the converse for the readership of epistles written, as Dibelius himself puts it, "mainly in the higher Koine."[49] While the *Armenstolz* of James and Judaism makes at least some showing in Hermas, its absence in the Pastorals is noticed even by Dibelius.[50] And in light of his comments about James and Hermas, what is remarkable about Dibelius' treatment of the passage on the rich in 1 Timothy 6 (verses 17-19) is how unproblematic their presence is—the rich simply assume their place alongside members of other social stations in the church. One does not know quite what to do with Dibelius' comment that it is only with a social ascent beyond that of Hermas that the church's preference for the poor

---

[45]Dibelius, *Hirt*, at Mandate 8. 10, p. 528.

[46]Dibelius, *Hirt*, at Similitude 4. 5-7, pp. 559-560.

[47]Dibelius, *Hirt*, from the Introduction, p. 425.

[48]Carolyn Osiek, *Rich and Poor in the "Shepherd of Hermas": An Exegetical-Social Investigation*, The Catholic Biblical Quarterly Monograph Series, No. 15 (Washington, D.C.: The Catholic Biblical Association of America, 1983).

[49]Dibelius/Conzelmann, *The Pastoral Epistles*, p. 3, *Die Pastoralbriefe* (1966), p. 2.

[50]Dibelius/Conzelmann, *The Pastoral Epistles*, p. 91, *Die Pastoralbriefe* (1966), p. 69, noting the lack of James' *Pauperismus*.

ends, as I find no comment as to his thoughts on which of the two, Hermas or the Pastorals, was written first. But one can observe that with the Pastorals no such preference is in existence, and this in correspondence that notes without embarrassment rich Christians among its readership.

Because Dibelius himself never addresses the subject directly, conclusions about his ideas on the social level of Christians in the Pastorals must remain tentative. Curiously, for one who worried a great deal about the social setting of earliest Christianity, he leaves it for others to infer that part of what he means by calling these epistles *bürgerlich* is that these Christians are socially ascendant, or more specifically, as Conzelmann puts it, members of a Christian bourgeoisie.

b. Culturally Accommodative

Though the lines of connection between social level and cultural engagement are not drawn by Dibelius, it is not surprising to find him placing the socially ascendant Christians of the Pastoral epistles among those Christians who accommodate themselves to the cultural milieu of the early Roman Empire. Dibelius notes that during the emergence of early Christianity, the worth and the nobility of the old Hellenistic bourgeoisie (*Bürgertum*) of the various city-states was in decline.[51] Under the new order of the Roman Imperium

> the internationalized man stood as an individual before the cosmos; but the new aristocracy of this world-bourgeoisie (*Weltbürgertum*) bestowed a new feeling of freedom and bid the slave to philosophize himself beyond his master and the poor to raise himself above the rich who is fettered by his pleasure. This new feeling for life is clear to us above all in Stoic philosophy, the most widespread teaching about life of the time.[52]

The Pastorals take their place alongside other Christian writings of the sub-apostolic age which adopt the language and concepts of those who, like the Stoics, were concerned to reconstruct the spiritual culture of a world in transition from the multiplicity of the Hellenistic order to the new reality of intellectual life under Roman political hegemony.

Particularly serious, in Dibelius' estimation, is the development that takes place among those Christians who, like the author of the

---

[51]Dibelius, *Urchristentum*, p. 10.
[52]Dibelius, *Urchristentum*, p. 10.

Pastorals, adopt the rational cultural education (*Bildung*) of their day, not in order to contrast it with the irrational faith of the gospel, but rather in order to show to this faith its place within the educational process (again, *Bildung*):

> The first preachers of the Christian message did not have this need. Paul saw the contrast with the world, the chasm between the wisdom of the Greeks and the foolishness of the cross; wisdom was for him a symbol of human achievement, which as with all human nobility becomes nothing before God's judgment; the cross is a sign of God's grace, which newly bestows a dignity grounded in eternity upon those who are degraded: "we, who have nothing and yet have all things." To be sure, a Christian of the second century, who wrote the so-called Pastoral epistles under the name of Paul, made the apostle into a preacher of doctrine that is "sound" or correct by virtue of being reasonable, and knows how to describe it in the language of Hellenistic *Bildung*; he has painted over the portrait of the apostle in the interest of his *Bildungschristentum*.[53]

This passage in *Urchristentum* sheds significant light on what Dibelius means when he speaks of an ethic of *christliche Bürgerlichkeit* in his commentary on the Pastorals. The notion of a pattern of Christianity dedicated to *Bildungschristentum* explains his referencing his excursus on *die christliche Bürgerlichkeit* when he comes to the author's expressing of the content of the Christian life as "educating us to lead a prudent, upright, and pious life in this age" (παιδεύειν ἵνα...σωφρόνως καὶ δικαίως καὶ εὐσεβῶς ζήσωμεν ἐν τῷ νῦν αἰῶνι, Titus 2:11-12).[54] It will be recalled that it is at this point that Dibelius also expresses his agreement with Eduard Meyer's assertion that the pattern of life advocated in the Pastoral epistles is "almost identical with 'the ideal of Greek ethics.'"[55] Indeed, he notes, παιδεύειν is being used in the normal Hellenistic sense, "to educate," as opposed to the consistent Pauline and general Septuagintal sense, "to discipline through punishment."[56] No less significant is the triad: σώφρων, δίκαιος, and εὐσεβής, since these comprise three of the four standard Greek virtues; only

[53]Dibelius, *Urchristentum*, p. 16.
[54]Dibelius/Conzelmann, *The Pastoral Epistles*, p. 142, and *Die Pastoralbriefe* (1966), p. 107.
[55]Dibelius/Conzelmann, *The Pastoral Epistles*, p. 142, and *Die Pastoralbriefe* (1966), p. 107.
[56]Dibelius/Conzelmann, *The Pastoral Epistles*, pp. 142-143, and *Die Pastoralbriefe* (1966), p. 107, citing 1 Corinthians 11:32 and 2 Corinthians 6:9; also 1 Clement 56.2, with copious quotations of Old Testament passages.

"courageous" (ἀνδρεῖος) is missing.[57] The abovementioned passage from the *Urchristentum* lecture speaks directly to what is *bürgerlich* about the Pastorals' appeal to the "reasonableness" of the gospel rather than its pneumatic power.[58] A function also of this adoption of the language of Hellenistic *Bildung* is the rationalistic approach to the conscience in the Pastorals. Paul, on the one hand, viewing the conscience as that faculty which chooses freely between relative values, contrasts a "strong" with a "weak" conscience; the Pastorals, on the other, seeing the conscience as something which implies a necessarily binding moral alternative, contrast a "good" with an "evil" conscience. This, according to Dibelius, belongs among the qualities which characterize *die christliche Bürgerlichkeit*,[59] because it is more nearly the way conscience is thought of in the Hellenistic world and spoken of in the vernacular.[60]

This *christliche Bürgerlichkeit*, asserts Dibelius, is part and parcel of a program of building a life in this world, of actually becoming a part of the world. And though he acknowledges that the attempt is made to found this program on Christian principles, he insists that the entire enterprise be contrasted with that of the actual Paul who had lived in the tension between this world and God's world, and who had "joyfully affirmed (in 2 Cor 6:4-10) the suffering of this existence as part of citizenship (*Bürgschaft*) in the other kingdom."[61]

---

[57]S.C. Mott, "The Greek Benefactor and Deliverance from Moral Distress," Ph.D. dissertation, Harvard University, 1971, discusses the use of the Hellenistic ethical triad in the Pastorals, arguing for dependence on Philo.

[58]Dibelius/Conzelmann, *The Pastoral Epistles*, p. 39, and *Die Pastoralbriefe* (1966), p. 24. Especially illuminating is the Excursus on 1 Timothy 1:10: "The Term 'To Be Sound' (ΥΓΙΑΙΝΕΙΝ) and 'Sound' (ΥΓΙΗΣ)," *The Pastoral Epistles*, pp. 24-25; *Die Pastoralbriefe* (1966), pp. 20-21. It is in this discussion that Dibelius offers a contrast with the acknowledged Paul. Paul's preaching is distinguished in two respects: 1) its efficacy is based on the power of the Spirit (in this sense it is pneumatic) rather than on human reason; 2) the ethics that flow from it are based on revelation and are thus a structural element of faith rather than a mere appendage to the message, the congruency of which the believer recognizes in an act that is separate from the faith that saves (suggesting the reader compare Romans 13:9 with 1 Timothy 1:10b,11: καὶ εἴ τι ἕτερον τῇ ὑγιαινούσῃ διδασκαλίᾳ ἀντίκειται κατὰ τὸ εὐαγγέλιον τῆς δόξης τοῦ μακα–ρίου θεοῦ).

[59]Dibelius/Conzelmann, *The Pastoral Epistles*, p. 20, and *Die Pastoralbriefe* (1966), p. 17.

[60]Dibelius/Conzelmann, *The Pastoral Epistles*, p. 19; and *Die Pastoralbriefe* (1966), p. 17.

[61]Dibelius/Conzelmann, *The Pastoral Epistles*, p. 39, and *Die Pastoralbriefe* (1966), p. 32.

But to leave *die christliche Bürgerlichkeit* at the level simply of "building a life in this world" or of "becoming a part of this world" is to fail to give it the significance it actually would appear to have for Dibelius. For in *Urchristentum* he sets the Pastorals' project of *Bildungschristentum* in a larger context: the struggle between two ever competing expressions of the faith, the one standing always in judgment over culture, the other taking its stand within and striving for the eventual perfection of human culture.

> On the one hand, as with Paul and later Marcion, there is Christianity, the message of the most paradoxical things, comprehensible from culture's point of view only as "wholly other," and at work in the world only through judgment over this world; on the other hand, there is the Christian spirit of the completion (or perfection) of spiritual things in general, fulfilling all culture and therefore stimulating every culture, making recruits in the world through the riches of its message and the power of its ethos.[62]

The impression, he says,

> which continually confronts us of the coexistence of culture-preparation and culture-criticism within early Christianity gains fundamental significance. A culture in the western sense of the word requires a means of aligning all individual aspects of the culture, but in the case of conflict a means of bringing them into judgment also. Ancient classical culture had such a means; one can best term it a particular ideal of humanity that was sketched out for the citizen (*Bürger*) of the polis as: "an image of what the citizen should become." Lacking such a measure and such a means, the world of late antiquity took them from Christianity—and that determined the Christian victory.[63]

What Dibelius would appear to mean, then, when he says that the significance of the Pastorals lies largely in their being the documents in the New Testament canon which most clearly enjoin a structuring of life under the banner of *das Ideal christlicher Bürgerlichkeit* is that they abandon the culturally critical posture of the historical Paul for a stance that is more accommodative. From the latter stance these letters point the way toward Christianity's resketching for the citizen of the world of late antiquity the ideal of human existence—and this not in terms that are "wholly other," but

---

[62]Dibelius, *Urchristentum*, p. 16.
[63]Dibelius, *Urchristentum*, p. 30.

rather in terms that are "the fulfillment of the educated person's intuitive expectations."[64]

This, by the way, appears to approximate the sense given to the term by those who bring Dibelius' *Bürgerlichkeit* over into English by using the language of "good citizenship." J.T. Sanders, for instance, says that in the Pastorals there is "an unreflected ethics that is indistinguishable from good citizenship,"[65] and "Christianity now moves in the direction of equating Christian ethics with good citizenship."[66] It is the practice of P. Buttolph and A. Yarbro so to render *Bürgerlichkeit* in the Hermeneia translation of Dibelius' commentary.[67] It is the case, as well, with H. Koester's translation of his own *Einführung in das Neue Testament*.[68]

c. Unheroically Conservative

There is an ethical conservatism to this project that is altogether alien to Christianity's original social stance. According to Dibelius, the basic posture of early Christianity with respect to social ethics was one of "apocalyptic pacifism, which anticipated the end of the world, not its reformation."[69] Corresponding to this attitude is Paul's advice to remain in that station in which one was called to be a Christian (1 Corinthians 7:17-24). The standpoint is undeniably socially conservative:

> But behind this advice stands, unexpressed but well understood, a
> great "for the time being," namely, "until the imminent end of the

[64]Dibelius, *Urchristentum*, p. 16.

[65]Jack T. Sanders, *Ethics in the New Testament: Change and Development* (Philadelphia: Fortress Press, 1975), p. 88.

[66]Sanders, *Ethics*, p. 89.

[67]Of the numerous examples, note their translation of the heading of Dibelius' second excursus on 1 Timothy 2:2 (*Die Pastoralbriefe* [1966], p. 32; *The Pastoral Epistles*, p. 39): *Das Ideal christlicher Bürgerlichkeit* becomes "The Ideal of Good Christian Citizenship." At one point (*The Pastoral Epistles*, p. 20; *Die Pastoralbriefe* [1966], p. 17; cf., *Die Pastoralbriefe* [1931], p. 12), Buttolph and Yarbro note that *bürgerliche Ethik* lies behind their rendering "generally acceptable standards." Interestingly, this phrase concludes one of Conzelmann's additions, an expansion (two sentences in German, four in English) explaining the theological context of Dibelius' phrase *christliche Bürgerlichkeit* (= "good Christian citizenship").

[68]Helmut Koester, *Einführung in das Neue Testament im Rahmen der Religionsgeschichte und Kulturgeschichte der hellenistischen und römischen Zeit* (Berlin and New York: Walter de Gruyter, 1980), pp. 741, 744. Helmut Koester, *Introduction*, 2:302, 305.

[69]Dibelius, *Urchristentum*, p. 17.

world," which gives to the apparently socially conservative posture a provisional character.[70]

Pressed to respond to the questions of daily life by the numerical growth and social ascent of the movement, the church sought rules for ordering the many-faceted, complicated life of Hellenistic culture from within the Hellenistic world itself as far as it was accessible to Christians. Persuaded that the provisional nature of the present order of things made a systematic reconstruction of the world fruitless, they sought a "for the time being" arrangement with the world using traditional material.[71] Thus appeared even as early as Paul's letter to the Colossians[72] the New Testament *Haustafeln*, recalling and likely dependent upon Stoic rules for governing the household under the guiding principle that each person should derive his or her duty from the position he or she receives in the world. The Stoic principle which is being borrowed is that individuals will best adapt themselves to the divine ordering of the world by accomplishing that which befits them and by renouncing everything which is alien to them; as well, they will, through their own existence, point the way to the good.[73] In the letter to the Philippians (4:8),[74] Paul himself even mentions the essentially non-Christian word "virtue" (ἀρετή), calling to mind natural law views according to which people as such possess knowledge of and capability to do the good.[75] But, says Dibelius, in the case of the apostle appearances are deceiving:

> For while the Stoic cries to every person the admonition to reflect upon the good, Paul demands it only of Christians, who know themselves to have been redeemed and removed from the press of the world. All these apparently rationalistic, natural law, *bürgerlich* demands are thus

---

[70]Dibelius, *Urchristentum*, pp. 17-18.

[71]Dibelius, *Urchristentum*, p. 18.

[72]See Dibelius' *A Fresh Approach to the New Testament and Early Christian Literature* (New York: Charles Scribner's Sons, 1936), pp. 167-171, for his acceptance of Pauline authorship for Colossians.

[73]Dibelius, *Urchristentum*, p. 19.

[74]In this verse, Dibelius sees a series of "unalloyed expressions of *bürgerlich* life." Martin Dibelius, *An die Thessalonicher I,II, an die Philipper*, Handbuch zum Neuen Testament, no. 11, 3rd edition (Tübingen: Verlag von J.C.B. Mohr [Paul Siebeck], 1937), p. 95.

[75]Dibelius, *Urchristentum*, p. 19. In his commentary on Philippians (*An Thess I,II, an Phil*, p. 95), he notes that ἀρετή is "the natural leitmotif of Greek *Bildungsgeschichte*."

made "in Christ"; their fulfillment thus takes place on another plain from that on which they originated among the Stoics.[76]

Where, however, the "for the time being" qualification of this ethical borrowing "sank into oblivion there arose the impression as though that which was to be undergone had been made into the conclusive and to a certain degree come to be spoken of as being holy."[77] With the loss of their eschatological conditioning, maintains Dibelius, "Christian social ethics were stamped with a conservative bent which according to their essence they did not possess":

> Decisive was the time in the second and third centuries when belief in the end receded. Now that which was final had to take the place of that which was provisional; now a handling of the world from a Christian viewpoint had to begin. But it was already too late for a Christian revolution of social ethics. The church had had too close dealings with the present conditions under the sign of the provisional not to have identified itself finally with them, with the given class rankings, with the prevailing distribution of power.[78]

Dibelius gives passing acknowledgement of the *bürgerlich* elements of Paul's ethics, but believes the weighty theological context precludes their misappropriation.[79] The Pastorals, however, reflect the second century church's relaxing of its eschatological vigil in the pursuit of a significantly more settled version of the faith. The letters portray a Christianity that is a matter of

> right teaching and good works; a dogma presupposed as a possession of the community and a bourgeois (*bürgerlich*) ethic combine into *a completely static Christianity*, in which the dynamic tension of the eschatological gospel of Paul is not to be found.... One who has a sense for the significance of clearer solutions and *relatively attainable goals* in the history of religion will not depreciate the valuing of this tendency in the Pastorals, which could almost be called rationalistic. But one does not need on this account to identify the ὑγιαίνουσα διδασκαλία with the completely different gospel of Paul which wants to transform people through the preaching of the most paradoxical of things: the

---

[76]Dibelius, *Urchristentum*, p. 19.

[77]Dibelius, *Urchristentum*, p. 22.

[78]Dibelius, *Urchristentum*, pp. 22-23.

[79]Dibelius, *An Thess I,II, an Phil*, p. 95, comments on Philippians 4:9.

crucifixion of the Son of God and the pardon of the sinner by the just God."[80]

His comment about not depreciating the Pastorals' rationalistic tendency notwithstanding, Dibelius does appear to find worrisome the fact that the loss of Paul's eschatological dynamism leads to a loss of ethical heroism. What makes for the Pastorals' *durchaus statischen Christentum* is its inability to challenge the social status quo. Accordingly, he notes, the Pastorals' treatment of the persecutions of the great witnesses, Paul and Timothy,

> stands in marked contrast to the unheroic tenor of the whole (cf. 2 Timothy 1:3-14). Thus the teaching of this bourgeois (*bürgerlich*) Christianity has a nature that is in no way heroic.[81]

While they may not stand at the endpoint of the process Dibelius describes in *Urchristentum*—one in which by the end of the third century the church has had such close dealings with the status quo that it cannot help but become identified with it—the Pastorals certainly point in that direction.

Note must be taken of the fact that in the 1955 (3rd) and 1966 (4th) editions of the commentary (Dibelius died in 1947), Hans Conzelmann elides these two passages that speak of Pastoral Christianity as being "thoroughly static," "unheroic," and as aiming

---

[80]Dibelius, *Die Pastoralbriefe* (1931), p. 3: *Es handelt sich um ein Christentum der rechten Lehre und der guten Werke; eine als Gemeindebesitz vorausgesetzte Dogmatik und eine bürgerliche Ethik verbinden sich zu **einem durchaus statischen Christentum**, in dem von der dynamischen Gespanntheit des eschatologischen Evangeliums des Paulus nichts zu finden ist.... Wer Sinn hat für die Bedeutung klarer Losungen und **relativ erreichbarer Ziele** in der Religionsgeschichte, wird den Wert dieser Tendenz in den Past, die man fast rationalistisch nennen könnte, nicht unterschätzen, wird aber deswegen die ὑγιαίνουσα διδασκαλία nicht zu identifizieren brauchen mit dem völlig anders gearteten Evangelium des Paulus, das die Menschen verwandeln will durch die Predigt der paradoxesten Dinge: der Kreuzigung des Gottessohns und der Begnadigung der Sünder durch den gerechten Gott* (emphasis mine). NB: this passage does not appear in Conzelmann's edition—cf., *Die Pastoralbriefe* (1966), pp. 3-4; and see comments below.

[81]Dibelius, *Die Pastoralbriefe* (1931), p. 24: *Freilich weiß auch er von Verfolgungen, die das Schicksal der großen Zeugen sind, des Pl und auch des Timotheus. Aber die Ausführungen des II Tim, die davon handeln, heben sich von dem unheroischen Gesamtinhalt der Past in bezeichnender Weise ab s. zu II Tim 1:3-14. So hat auch die Lehre dieses bürgerlichen Christentums keinerlei heroische Art.* NB: this passage does not appear in Conzelmann's edition—cf., *Die Pastoralbriefe* (1966), p. 32; and see comments below.

at "relatively attainable goals."[82] In what must be considered a significant revision of Dibelius, Conzelmann argues for seeing the ethical adaptation to the loss of imminence as a necessary thing, urging
that a value judgment (i.e., Dibelius' value judgment) not be made
when the Pastorals are compared with Paul.[83] Rather, he would see
the ethics of *christliche Bürgerlichkeit* in the situation of a toned down
eschatology as being a historically necessitated *via media* between
"the path of salvation by works that lies to the right, and the way of
world-renunciation and speculation that lies to the left."[84] Conzelmann's version of the Pastorals' ethical conservatism thus stresses
the moderation of the epistles in the face of radical answers to the
question of how the church is to live in a world that is not, after all,
quickly passing away. He is consciously supplying theological
reflection not in the original,[85] though he takes as his starting point a
theologoumenon that legitimately stems from Dibelius, i.e., the
absence of the historical Paul's apocalyptic viewpoint.

All the same, one cannot help but conclude that in his attempt to
refine Dibelius, Conzelmann gives up something important to the
original. Given Dibelius' worrying in *Urchristentum* about the process that saw the caving in of early Christianity's apocalyptic and
critical conservatism to a brand of conservatism supportive of the
powers that be, and in light of his identifying the Pastorals among
those writings which sought to recruit precisely through the power
of its ethos, one cannot help but wonder if Dibelius' verdict that the
Pastorals ethics are "unheroic," "thoroughly static," and content
with "relatively attainable goals" should have been allowed to
stand.

At any rate, we are prepared to treat Dibelius' epithet *bürgerlich*
when applied to the Pastorals as having the following three layers of
meaning:

---

[82]He elides a third passage as well, one in which the expression "good conscience" (a mark of *christliche Bürgerlichkeit*) is spoken of as characteristic of the
Pastorals' "static Christianity": *Er* (the expression ἀγαθὴ συνείδησις) *ist
charakteristisch für das statische Christentum der Past* (Dibelius, *Die Pastoralbriefe*
[1931], p. 12—cf., *Die Pastoralbriefe* [1966], p. 17).

[83]Dibelius/Conzelmann, *Die Pastoralbriefe* (1966), p. 17; *The Pastoral Epistles*,
p. 20.

[84]Dibelius/Conzelmann, *Die Pastoralbriefe* (1966), p. 9; *The Pastoral Epistles*,
p. 10.

[85]Dibelius/Conzelmann, *Die Pastoralbriefe* (1966), *Vorvort*; *The Pastoral Epistles*, p. xii.

a. *Socially Ascendant.* Taken in a socially descriptive sense, *bür-gerlich* brings into view Christianity's emergence from its origins in the time of Jesus and Paul among the lowest class of people.

b. *Culturally Accommodative.* With an eye to early Christianity's encounter with Greek and Roman culture, the term suggests the adopting of an accommodative posture as opposed to Paul's critical stance, especially in using the thought-forms of *Bildungsmensch,* an ideal of humanity sketched out for the *Bürger* of the ancient polis.

c. *Unheroically Conservative.* With regard to social ethics, the epithet points to a hardening of Paul's apocalyptic pacifism into a conservatism that in a subsequent generation embraces present conditions and is identified with the given class rankings and the prevailing distribution of power.

2. *Ceslas Spicq*

That what one means by referring to the "bourgeois" nature of the Pastorals' Christianity is not unambiguous becomes evident when Dibelius' approach is compared with that of Ceslas Spicq, the conservative Roman Catholic commentator. The latter bristles at the notion that the *morale bourgeoise*[86] to which Dibelius points represents a falling away from Paul's gospel. He attempts to show the Pastorals' accommodation to Hellenistic ethics to be something of which Paul himself was quite capable. In doing so he wants both to acknowledge the singularity of the Pastorals' approach to ethics and to demonstrate a basic continuity with the acknowledged Pauline corpus.

As to continuity, he points out that at the same time Paul's earlier letters had exalted the foolishness of the cross and the necessity of sacrifice, they had nonetheless depicted the Christian "under the most amiable of traits in the enumeration of the fruits of the Spirit and in the encomium on charity (Galatians 5:22; 1 Corinthians 13:4-7)."[87] In the captivity epistles the winsome portrait of the Christian is more pronounced. There Paul enjoins relations imbued with agreeableness (*beauté*) and wholesome joy, encourages the adoption of everything that is honorable, just, and agreeable, and calls for the maintenance of a faultless deportment.[88] What Spicq finds in the Pastorals is simply movement in the same direction.

---

[86]Spicq, *Pastorales,* p. 175.

[87]Spicq, *Pastorales,* p. 294.

[88]Spicq, *Pastorales,* p. 294, citing Philippians 4:8,9; Colossians 4:5,6; 2:5.

The discontinuity lies less in the exclusive insistence on such norms as in their formulation. Here Spicq makes it clear that he sees the watershed dividing the Pastorals from the earlier Pauline corpus to be less a changed eschatology than an abandonment of Jewish for European thought forms—an abandonment occasioned by the final rift with Judaism Spicq believes to have already occurred within Pauline Christianity by A.D. 66-67.[89] What has become more than a doctrinal, religious, and cultic, but also a psychological break as well, has brought about the need to "think" the new faith in terms accessible to the Greek mentality:

> This is why St. Paul—this is one of the finest accomplishments of his genius for adaptation—presents Christian ethics under the heading of beauty,[90] defines it by good sense and the golden mean, and preaches order, decency, and deportment. His disciple is a cultivated, refined man who has a sense of *decorum* and is solicitous for his own reputation. His relationships are not strained; he is neither harsh nor surly. With thanksgiving he uses everything God gives him, and is suspicious of supererogatory abstinences; he drinks wine, moderately, if his health requires. He is convinced that piety is useful for everything; it possesses promises for the present life as well as for the future. Christ Jesus *has illuminated life!*[91]   The pastoral epistles are the charter of Christian humanism.[92]

Herein lies the twist Spicq would give to Dibelius' claim that the Pastorals mark an accommodation to Hellenistic ethics: it is not so much that the ethics are unheroic but that they are humanistic. Again, Spicq:

> If the Pastorals state as strongly as the earlier epistles the contrast between Christianity and paganism, they no longer isolate the church from the profane world; to the contrary, they plant within it a remark-

---

[89]Spicq, *Pastorales*, p. 294, n. 4, for discussion of his views on the movement away from the Jewish preoccupation of Galatians and Romans (pre-captivity epistles) to the notion of the unity of Jew and Gentile in Colossians/Ephesians (epistles of Paul's first captivity) to the assumption that Jews are outsiders to the Christian community in the Pastorals (epistles of the second captivity). Spicq believes the Pastorals could have been written as late as the outbreak of the Jewish-Roman war in A.D. 66.

[90]*Beauté* = καλός. See Spicq's Excursus VIII, "Vie chretienne et Beauté," *Pastorales*, pp. 676-684.

[91]This is a reference to 2 Timothy 1:10. In a footnote (*Pastorales*, p. 295, fn. 2), Spicq explains that he understands φωτίζω (transitive) to indicate not only that in the gospel a bright source of light radiates, but that the gospel actually sheds light on an object (in this case, on life).

able optimism and security. Experience has proven that every Christian is called to live in the midst of his former companions in error and sin. Far from hating and combatting them, he is to show them a man who has been transformed by grace, not at all (transformed) to lead an exceptional life, but to realize the ideal of the noble and good man,[93] of the good father, of the faithful citizen. Exhortations such as: ἵνα μὴ τὸ ὄνομα τοῦ θεοῦ καὶ ἡ διδασκαλία βλασφημῆται (1 Timothy 6:1), ἵνα μὴ ὁ λόγος τοῦ θεοῦ βλασφημῆται (Titus 2:5; cf. 8,10) can be understood as litotes, and explain how, despite all obstacles and opposition, the world was so swiftly won to Christianity.[94]

Thus, by virtue of their embodying a Christian humanism that strives for a rapprochement between Christian discipleship and the Greek ideal of "the noble and good man, the good father, and the faithful citizen," the Pastorals are not

> a bourgeois Christianity, as expressed by Dibelius, but the pure gospel taught to Christians living in society, in the church, making an open confession of their faith, expressing it in a new language and translating it into works.[95]

This denial does not, however, stop Spicq from taking up the matter as to whether the Christians of the Pastorals may be said to come from a "bourgeoisie" proper. Surprisingly perhaps, he answers in the affirmative.

Spicq calls attention to the fact that 1 Timothy contains the apostle's severest words about riches (2:10; 6:5-10; 6:17-19).[96] He supposes this may have something to do with Luke's influence, but says that it surely is a function of the need to combat the lust for money that was so developed in Ephesus,[97] especially in light of the fact that the Ephesian church drew its membership from the well-to-do. He acknowledges the general poverty of the Corinthian church, which is often offered as the benchmark for the social level of Paul's churches. But he believes the Corinthian church to have been the exception.[98] In addition, he points out that even there rich Chris-

---

[92]Spicq, *Pastorales*, p. 295.

[93]*Le parfait honnête homme.* See Spicq, *Pastorales*, p. 227, where the phrase is defined by the appositional καλὸς κἀγαθός.

[94]Spicq, *Pastorales*, p. 296.

[95]Spicq, *Pastorales*, p. 243.

[96]For this entire paragraph, see Spicq, *Pastorales*, p. 292, n. 3.

[97]See Spicq, *Pastorales*, p. 425 for his views on the wealth of Ephesus.

[98]See Spicq, *Pastorales*, p. 424, where he claims that Corinth and Smyrna (Revelation 2:9) were the only two poor churches in the diaspora.

tians had come into at least casual contact with poor Christians (citing 1 Corinthians 11: 21-22) and that the Apostle had had to rely on the generosity of the former for the success of his collection (2 Corinthians 8-9). Even so, according to Spicq, if the rich were in the minority in the church in Corinth, they were in the majority in Ephesus. And, he asserts, it appears that at the time of the writing of the Pastorals, the rich were becoming more and more numerous.

Particularly illuminating, he feels, is the case of the lavishly clothed women of 1 Timothy 2:9. Spicq asserts that during his more than three year ministry in Ephesus—"the economic, industrial, financial, administrative, and religious center of Asia Minor"—Paul would have found among his constituency the wives and daughters of the city's shipowners, merchants, importers and exporters, proprietors of the commercial houses and great warehouses, goldsmiths and jewelers, and businessmen and bankers.[99] It would have been upon the conversion of such men and their wives and the selling of their magical papyri and amulets that the church would have gained the 50,000 drachmas which Acts 19:19 relates. The paraenesis on the virtues and the deportment of these women who would henceforth be making a religious profession (1 Timothy 2:10) can only be understood in this economic, social, and cultural context, which is evoked again at the end of the epistle, τοῖς πλουσίοις ἐν τῷ νῦν αἰῶνι (6:17). To Spicq it would appear that Paul exercises good judgment in defining the Christian ethic of riches for this particular community:

> The psychological indications of our epistles presuppose a high social level. It is not a matter of an aristocracy, but this is not the coarseness of the Corinthians either: (these people) have a sense of nuance, of taste, love of beauty, severity of deportment. In this sense, M. Dibelius is correct: these are the virtues of the Christian bourgeoisie.[100]

Indicative of the humanistic or life-ennobling nuance which Spicq wants to bestow upon the epithet "bourgeois" is the way language of nobility or aristocracy finds its way into his comments on the ethics of these epistles. Among the virtues to which he is able to attach a sense of nobility are "prudence" (σωφροσύνη),[101] "piety" (θεοσέβεια),[102] and "reverence" (σεμνότης).[103] The man who so

[99]For this paragraph, see Spicq, *Pastorales*, pp. 424-425.
[100]Spicq, *Pastorales*, p. 292, n. 3.
[101]Spicq, *Pastorales*, p. 289.
[102]Spicq, *Pastorales*, p. 405.
[103]Spicq, *Pastorales*, p. 406.

regulates his life and governs his home as to assume the καλὸν ἔργον of the episcopacy exercises a *noblesse oblige*.[104] In his eighth excursus, *Vie chretienne et Beauté*, Spicq goes to some lengths to make it clear that καλόν is a lofty ethical term; the section is peppered with *noblesse*.[105] The virtues urged upon the "rich in this world" at 1 Timothy 6:18 are a transposition of "the aristocratic virtues required of men of property by Aristotle."[106] Thus, while the people of the Pastorals may not be members of an aristocracy, the virtues in which the gospel is to educate them are those belonging to people with upper class sensibilities.

Unlike Dibelius, then, Spicq does explicitly assign Pastoral Christians to a bourgeoisie. And the terms in which he does so are instructive: he asserts that their considerable wealth places them somewhere between an aristocracy and "the coarseness of the Corinthians"—i.e., they are a middle class. Like Dibelius, though, Spicq's primary interest is less with social description than with characterizing the ethos of these epistles. And precisely here is his largest quarrel with Dibelius: to the extent that "bourgeois" connotes a static Paulinism that uncritically makes its peace with the world, it is unsatisfactory to Spicq. But to the extent that it describes a community of prosperous Christians who are in a position to be taught that the gospel ennobles human existence, and that it does so at many points by affirming values that are already familiar, the term is serviceable.

D. POINTS OF COMPARISON AND ISSUES TO PURSUE

The juxtaposition of these two authoritative commentators' reflections on the *bürgerlich* nature of the Pastorals provides the backdrop against which we map out our project and its parameters. Dibelius is chiefly responsible for our decision to pursue three tracks: social description, cultural engagement, and social ethics.[107]

---

[104]Spicq, *Pastorales*, p. 429.

[105]Spicq, *Pastorales*, pp. 676-684. For example: "*kalos* designates purely and simply virtue, τὰ τῆς ψυχῆς καλά, punctuating *aréte* with that nuance of nobility which is appropriate to it" (p. 678).

[106]Spicq, *Pastorales*, p. 577.

[107]At this point, a terminological note is in order. When referring to the socially descriptive sense of Dibelius' epithet, I shall generally use the term "middle class" or the English cognate noun "bourgeoisie." Although I recognize that "bourgeoisie" and "middle class" are not exact equivalents, I nonethe-

1. A Christian Bourgeoisie?

In the first place, Dibelius and Spicq raise the question of the social provenance of early Christians. The former obliquely and the latter straightforwardly place Pastoral Christians in a bourgeoisie, or a middle class. What it means to speak of a bourgeoisie in an ancient economy is not at all self-evident, nor is it clear how such a placing of Pastoral Christians locates them vis-à-vis other early Christians. Our first efforts, then, are aimed at gaining clarity about whether Dibelius' epithet is helpful in a socially descriptive sense.

Dibelius offers any number of starting points for evaluating the *bürgerlich* (= middle class) mode of existence of the Pastorals,[108] but

---

less understand them to be synonymous in general usage and will use them that way. To anticipate, I conclude that the language of a "middle class" or "bourgeoisie" is not helpful for social description in the early imperial period in general. Nor, specifically, is it helpful for locating the social provenance of Christians in the Pastorals or the acknowledged Pauline letters, and that is partially by virtue of the term's aiming too low.

Where I understand the issue in Dibelius to be the Pastorals' degree of cultural engagement, I preserve his German *"bürgerlich,"* this because I believe Dibelius' standard of measure for the degree of cultural engagement to be that of antiquity's "ideal citizen" (*Bürger*). I would speak (as do the Hermeneia translators) of a "citizenship ideal," but am not confident that this language can be sufficiently insulated from what citizenship has come to mean in the modern democracies where enfranchisement is a nearly universal phenomenon. Furthermore, the Pastorals do not take up the matter of political responsibility in any more direct a fashion than to urge prayer for and obedience to civil authorities. Therefore, I cautiously forward *bürgerlich* with hopes that its alienness to the English reader and its etymological tie to Dibelius' ideal *Bürger* of antiquity will allow us to provide it a particular nuance.

As much as possible I avoid the term "bourgeois" when speaking of the social ethics of the Pastorals, as it is fraught with evaluative connotations. Where it is synonymous with "banal," "mundane," "pedestrian," or even the more refined "quotidian," the adjective "bourgeois" imposes premature closure on the discussion of the social-ethical style of the Pastorals. My terminological preference is to focus on what I acknowledge to be the essential "conservatism" of the Pastorals' ethics, asking as to whether the Pastorals are more or less so relative to the acknowledged letters. Following Dibelius' lead, I qualify the ethical conservatism as being either "heroic" or "unheroic" in order to evaluate his contention that Paul's ethical reserve is apocalyptically conditioned and the Pastorals' is not.

[108]See the issues outlined in his second excursus on 1 Timothy 2:2, *das Ideal christlicher Bürgerlichkeit*, ad loc.; and see p. 17 above. Additionally, Roland Schwarz's *Bürgerliches Christentum im Neuen Testament? Eine Studie zu Ethik, Amt und Recht in den Pastoralbriefen*, Oesterreichische Biblische Studien, no. 4

few are as promising as the one employed by Spicq, i.e., wealth.[109]
To be sure, it is not the only measure of social station, nor did there
emerge within antiquity, any more than there has in the modern
world, a univocal "middle class" view of wealth. Nonetheless
wealth was perceived as a central measure of social location. The
desire to laud or the need to chide the wealthy pervades the
literature, the orations, the inscriptions, and the papyri of our
period. So much so that it should be possible, at least on this matter,
to ask where within the "everyday world" of Hellenistic civic life the
social reality of the Pastorals fits. We understand wealth, then, to be
a leading index of social provenance, and choose it to be our central
focus in trying to understand the contours of these communities.

Accordingly, the second chapter assumes the following form:
first we explore the traditional categories used to talk about social
level in the ancient world, viz., rank, class, and status, with an eye to
the applicability of these categories to our documents. Second, we
consider two suggestions made by social historian E.A. Judge: 1)
that the social structure of the Hellenistic municipalities in the early
Roman Empire ought to be conceived of in terms of three overlapping institutions: household, association, and citizenship; and 2) that
the longheld assumption that the churches in the Pauline orb were

---

(Klosterneuburg: Verlag Oesterreichisches Katholisches Bibelwerk, 1983) ranges
the *Episkopenspiegeln*, ethics, and concepts of "office" and "law" in quest of the
bürgerlich elements of the Pastorals. While his is an invaluable study on the
cultural and ethical senses of Dibelius' epithet, he does not pursue the question
of social description. Jouette Bassler's, "The Widows' Tale: A Fresh Look at 1
Timothy 5:3-16," *Journal of Biblical Literature* 103 (1984): 23-41, and Dennis
Ronald MacDonald's, *The Legend and the Apostle: The Battle for Paul in Story and
Canon* (Philadelphia: The Westminster Press, 1983) represent the promise of the
issue of women for a social description of these epistles.

[109]Because it is our intention to isolate the Pastorals' own social reality and
because Acts is often associated with the Pastorals as being too "middle class"
to be descriptive of the original Pauline communities, we will not appeal to the
portrait of the Ephesian church in Acts in quite the way Spicq does. Some of
the more striking parallels between Luke-Acts and the Pastorals do happen to
intersect our interests, however. Wilson's monograph (*Luke and the Pastorals*),
defending common authorship for Luke-Acts and the Pastorals, includes a
chapter on "The Christian Citizen," in which a common approach to wealth is
central (pp. 36-52, esp. 49-50); especially instructive is his discussion of the
speech to the Ephesian elders in Acts 20 (pp. 117-118; with Acts 20:33-35
compare 1 Timothy 6:9-10 and Titus 1:11). All the same, we are not prepared to
make a case for a specific relationship between Luke-Acts and the Pastorals,
and will thus not treat the material in Acts as being directly descriptive of the
Pastorals' social situation.

impoverished is erroneous. Third, we explore the indications of wealth in the Pastoral communities, asking about the implications for social description: are we dealing here with something usefully thought of as a Christian bourgeoisie?

2. Cultural Accommodation?

In the second place, both Dibelius and Spicq presuppose a certain posture vis-à-vis the classical ideal of the citizen: Dibelius speaks of *Bildungsmensch* and Spicq of the καλὸς κἀγαθός. This raises the question of the social history of early Christianity. For the view of wealth in these letters presupposes the dynamic relationship between economic superiors and inferiors in early imperial municipal life. By studying the role of the wealthy *Bürger* as benefactor in this social world, we attempt to understand whether the Pastorals accommodate or criticize their *bürgerlich* cultural milieu.

The impetus for this tack is shared by the social historian Ramsay MacMullen and the New Testament scholar and philologist Frederick W. Danker—by MacMullen for pointing up the singular importance to ancient societies of what he calls the "sheer willingness" of their elites to lavish benefactions on their communities;[110] and by Danker for assembling in his study *Benefactor* a laboratory in which this phenomenon can be placed, so to speak, under the microscope.[111] In large measure the present study is an attempt to verify Danker's contention that the person of the benefactor and the phenomenon of benefactions—reciprocal relationships established between social superiors and their inferiors—are as pivotal to an understanding of some parts of the New Testament—among which are the Pastoral epistles—as he contends.[112]

In the third chapter, then, following an outlining of what we understand to be a recognizable, *bürgerlich* cultural ideal of the wealthy person's responsibilities, rewards, and hopes, we ask to

[110]Ramsay MacMullen, *Roman Social Relations: 50 B.C. to A.D. 284* (London: Yale University Press, 1974), pp. 61, 125.

[111]Frederick W. Danker, *Benefactor: Epigraphic Study of a Graeco-Roman and New Testament Semantic Field* (St. Louis: Clayton Publishing House, 1982). (Benefactor documents collected and translated in Danker's *Benefactor* are cited according to his numbering; in some cases a source for the text is provided parenthetically; lines are cited according to the source. Except where noted I follow his translation of the documents.)

[112]Danker notes that the language of benevolence clusters in those New Testament books which bear the most noticeable Hellenistic stamp; cf. *Benefactor*, p. 46 where he cites "Luke-Acts, the Pauline Letters (especially the Pastorals), and 2 Peter."

what extent the Pastorals share and to what extent they repudiate such a social world.

3. An Unheroic Ethic?

Dibelius and Spicq raise a third and final question, that of the social ethics of these letters and their relationship to the ethics of the acknowledged Pauline letters. Dibelius finds a change in social ethics that is a function of a changed eschatology. Spicq defends the ethics of the Pastorals as being a legitimate extension of elements of the apostle's own thinking. It might have been profitable to pursue this matter through that part of the sociology of knowledge which is concerned with the fit between "social world" and "ethos," with the affinity between a symbolic communal perception of reality and the concrete life lived out according to that reality.[113] However, at this point in the investigation we have found it expedient to frame the question in more conventional, historical-critical terms. Before surrendering the discussion to the sociology of knowledge we would like to have a better sense of whether the data of the epistles themselves support the thesis that the Pastorals present a more "conservative" ethic, and especially whether their brand of ethical conservatism is conditioned by a post-Pauline, non-apocalyptic eschatology.

Thus the fourth chapter begins with a comparison of the social ethics of the Pauline homologoumena and those of the Pastorals, with an eye to answering whether the Pastorals evidence a drift that is too conservative for Paul. From there we ask whether the ethics in the Pastorals have a different relationship to eschatology than in the acknowledged letters, and whether the eschatology itself has moved away from Paul's vibrant apocalypticism.

Finally, just as Celsus' and Origen's (albeit one-way) conversation sounded the overture to our study, so it provides the background music against which we offer conclusions about the "bourgeois" nature of Pastoral Christianity: 1) about the relative

---

[113]See John H. Schütz, "Ethos of Early Christianity," *Interpreter's Dictionary of the Bible*, Supplementary Volume, 1975, pp. 289-293; especially governed by attention to the sociology of knowledge is Kee's *Christian Origins*. In her *The Pauline Churches: A Socio-historical Study of Institutionalization in the Pauline and Deutero-Pauline Writings* (Cambridge, at the University Press, 1988), Margaret Y. MacDonald lays out a methodologically rigorous agenda for a comparative reading of various sections of the Pauline corpus sociologically; hers is an important work and I regret that it did not come to my attention in time to be taken into consideration in this dissertation.

social provenances of the Pauline homologoumena and the Pastorals; 2) about how accommodative and how critical the Pastorals are of their culture's idea about how rich people ought to live; and 3) about whether the Pastorals take "the enduring structures of this world" so much more seriously than do the homologoumena that their brand of ethical conservatism must be distanced from Paul's.

CHAPTER II

The Social Provenance of the Pastoral Epistles: A Christian Middle Class?

A. ARISTOTLE AND THE PERILS OF COMMON SENSE

The Roman Empire was an urbanized society (rather, collection of societies) vastly differentiated in wealth, power, and prestige. It is altogether understandable, perhaps even inevitable, that such a social universe would be talked about in terms of an elite, aristocratic upper class at the top, an impoverished peasant and proletarian lower class at the bottom, and a reasonably, though not fabulously, wealthy and powerful bourgeoisie in the middle. Indeed, somewhere between the roughly one percent of the Empire's 50 or so million who comprised the senatorial, equestrian, and curial orders on the one hand and the unnumbered masses who manned the mines, sweated in the shops, and begged in the plazas on the other there was a similarly unnumbered, but undoubtedly significant, range of people who belonged neither to the aristocracy nor to the dispossessed.

To name this group a middle class would not only appear to be a matter of common sense, it would be to adopt the language of antiquity's most perceptive social thinker. For with an eye to the link between government and its social nexus, Aristotle had envisioned an ideal state run not by the exceedingly wealthy (οἱ εὔποροι σφόδρα) nor the overly poor (οἱ ἄποροι σφόδρα), but by those of middling prosperity (οἱ μέσοι τούτων). The rich are unable to submit to government and are contemptuous (καταφρονεῖν) of those beneath them, while the poor are able only to be servile and are envious (φθονεῖν) of those above them (*Politics* 1295a25-1297b34). Aristotle's ethical mean finds its social locus in the group living between the extremes of wealth and poverty, those who are rich enough not to be covetous of their superiors and poor enough not to be contemptuous of their inferiors. It is readily apparent, however, that in this conceptualization it is Aristotle the ethicist, not Aristotle the student of political life, who writes. His normal picture is of a two-tiered society, pulled back and forth between the interests of the rich and the poor, in whose respective names oligarchy and radical democracy are championed. M.I. Finley summarizes:

> In the *Politics*, τὸ μέσον appears only in a few normative generaliza-
> tions—"The larger πόλεις are more free from civil disturbance
> (στάσις) because τὸ μέσον is numerous"—of little practical signifi-
> cance, for "in most states τὸ μέσον is small" (1296a9-24).[1]

Here, as elsewhere, Aristotle seeks the mean—in this case an ideal class of men who would be able to govern without being seduced into serving their own interests.

Aristotle's remarks are important for the modern Western student of ancient social structure because they suggest the diamond-
shaped model that is the working ideology and, to a marked degree,
the reality of modern Western societies: a small super-wealthy and
powerful elite at one extreme, a similarly small but quite impoverished and powerless group at the other extreme, and sandwiched
between the two a vast expanse of the relatively prosperous and
powerful. Because its history is uniquely colored by the absence of
both aristocracy and Old World peasantry, the United States is
probably distinctive in presenting a system of stratification that is
perceived as being focused on a middle class.[2] But, as Talcott

---

[1]Moses I. Finley, *Politics in the Ancient World* (Cambridge, at the University Press, 1983), p. 10; cf., A.R. Hands, *Charities and Social Aid in Greece and Rome* (Ithaca, NY: Cornell University Press, 1968), pp. 71f.

[2]Paradigmatic is the following remark of Talcott Parsons (*The Evolution of Societies*, ed. and intro. by Jackson Toby [Englewood Cliffs, NJ: Prentice Hall, Inc., 1977], p. 224): "The American stratification system is focused on the middle class. The position of the upper class is tenuous. Where it has survived, it has been more as a power elite. Furthermore, there are now few working-class people in the traditional sense, only the poor." Cf. p. 186 where he points to the following factors' influence in shaping the American experience: the generally nonaristocratic origins of the American population, the emigration of a considerable proportion of upper-class elements during the American Revolution, the Constitution's forbidding of the granting of titles, the lack of recognition of landed proprietorship or wealth as a criterion for government office and authority, the ability of new wealth and education to provide political mobility, the appearance of an industrial class on a landscape in which the lack of an aristocracy or a peasantry discouraged a keen sense of class consciousness. For the American experience: Alexis de Tocqueville's *Democracy in America*, 2 vols., ed., Phillips Bradley (New York: Vintage Books, 1945) is a classic description of a bourgeoisie as a ruling class; Digby Baltzell's work on the American upper class (chiefly *The Protestant Establishment: Aristocracy and Caste in America* [New York: Random House, 1964; Vintage Books, 1966] and *Puritan Boston and Quaker Philadelphia: Two Protestant Ethics and the Spirit of Class Authority and Leadership*

Parsons notes, the evolution of the European democracies has also been in the direction of expanding the power of the middle classes at the expense of the upper and through the elevation of the lower classes.[3] What is distinctive about the modern middle class is the fact that an industrial, commercial economy has combined with a constitutional, democratic form of government to enable this group's numerical strength and its economic and political clout to approximate each other.[4]

In short, what can only have been wishful thinking for Aristotle is probably taken for granted by most citizens of the Western industrial democracies. The rub is that just as the diamond-shaped model failed to capture for Aristotle the contours of fourth century B.C. Greece, so it now may fail those who, almost intuitively, would

[New York: MacMillan, The Free Press, 1979]) explores the conflicting values of hierarchy and egalitarianism in American social history; on the relationship between individual and group in the American middle class experience, note Robert N. Bellah et al., *Habits of the Heart: Individualism and Commitment in American Life* (Berkeley and Los Angeles: University of California Press, 1985), esp. pp. 118-119, 148-152.

[3]Parsons, *Evolution*, p. 224. For an outline of the emergence of the modern European middle classes from the medieval boroughs, and for the different nuances of "bourgeois" in the European democracies, see Carl Brinkmann, "Bourgeoisie," and Alfred Meusel, "Middle Class," in *Encyclopaedia of the Social Sciences* (New York: The MacMillan Co., 1930), 2:654-656; and 10:407-415, respectively. On the French experience: Bernard Groethuysen's catologuing of the crisis of the Catholic spirit in France during the period of the enfranchisement of the middle class (*The Bourgeois: Catholicism vs. Capitalism in Eighteenth-Century France*, trans. Mary Ilford [London: Barrie & Rockliff, the Cresset Press, 1927, 1968]) is testament to the revolution in mindset the onset of modern European capitalism brought in its wake; see also Robert Darnton's essays, *The Great Cat Massacre and Other Episodes in French Cultural History* (New York: Basic Books, Inc., 1984). On the German (and American) experience: Max Weber's *Protestant Ethic and the Spirit of Capitalism*, trans. Talcott Parsons (New York: Charles Scribner's Sons, 1958) in tandem with Marianne Weber's biography of her husband (*Max Weber: A Biography*, trans. and ed. Harry Zohn [New York: John Wiley & Sons, 1975]) are seminal works on the rise of the bourgeoisie, and the interpenetration of the worldviews of historic Protestantism and modernity.

[4]For a theological protest against the hegemony of this ethos, see Johann Baptist Metz, ed., *Christianity and the Bourgeoisie* (New York: The Seabury Press, 1979). In celebration of it, Robert Benne, *The Ethic of Democratic Capitalism: A Moral Reassessment* (Philadelphia: Fortress Press, 1981); Michael Novak, *The Spirit of Democratic Capitalism* (New York: American Enterprise Institute and Simon & Schuster, 1982); and Franky Schaeffer, ed., *Is Capitalism Christian? Toward a Christian Perspective on Economics* (Westchester, IL: Crossway Books, A Division of Good News Publishers, 1985).

apply it to the social structure of the first century Roman world. And for the same reason: the absence of τὸ μέσον, the lack of a middle.

Our investigation of the social provenance of the Pastoral Christians has as its goal the establishing of whether or not they were members of a bourgeoisie—what Aristotle would have called τὸ μέσον τῶν εὐπόρων καὶ τῶν ἀπόρων, and what we would envision as the bulge in the middle of a diamond-shaped stratification system.

We shall proceed, first, to discuss the standard terminology employed in social description of the Roman world; second, to examine E.A. Judge's contention that stratification in ancient societies must be studied in an institution-specific way; and third, to assess his claim that Pauline Christianity was not as "lower class" a phenomenon as it is usually made out to be.

B. *ORDO*, CLASS, AND STATUS

1. Ordo

Romans themselves recognized their stratified world, and legally and officially divided it up into orders or estates:

> juridically defined group(s) within (the) population, possessing formalized privileges and disabilities in one or more fields of activity, governmental, military, legal, economic, religious, marital, and *standing in a hierarchical relation to other orders*.[5]

No configuration of first century societies can ignore the juridically defined groups into which people fell. The legal designation of senator, equestrian, curial, citizen (of the Roman citizen-body or of a provincial municipality), free person, freedperson, or slave provided an objective index to at least part of one's social standing, and defined a section of the population to which a person belonged to the exclusion of other sections. Nonetheless, the system of orders did not exhaust and at points obscured social position.

The system was elitist. That is to say, despite the official recognition of freeborn plebians and freedpersons as *ordines*, the system functioned primarily to define the boundaries between, on the one

---

[5]M.I. Finley, *The Ancient Economy*, 2nd ed. (Berkeley and Los Angeles: University of California Press, 1985), p. 45, emphasis his.

hand, these lower orders, and, on the other, Roman senators and equestrians and elite provincial families (curials, upon whom Roman citizenship was being conferred and who were progressively being drawn into the mother city's aristocracy). There was, in short, no provision for a "middle rank" in the Roman system, as the intent throughout was to fence off the elite from those beneath them.[6] Further, despite their intent, the *ordines* were not sure measures of power, prestige, and wealth. Depending on the resources and influence of their masters, slaves could very well rise to positions of such eminence that even members of the upper orders would be obligated to traffic with them, if begrudgingly.[7] And while a free born citizen was technically the superior of a freedperson, the nature of the client relationship the latter still maintained with a former master might be a source of security and wealth unavailable to a patronless person of free birth.

Finally, as illustrated by the facts that from within the senatorial ranks an unofficial "nobility" emerged or that a Pompeian could brag that he was *princeps libertinorum*, "first among freedmen,"[8] the juridical definitions simply did not exhaust the strata within strata in which people actually lived.

When the official orders are taken as the sole measure of social stratification, early Christianity is almost by definition—but no less misleadingly—dubbed "lower class." This is the case most strikingly in the work of John Gager. His description of Roman social structure is a rehearsal of the *ordines*: senatorial aristocracy, equestrian order, municipal bureaucracies, plebs, freedpersons, slaves. He maintains that even though some early Christians may have had wealth and education, their exclusion from the higher orders meant they were lower class, and that consequently "for more than two hundred years Christianity was essentially a movement among disprivileged groups in the Empire."[9]

---

[6]See the comments of Stanislaw Ossowski, *Class Structure in the Social Consciousness*, trans. from the Polish by Sheila Patterson (London: Routledge and Kegan Paul, 1963), p. 35, on the use of ranking definitions by privileged classes to contrast themselves with the rest of society.

[7]Thomas Wiedemann, *Greek and Roman Slavery* (Baltimore and London: The Johns Hopkins University Press, 1981), p. 69.

[8]CIL 4.117. I owe this reference to Osiek, *Rich and Poor in Hermas*, p. 92. Inscriptional and papyrological sigla and the documents and collections to which they refer can be found in Danker, *Benefactor*, pp. 9-25.

[9]John G. Gager *Kingdom and Community: The Social World of Early Christianity* (Englewood Cliffs, NJ: Prentice-Hall, Inc., 1975), pp. 93-113, esp. p. 96; and "Review of *Early Christianity and Society: Seven Studies*, by R.M. Grant; *Social*

2. Class

To compensate for the inadequacy of the *ordines* alone modern observers often appeal to categories of social class. As distinguished from an order, a class is a non-juridically defined group which the modern observer perceives and into which he or she heuristically places people.[10] While a host of criteria for division into classes could be and have been forwarded, Stanislaw Ossowski maintains, and plausibly so, that three are basic: 1) political power, "the rulers and the ruled"; 2) property ownership, "the propertied classes and the propertyless classes," "the haves and the have-nots," "rich and poor"; and 3) labor expropriation, "those for whom others work and those who work," "masters and slaves."[11] Ossowski further contrasts *gradational* class schemes, which position people on the basis of their possessing more or less of an item (e.g., wealth, power, leisure—though wealth is generally the prime consideration), from *relational* class schemes, which concentrate on structured interactions between people in positions of greater and lesser power (e.g., master/slave, seller/buyer).[12] When the object of study is an ancient society there is the additional necessity of defining categories in such a way as to avoid projecting modern dynamics back into an alien environment. In this regard, there are two persistent problems attendant to the use of social class language: 1) the supposition that there was an industrially and commercially based economy which supported a capitalist class, and 2) the smuggling in of the diamond configuration idealized by Aristotle and familiar to modern democratic societies.

Aspects of Early Christianity, by A.J. Malherbe; and *Sociology of Early Palestinian Christianity*, by G. Theissen," in *Religious Studies Review* 5 (1979): 174-180, p.180. See Wayne A. Meeks' critique of Gager's collapsing the categories of *ordo* and class, in the former's *The First Urban Christians: The Social World of the Apostle Paul* (New Haven: Yale University Press, 1983), p. 215, n. 20.

[10]In this I am following Finley, *Ancient Economy*, pp. 48-49. He says: "In principle, of course, the members of any classification system are 'classes' by definition. However, there is a distinction we must express somehow in language, between groups which are and groups which are not juridically defined, and some students have suggested 'order' for the first, 'class' for the second."

[11]Ossowski, *Class Structure*, p. 23.

[12]Ossowski, *Class Structure*, passim; summarized and put to good use in Richard L. Rohrbaugh, "Methodological Considerations in the Debate Over the Social Class Status of Early Christians," *Journal of the American Academy of Religion* 52 (1984): 519-546.

a. Gradational Approaches to Class

Both the strengths and the weaknesses of the use of what Ossowski would call gradational class categories are illustrated in the work of M.I. Rostovtzeff, by far the most influential modern student of the social and economic history of the Roman Empire, and an ardent advocate of the importance to Roman social history of its "bourgeoisie." He uses the term to refer to a stratum of provincial urban society which, though invisible to the system of *ordines*, nonetheless possessed sufficient wealth and prestige and evidenced sufficient economic activism to enable it to stand between the elite Roman orders and the proletarian masses of its various cities.

Under the emperors, he notes, provincial municipal life flourished, partly due to the attractiveness of a high standard of living available in the cities after the imposition of the *pax Romana*, and partly due to early imperial policies which favored privileged provincials.[13] From an economic point of view the process of urbanization which the imperial provinces underwent from Augustus through the Flavians

> meant the formation of a city *bourgeoisie*, of a class of landowners, traders, and industrialists, who resided in the city and who developed an energetic business activity on capitalistic lines.[14]

Elsewhere he refers to them as

> the higher, that is, the most civilized and best educated, classes of the urbanized parts of the Empire. (They were) *bourgeois*, to use a modern word much abused by the socialists, ...the propertied classes of the provincial cities, the landowners and farmers—whether they lived in the cities or continued to reside on their farms and in their country houses—not from the city or the rural proletariate....
>
> They formed an almost pure plutocracy: the municipal administration could be undertaken only by wealthy people, since office was elective ... and unpaid, and involved obligatory gifts to the city and a far-reaching financial responsibility towards the central government.... Most of them were well-to-do landowners. In the industrial and commercial cities, side by side with this aristocracy of landowners, a new class was gradually springing up and taking the leading part in

---

[13]M.I. Rostovtzeff, *The Social and Economic History of the Roman Empire*, 2 vols., 2nd ed. revised by P.M. Fraser (Oxford, at the Clarendon Press, 1957), pp. 83-84.
[14]Rostovtzeff, *Roman Empire*, p. 93.

civic life, a class of rich merchants and shopkeepers, who were partly freeborn but mostly freedmen and their descendants.[15]

Though he acknowledges that ancient forms were different from modern ones, Rostovtzeff nonetheless insists that "capitalistic" modes of production did exist in antiquity, where profit and not consumption were the goal of economic activity.[16] Finley has argued that Rostovtzeff mistakes scattered archaeological relics for a ubiquitous factory system with interdependent markets and thus overestimates the importance of manufacturing and trade to the ancient economy.[17] The point of the objection is that Rostovtzeff has allowed the way modern economics have created a large, wealthy, and powerful middle class to blind him to the actual conditions of the first century. Says G.W. Bowersock:

> Rostovtzeff could not bring himself to admit the importance of agriculture in antiquity, and he refused to recognize that what he saw as his beloved middle class was not a middle class at all but a ruling class. Indeed, it is arguable that there was no middle class whatsoever in antiquity. The senators of Antonine Rome and the leading citizens of the provincial cities were no bourgeoisie. They were the upper class, and enjoyed its many privileges—legal and otherwise. A substantial number of them were fabulously wealthy.[18]

Some have suggested that Rostovtzeff's overestimation of the Empire's middle class can be better appreciated against the backdrop of his own native Russia's transition to the Soviet regime. Says Reinhold Meyer:

> His understanding of the term "bourgeoisie" must also be placed in the context of pre-Soviet Russian society, predominantly agricultural, under the sway of a decaying feudal landed aristocracy, emerging into the dawn of industrial capitalism, and generating an enterprising bourgeoisie and a growing industrial proletariat. Situated socially and economically in an intermediate position between the declining but politically dominant ruling nobility and the increasingly class-conscious peasants and industrial workers, the Russian bourgeoisie was truly a *middle class*, drawing its income both from commercial and industrial enterprise and from rationalized agriculture. But it never

---

[15]Rostovtzeff, *Roman Empire*, pp. 107, 186.

[16]Rostovtzeff, *Roman History*, p. 543, n. 1.

[17]Finley, *Ancient Economy*, pp. 58-60, 191-196.

[18]G.W. Bowersock, "Review of *The Social and Economic History of the Roman Empire* by Michael Ivanovitch Rostovtzeff," *Daedalus* (1974): 19.

succeeded, as did its counterparts in the more advanced capitalist countries, in becoming a ruling class.[19]

What is particularly problematic about Rostovtzeff's use of social class language is that his bourgeoisie, or middle class, comprise the tiny ruling elites of their cities. They are barely a larger section of the Empire's populace than their senatorial and equestrian superiors—but Rostovtzeff inflates their numbers by making them into capitalists who presided over a nonexistent market economy. Not always by the standards of Roman senators and equestrians, but certainly by the standards of their own cities, they were quite, not merely relatively, rich.[20]

Beneath this upper stratum of urbanites, Rostovtzeff locates a lower bourgeoisie. There is, as we have seen, the provincial municipal aristocracy, standing as it does between the Roman elite and everyone else, from ordinary municipal citizen on down. But on the local level—that is, the level of the provincial municipality—the class in the middle is what he calls "the petty bourgeoisie." This group stands between the municipal aristocracy (a.k.a. the wealthy bourgeoisie, the upper classes of the cities) and the urban proletariat, or working classes. This petty bourgeoisie was composed of

> the shopowners, the retail-traders, the money-changers, the artisans, the representatives of liberal professions, such as teachers, doctors, and the like. Of them we know but little. We cannot say how large their numbers were as compared with the municipal aristocracy on the one hand and the city proletariate on the other. The ruins of the ancient cities of Italy and the provinces, with their hundreds of smaller and larger shops and hundreds of inscriptions, mentioning individual members of this class and their associations, lead us to believe that they formed the backbone of municipal life. But we shall never be able to say how many shops were owned by this petty *bourgeoisie* and how many were run by slaves and freedmen (*institores*) for the members of

---

[19]Meyer Reinhold, "Historian of the Classic World: A Critique of Rostovtzeff," *Science and Society* 10 (1946): 361-391.

[20]Rostovtzeff, *Roman Empire*, pp. 125f, 589f, n. 32. As principal spokesmen for his bourgeoisie, Rostovtzeff selects Dio Chrysostom and Plutarch. Aelius Aristides, Pliny the Younger, and Opramoas (the Lycian millionaire whose inscriptions appear as Danker No. 19) should also be mentioned (p. 151). See also the list of rich men who were municipal benefactors on p. 601f, n. 13. There he claims that the phenomenon of the increase in the number of large benefactors begins in the East with the second half of the first century A.D., and reaches its climax in the first half of the second. Still, his first century bourgeoisie is a bit more difficult to find. Dio's family is included (p. 574, n.

the municipal aristocracy. Moreover, we have no means of drawing a line between the higher and the lower *bourgeoisie*, as the former was certainly recruited from the latter.[21]

By virtue of its failure to leave behind a literature or anything more than the mention of the names of some of its members in the inscriptions, this so-called petty bourgeoisie ceases to exist for Rostovtzeff. It may have been "the backbone of municipal life," but it simply has no place in his analysis of the social history of the Roman Empire. When he speaks of the empire-wide "strong and numerous city-*bourgeoisie*" as being "the leading force in the Empire,"[22] it is the wealthy bourgeoisie as opposed to the petty bourgeoisie that he has in mind.

And here is the point of inevitable confusion. For quite aside from the question as to whether the rise of a bourgeoisie is not historically a function of the rise of a capitalistic and industrial economy, Rostovtzeff's language of a "strong and numerous city-*bourgeoisie*" irresistibly invites the reader to envision his "wealthy bourgeoisie" as the bulging middle stratum of a diamond-shaped society when in fact they stood at the pinnacle of a steep pyramid. Nor can Rostovtzeff's petty bourgeoisie, as he rightly appears to suspect, be identified with a bulging middle class, as the record they have left behind is not commensurate with the supposition that they brokered power between the municipal aristocracy above them and the so-called working classes beneath them.[23] Statistically, the range of municipal inhabitants who fell, by whatever measure, somewhere between the members of their city's elite and its dregs may very well have been in the majority. But there is real question whether there are any criteria by which these "petty bourgeoisie" warrant being positively labeled as a class. For, other than the obvious fact that they were urbanites who were neither aristocrats nor beggars, data which would indicate that they operated with any political or economic self-understanding vis-à-vis those above or beneath them are lacking.

For all its faults, the sort of gradational scheme Rostovtzeff employs at least allows a point of entry into the debate over the "bourgeois" social origins of early Christians, and for our purposes,

---

10); but Rostovtzeff relies heavily on Petronius' satirical portrait of Trimalchio (pp. 57, 562, n. 18).

[21]Rostovtzeff, *Roman Empire*, p. 190.

[22]Rostovtzeff, *Roman Empire*, p. 103.

[23]See Rostovtzeff, *Roman Empire*, pp. 190, 346, for his description of the Empire's "working classes."

especially of the Pastoral Christians. Martin Hengel claims that the
introduction of the theme of self-sufficiency or contentment (αὐτάρ–
κεια) in the Pastorals (1 Timothy 6:6-9) points to a certain *Verbürgerlichung* in the early Christian community. But, he maintains, this
accommodation to *bürgerlich* life is simply consistent with the fact
that from the very beginning early Christianity was essentially *eine
'kleinbürgerliche' Bewegung*.[24] That he has in mind precisely the kind
of people whom Rostovtzeff names as a petty bourgeoisie becomes
evident when Hengel both acknowledges that early Christians were
not well-to-do but also asserts that they did not come primarily from
the *Lumpenproletariat* either. "The early Christians were petty bourgeois: manual workers and craftsmen, small businessmen and
workers on the land, all of whom had a great respect for honest
labour...."[25] Rostovtzeff's categorization also provides a basis for
understanding Rudolph Bultmann's location of the Pastoral Christians. Bultmann, in conscious dependence upon Dibelius, freely
refers to the Pastorals' *bürgerliche Ethik*.[26] He understands the Pastorals to belong to that stratum of developing Christianity[27] which
directs its moral reflection and paraenesis toward a decidedly limited range of issues (family, property, slavery, relation to the state):

> This is only natural because the Christian faith is in the main still
> restricted *auf die Kreise kleiner Leute oder doch des kleinen Bürgertums.*
> Their interests, it is true, already include, in addition to those of their
> own immediate circle of living, those of property and business. There
> are even slave-holders among them. But to undertake great enter-
> prises, in particular to take a responsible part in politics, is still far
> from their mind, nor have they any such ambition. They also lack any
> regard for the problems and tasks of social life.[28]

Rostovtzeff's scheme is equally helpful in understanding what
Spicq means when he construes the "bourgeois" social location of

---

[24]Martin Hengel, *Eigentum und Reichtum in der frühen Kirche* (Stuttgart:
Calwer Verlag, 1973), p. 63.

[25]Martin Hengel, *Property and Riches in the Early Church: Aspects of a Social
History of Early Christianity*, trans. of *Eigentum* by John Bowden (Philadelphia:
Fortress Press, 1974), p. 60.

[26]Rudolf Bultmann, *Theologie des Neue Testaments*, 5th ed., (Tübingen, 1965);
idem, *Theology of the New Testament*, refs. to English, 2: 114, 116, 183, 186, 226,
229.

[27]According to Bultmann, other expressions of this stage of Christianity's
development are the *Haustafeln*, the Catholic epistles, the Apocalypse, and the
Apostolic Fathers.

[28]Bultmann, *Theologie des Neue Testaments*, p. 566.

the Pastorals in more elevated terms. For him the presence of rich
people in the congregation, and the peppering of ethical exhortation
with language of *noblesse* is a function of their being members of
what Rostovtzeff calls "the higher, that is, the most civilized and
best educated, classes of the urbanized parts of the Empire," "the
propertied classes of the provincial cities," "the almost pure plutoc-
racy," "the aristocracy of landowners, and new class of rich merchants and shopkeepers." This would also appear to be the point of
Koester's naming among the grounds for a dating of the Pastorals
well into the second century the need to allow sufficient time for
"the strong growth of Christianity in the middle classes of the
cities."[29]

b. *Relational Approaches to Class*

A student of class stratification can take a different tack. Instead
of concentrating on the horizontal boundaries that separate one
class from another, one can define a particular class in terms of the
way it relates to groups above or below it. The point of such a *relational* approach to class analysis is not so much to ask: "How much
must one have to be considered rich, and how little to be poor?",
but: "How is one person's wealth conditioned by another's
poverty?" Marxist scholars like Ossowski and G.E.M. de Sainte
Croix envision a social fabric made up of two-term asymmetric
relations in which one side is privileged at the expense of the other.
Rulers, for instance, cannot be thought of apart from those who are
ruled. Nor can masters be thought of apart from slaves. Since,
however, it is at least in principle possible to think of the rich
without reference to their relation to the poor, it is not so obvious
that wealth and poverty are correlative. Nonetheless, Ossowski
argues:

> The dichotomic conception of the relation of property is in fact an
> expression of the belief that we are here concerned with real, correla-
> tive and opposed relations and not only with different ways of formu-
> lating them; and that the existence of the rich is conditioned by the
> existence of the poor and conversely.[30]

He points to a twofold basis for the notion that one person's wealth
is based on another's poverty: 1) the belief in a limited amount of

---

[29]Koester, *Introduction*, 2:305; this statement appears for the first time in the
English edition.
[30]Ossowski, *Class Structure*, pp. 31-32.

wealth (if one person owns too much, another must go without);[31] and 2) the causal connection between property ownership and the other two dimensions of stratification: political power and labor expropriation.

In this mode, class analysis can scarcely avoid the language of "conflict," "exploitation," and "domination" to describe over-and-under relationships. But if prior ethical and world view commitments peer through such relational attempts at social description, they do not prevent important emphases in the ancient sources themselves from being honored. Sainte Croix, for instance, argues convincingly that Aristotle saw the fundamental task of government to be the reconciling of the fundamentally opposed interests of the propertied and the non-propertied.[32] And Ossowski points to John Chrysostom's declaration that the root and origin of private riches was always to be found in some injustice or rapine.[33]

However, the ancient data are not entirely amenable to such a construal of the rich and poor dichotomy—that is, that the mutually conditioning relation between the two orders is necessarily one of conflict and domination. Aristotle, after all, goes about designing means whereby rich and poor can live together under a just government; and he does so by protecting the interests of the rich as well as of the poor. For example, he argues that the best compromise between the aristocratic and democratic governing principles is struck when municipal office is unpaid:

> for the poor will not want to hold office because of making nothing out of it, but rather to attend to their own affairs, while the wealthy will be able to hold office because they have no need to add to their resources from the public funds; so that the result will be that the poor will become well-off through spending their time upon their work, and the notables will not be governed by any casual persons (οἱ τυχόντες, *Politics* 1309a5-9).

---

[31]See Bruce Malina, *The New Testament World: Insights from Cultural Anthropology* (Atlanta: John Knox Press, 1981), Chapter 4, "The Perception of Limited Good," pp. 71-93, for an analysis of the biblical world's perception that wealth was a zero-sum commodity.

[32]G.E.M. de Sainte Croix, *The Class Struggle in the Ancient Greek World from the Archaic Age to the Arab Conquests* (Ithaca, NY: Cornell University Press, 1981), pp. 75f, quoting *Politics* 5. 8 (esp. 1308a3-11, 1308b25-31, 1308b34-9a9, 1309a14-32).

[33]Ossowski, *Class Structure*, p. 32, citing Homily 12 of John Chrysostom *1 Timothy*.

To be sure, Aristotle frankly accepts the existence of economic inequality, and assumes the interdependence of rich and poor—but he rejects the zero-sum proposition. Through a system of reciprocities, both sides can be winners: the poor are afforded opportunities to better themselves economically, and the wealthy are induced through the promise of honors (τιμαί) to hold office without pay (1309a14). Says he, oligarchies (rule by the rich) as well as democracies (rule by the poor) would do well to compensate their non-ruling classes by providing them with equality or precedence (ἢ ἰσότητα ἢ προεδρίαν) in all other areas of life, ἐν μὲν δήμῳ τοῖς εὐπόροις ἐν δ' ὀλιγαρχίᾳ τοῖς ἀπόροις (1309a28). Sainte Croix appreciates the problem Aristotle's ameliorative spirit presents to making him into a proto-Marxist. He says we must be satisfied with Aristotle's acute understanding of the structural defects of his society and his often astute measures for palliating the evil consequences of those defects. We must not sneer at him for not championing a radical transformation of society for the better. It is only in our own time that

> the prolonged death-throes of capitalism encourage us to look forward to a fully socialist society. For Aristotle and his contemporaries there were no prospects of fundamental change that could offer any expectation of a better life for even a citizen of a *polis*, except at the expense of others.[34]

The inveterate resolve of Marxist social analysis to refuse to allow the presence of a class that ameliorates the tension between rich and poor ever to be more than a passing thing (NB: "the prolonged death-throes of capitalism") can be a strength. For this resolve corresponds to the awareness even of non-Marxist students of antiquity that when it came to the proportions of the social scale:

> 'Verticality' is the key to the understanding of it. Great were the differences between the extremes, attenuated the middle parts. The sense of high and low pressed heavily on the consciousness of both.[35]

The tendency to view such a society as a system of asymmetrical and mutually conditioning, dichotomous relationships is true to this sense of "verticality." But an approach that makes rich and poor enemies by definition cannot take seriously the extent to which both sides may have construed their relationship to be cooperative rather than adversarial.

---

[34]Sainte Croix, *Class Struggle*, p. 76.
[35]MacMullen, *Relations*, p. 94.

When one has locked in on the problem of the exploitation of people on the lower end of a two-term relationship, one can be made positively blind to one of the most important social dynamics of the ancient world: the expressed need of social bodies to entice their superior members into the service of those beneath them for the sake of the common good. Behind Aristotle's provision of τιμαί to entice into service people who by virtue of education, birth, and wealth were worthy to lead there stood an elaborate system of the exchange of rights, prizes, and perquisites.[36] Due note should be taken of the constantly recurring inscriptional formula: "Such and such an honor is being bestowed and (perhaps more importantly) displayed in order to make it manifestly clear that such and such a municipality or association expresses gratitude to its benefactors."[37] The ubiquity of the need to express gratitude and thus attract further benefactions and new benefactors should make it apparent that something more subtle, more complex, and more reciprocal is going on here than the language of "domination" and "exploitation" would suggest.

In an interesting episode, Dio Chrysostom, a late-first-century magnate of the municipality of Prusa in Bithynia—and, incidentally, held up by Rostovtzeff as a typical bourgeois of the early Empire[38]—finds a mob at his doorstep. The grievance appears to be that Dio is withholding grain from the marketplace. In denying the charge, Dio points to the benefits he and his family have bestowed on the community, excoriating the mob for its lack of gratitude and trust. What is revealing is his threat of reprisal: withdrawal (ἀποχωρεῖν) from the city (*Oration* 46.12,13). This is not the last time Dio is to make this threat.[39] Nor, as C.P. Jones points out, is it a meaningless one:

> for the loss of a wealthy citizen meant one less benefactor for the people, and even in Dio's day this flight of the rich was beginning to disturb those who thought: in the late empire it was to become a grave problem for the emperors.[40]

---

[36]See chapter III, below, passim.

[37]E.g., Danker No. 1.25-27; No. 2.10-12; No. 4.7-10 (= *ZPE* 25 [1977]: 265-272; 274-275); No. 12.42-43 (= *SIG* 762).

[38]Rostovtzeff, *Roman History*, p. 574, n. 10.

[39]See *Oration.* 47.2,19; 49.15; esp., 50.7. References from C.P. Jones, *The Roman World of Dio Chrysostom* (Cambridge, MA: Harvard University Press, 1978), p. 139. See also Jones' discussion of the riot at Prusa, pp. 19-25.

[40]Jones, *Dio*, p. 24.

In a word, a class model that is committed to the unmasking of exploitation by social superiors is inadequate for a world in which the withdrawal of benefits would be perceived as a greater threat than exploitation. If this social world is to be understood in its own right, it will be necessary for us to allow over-and-under relationships—particularly between benefactor and beneficiary—to stand without prejudice to their inherent justice. And while grateful to the Marxist model championed by Ossowski and Sainte Croix for calling attention to the fact that the important thing about wealth is less its sheer possession than the opportunities for social power its possession bestows, we find it necessary to correct the correlative model of class by providing for the reciprocal and functional nature of such relationships.

In any event, the invitation to consider concrete over-and-under relationships is a particularly attractive one to us, for the Pastoral epistles are full of them: church leaders and everyone else in the community, God and kings, governmental leaders and their populace, God and the rich, the rich and the rest of the community. At the same time, these letters are light on the sort of data—e.g., level and source of income—that would allow the placing of anyone in a particular stratum, à la Rostovtzeff.[41]

3. Status

The mention of the provision of honors (τιμαί) to gain the community service of citizens at the upper end of the social scale leads to the third term often employed in the study of ancient social structure: status. Analytically distinct from membership in juridically and non-juridically defined groups (orders and classes), status brings into view the role social actors' quest for prestige and honor plays in the molding of social structure. It has less to do with actual membership in particular groups than with motives (e.g., self-

---

[41]Some of the super-rich of antiquity were kind enough (often eager) to leave a record of their prosperity. There was in fact a property requirement for membership in the senatorial, equestrian, and curial orders. But a perusal of Richard Duncan-Jones' exhaustive (and exhausting) work on the Roman economy (*The Economy of the Roman Empire: Quantitative Studies,* 2nd ed. [Cambridge, at the University Press, 1982]) makes it readily apparent that data available for a statistical measuring of ancient wealth and its sources are exceedingly spare, and the data that exist are at times oblique. And of course, the further down the social scale one goes the worse the problem gets. Rostovtzeff tacitly acknowledges the problem when he subtly shifts from designating class membership on the basis of wealth (senators, equestrians, the upper class bourgeoisie) to doing so on the basis of occupation (the petty bourgeoisie).

understanding and the desire for respect from others) behind actions which, in turn, do give shape to groups. The name of Max Weber is often associated with attempts to analyze ancient social structure under the rubric of status-groups rather than classes or orders.[42] It is perhaps not accidental that Weber took as the primary task of the sociologist the understanding of the goals of social actors, and that he was interested in the ways individual actors' values and ideas influenced social structure. For us, the category of status provides a way to talk about social standing: a) from the point of view of the actor's self-understanding; and b) with a view to the respect and esteem that are bestowed upon or withheld from him or her by others.

I employ status less ambitiously than do those who would attempt a calculus for measuring the various indices of status in order to posit a "generalized status" of each person, a composite of all the crisscrossing categories.[43] Nor do I believe it to be particularly promising to attempt to account for behaviors and ideas (e.g., the attraction to Christianity by people of mixed status) as means of overcoming feelings of relative deprivation and achieving "status crystallization."[44] I note Ossowski's[45] and, in his wake, Rohrbaugh's[46] criticism that the attempt to weigh the several variables in order to show how high standing in one may be at odds with low standing in another and so account for such-and-such a behavior leaves analysis at the mercy of the "predilections of the evaluating individual."[47]

---

[42]Max Weber, *Economy and Society: An Outline of Interpretive Sociology*, 2 vols., ed. by Guenther Roth and Claus Wittich (Berkeley: University Press, 1978), 1:302-307 ("Status Groups and Classes"), and 2:926-940 ("The Distribution of Power Within the Political Community: Class, Status, Party"). See also, Meeks, *Urban Christians*, p. 53.

[43]See the summary in Meeks, *Urban Christians*, pp. 54-55. He offers the following as variables that should be taken into account in such analysis: power (defined as "the capacity for achieving goals in social systems"), occupational prestige, income or wealth, education and knowledge, religious and ritual purity, family and ethnic-group position, local-community status (evaluation within some subgroup, independent of the larger society but perhaps interacting with it), *ordo*, citizenship, personal liberty, age, and sex.

[44]While Meeks is mildly friendly toward theories of status dissonance and crystallization, Gager is straightforwardly dependent upon them (*Kingdom*, pp. 37ff).

[45]Ossowski, *Class Structure*, p. 55.

[46]Rohrbaugh, "Debate," pp. 530-531.

[47]Ossowski, *Class Structure*, p. 55.

The subjectivity of the observer, in my view, is less problematic than the gap between modern and ancient societies. Theories of status dissonance and crystallization have arisen in response to the demand for a framework for understanding post-medieval Western societies.[48] But in modern societies the idea of status crystallization presupposes, among other things, a social structure that makes widescale, upward social striving possible and an ethos that makes it virtuous; in a word, it presupposes modern industrial capitalism and so-called bourgeois civilization. The theory's ability to account for social behavior in other settings is not indisputable.[49]

Instead, I use the language of "status," "honor," or "prestige" in a broad way to cover things like the difference between officially *qualifying* for admission to the senatorial order on the one hand, and *enjoying* the deference the scarlet hemmed toga attracted on the other. "Status" also covers the pride of place the senatorial "nobility" enjoyed over their senatorial peers,[50] and the willingness of municipal benefactors to pay even for the statues erected in their honor.

Finley argues, correctly I think, that status considerations go far in accounting for the difference between the ancient and the modern economy. He points to powerful social and psychological pressures against production for profit rather than for consumption—pressures having to do with the dishonor attached to certain occupations—e.g., tax collecting, moneylending, trade—and ways of dis-

---

[48]Robert K. Merton, *Social Theory and Social Structure*, 1968 enlarged ed. (New York: MacMillan, The Free Press, 1968); Baltzell, *The Protestant Establishment*.

[49]Through an intriguing discussion of several papyri, Judge warns: 1) that the actual working of status and rank (*ordo*) in Roman society remains largely unknown to us; 2) that it offers some surprises where it is in evidence (high rank, or *ordo*—e.g., curial membership—could be something to be avoided by people whose wealth gave them high status, when high rank simply meant a tax on wealth—*Rank and Status in the World of the Caesars and St. Paul* [Christchurch, NZ: University of Canterbury, 1982], pp. 14-17; see POxy 3273); and 3) that the working of status and rank should be reconstructed on the basis of an analysis of first century sources themselves (esp. the papyri), not on the basis of extrapolations from other types of societies. For a contrary opinion, see Victor Turner's analysis of status-elevating-and-reversing ritual based on central African tribal life (*The Ritual Process: Structure and Anti-Structure* [Ithaca, NY: Cornell University Press; Cornell Paperbacks Edition, 1969, 1977]), and Chapter 5 in Meeks' *Urban Christians*, where he attempts an analysis of early Christian ritual in the light of Turner's work.

[50]Finley, *Economy*, pp. 46-47.

posing of wealth.[51] He grants there was a strong drive to acquire wealth, but insists that this drive was not translated into a drive to create capital; "stated differently, the prevailing mentality was acquisitive but not productive."[52]

Peter Brown mounts a similar argument.[53] His thesis is that the early Empire was an "age of equipoise" in which social and psychological pressures on urban elites channeled potentially community-destructive drives into a community-building contest of giving. During the early Empire, urban economic activists lived under a set of values that discouraged the reinvestment of profits toward greater profitability (the *sine qua non* of modern capitalism). The same values also moderated material consumption. Instead, economic activists were encouraged to return wealth won through landowning or industry back into their communities in the form of benefactions. Further, they lived under the pressure to invest a significant portion of their time and energy (time and energy which could otherwise have been employed in the pursuit of material profit) in the oversight of municipal affairs—all of which was rewarded by various expressions of thanks and the conferring of honors. Brown argues that the competition of urban elites to outdo one another in the investment of wealth and personal energy in the welfare of their communities under the imperative of φιλοτιμία, "love of honor," acted as a governor on the ancient economy.[54]

---

[51]Finley, *Economy*, pp. 50-61. Note also the comments of Weber on the way status considerations subdued economic activism among people of high status in ancient (and medieval) society: "As to the general *effect* of the status order, only one consequence can be stated, but it is a very important one: the hindrance of the free development of the market.... From the conflict between the status order and the purely economic order..., it follows that in most instances the notion of honor peculiar to status absolutely abhors that which is essential to the market: hard bargaining. Honor abhors hard bargaining among peers and occasionally it taboos it for the members of a status group in general. Therefore, everywhere some status groups, and usually the most influential, consider almost any kind of overt participation in economic acquisition as absolutely stigmatizing.

"With some over-simplification, one might thus say that classes are stratified according to their relations to the production and acquisition of goods; whereas status groups are stratified according to the principles of the *consumption* of goods as represented by special styles of life" (Weber, *Economy*, 2:937).

[52]Finley, *Economy*, p. 144.

[53]Peter Brown, *The Making of Late Antiquity* (Cambridge, MA: Harvard University Press, 1978).

[54]Brown, *Making*, chapter 2, "An Age of Ambition," pp. 27-53.

Brown's treatment of the early imperial "age of equipoise" is largely an exegesis of a passage in Ramsay MacMullen's *Roman Social Relations*.[55] MacMullen claims that imperial civilization relied on the "sheer willingness" of its elite citizens to lavish beneficences upon their cities. Actually, this was a "willingness" that was less than "sheer," for the return on the elite person's gifts was not insignificant. If members of the elite behaved toward their inferiors out of deference and generosity, they in turn were granted the right to command:

> Ultimately, that right rested on wealth. Modern historians may be right in thinking that what made the sharp inequities in the ancient economy bearable and kept social tensions within control was the willingness of the rich to supply to their fellow citizens the good things in life unconstrained.... In the Empire, (the rich provided) the amenities of a higher civilization: public banquets, theatrical presentations, temples, and the rest. An electoral slogan painted upon a Pompeian wall tells the whole story: "The united street-neighbors urge the election of So-and-So for magistrate. He will provide a four-pair gladiatorial show." What motive in turn inspired the candidate? Simply the love of status, *Philotimia*. No word, understood to its depths, goes farther to explain the Greco-Roman achievement. So far as I know, it has yet to receive the compliment of a scholarly treatise.[56]

The promise of status, φιλοτιμία, to an analysis of early Christians' place in imperial bourgeois life is great. To mention for now but one candidate—though as likely as any—for helping to unearth the role of philotimic considerations in placing early—but especially Pastoral—Christians within this social world, there are the *Orations* of Dio Chrysostom.[57]

One area that offers provocative points of comparison and contrast between Dio and the Pastorals is their mutual concern that those who provide a service be adequately recompensed. While Dio's seventy-fifth oration is titled "Concerning Law" (περὶ νόμου), it would be more accurate to see in it an encomium on the principle of reciprocity which written law or unwritten custom codifies. One of the ways "law" protects the delicate fabric of social life is by ensuring that benefactors receive "thanks in full for the kindnesses which they show to others" (ὁ νόμος πᾶσιν ὧν ἂν εὐεργετήσωσιν

[55]Brown, *Making*, pp. 30-31.

[56]MacMullen, *Relations*, p. 125.

[57]As part of the Novum Testamentum project, G. Mussies (*Dio Chrysostom and the New Testament* [Leiden: E.J. Brill, 1972]) has assembled texts in Dio that may be profitably compared with New Testament texts.

ἑτέρους ἐκτίνει τὰς χάριτας, *Oration* 75.6). He mentions three distinct relationships within which the bestowal of benefactions establishes an obligation of thanksgiving: to parents from children (γονεῦσι παρὰ παίδων), to private benefactors from their beneficiaries (τοῖς ἰδίᾳ τινῶν εὐεργέταις παρὰ τῶν εὖ παθόντων), and to "those who love public honor" from their cities (τοῖς κοινῇ φιλοτι-μουμένοις παρὰ τῆς πόλεως). "Law," so conceived, further stipulates rewards for benefactions (τὰ ἆθλα τῶν εὐεργεσιῶν): crowns, public proclamations, and seats of honor (στεφάνους καὶ κηρύγματα καὶ προεδρίας); "law" even has the power to transform inexpensive things into valuable objects: the parsley, pine, and olive of which crowns are made, and the three words which are used in public proclamations (*Oration* 75.7-8).[58]

Though difficult to measure, status or φιλοτιμία enables us to talk about a currency that allowed the creation of social power through the investment of wealth and energy in return for honor and heightened status. By its triple use of the τιμ– root to refer to rewards for superiors or for those who have rendered a service (1 Timothy 5:3,17; 6:1),[59] as well as by its reference to the nobility of aspiration to office and the promise of the high standing that follows praiseworthy service (1 Timothy 3:1,13),[60] at least one of the Pastoral epistles promises to yield fruit to the one who asks about the role of status considerations in the shaping of social structure.

4. Summary

Notice of the fact that the Roman world was ordered according to a legal ranking system alerts us to the fact that social life was consciously hierarchical. But the ranking system was all but blind to

---

[58]H.L Crosby, the editor of this Loeb volume (and whose translation I follow when quoting Dio), notes that the crown of olive was awarded at the Olympic games, the parsley at Nemea, and the pine at the Isthmian games. Further, distinguished public service at Athens was rewarded by the olive crown (Aeschines 3.187). He surmises that the three words in question may be ἀνὴρ ἀγαθὸς ἐστί, a phrase which occurs regularly in honorific decrees. Crosby does not provide examples, but they are abundant; from Danker, for example: No. 15.13-14 (= SIG3 174), of Menelaos of Pelagonia; No. 17.26,100 (= OGI 339), of Menas of Sestos; and No. 19.1.1.32-33; 4.14.19-20 (= IGR III), of Opramoas of Rhodiapolis; see Danker's discussion, pp. 318-319.

[59]On the widows of 1 Timothy 5:3-16, see below, II.D.3.c., pp. 100ff; on the elders, II.D.3.d., pp. 106ff; on (non-Christian?) slave owners, III.B.2.e., pp. 137ff; and on all three, III.B.2.e., pp. 137ff.

[60]On the deacons' "high standing," see below, II.D.2.b.2), pp. 84f.

the "lower orders," and its legal parameters were not literally socially descriptive.

Gradational class analysis allows a partial correction of the elitism of the orders, and it can compensate for the legal definitions of rank that would have made a free but poor artisan the formal superior of a wealthy imperial slave. But gradational class analysis finds the evidence for the actual social, political, and economic situation of everyone outside the Empire's tiny literary elite to be slim. The positing of a bourgeoisie by analogy with modern society can be a misleading consequence.

Relational class analysis is independent of scarce statistics and is consonant with the dichotomous tendencies of so many of our sources (rich and poor, rulers and ruled, masters and slaves, citizens and noncitizens). But its proclivity to divide the world into winners and losers (often in league with the sources themselves) masks trade-offs and reciprocities. And it smuggles in evaluative assumptions through its language of domination, exploitation, and oppression.

Status is important in the social description of first century communities because it brings the goals of social actors into view—specifically the willingness of inferiors to bestow honors in exchange for benefits, and of superiors to invest their time and wealth in those beneath them in quest of heightened status.

Once *ordo*, class, and status have been considered, the specific venues or institutions within which people lived in quest of status as members of *ordines* or classes need to be brought into view.

C. E.A. JUDGE AND EARLY CHRISTIANITY'S SOCIAL WORLD

The Australian social historian E.A. Judge has been a catalytic, even dominant, force in the modern pursuit of the social world of the New Testament. In 1960 and 1961 he published a brief monograph[61] and two articles[62] questioning two common assumptions: 1) that modern ways of conceptualizing social reality can be casually

---

[61]E.A. Judge, *The Social Patterns of the Christian Groups in the First Century: Some Prolegomena to the Study of New Testament Ideas of Social Obligation* (London: Tyndale, 1960).

[62]E.A. Judge, "The Early Christians as a Scholastic Community," *Journal of Religious History* 1 (June 1960): 4-15; idem, "The Early Christians as a Scholastic Community, Part II," *Journal of Religious History* 3 (June 1961): 125-137.

brought to bear on the ancient world, and 2) that early Christianity was dominated by and reflected the interests of the socially dispossessed. These articles have occasioned the most significant realigning of thought about the early Christians and their social world since the beginning of the century when in his *Light from the Ancient East* Adolf Deissmann won for the assumptions their tenured status.[63]

1. *Institutional Differentiation and Client Relationships*

Judge believes it is misleading to conceive of the ancient societies within which Christianity emerged as undifferentiated wholes which can then be divided by horizontal lines of class interest. It is not that there was no stratification, but rather that the dimensions and the dynamic of stratification can be appreciated only when specific venues (he would say institutions) are taken into account. He proposes that the social world of the Hellenistic republics be conceived as a series of overlapping but not systematically related circles.[64] His "contextual description of the early churches" presupposes

> first the small republican state, which provided the effective framework of civil life for most people in the Roman Empire, repeated as it was many hundreds of times over throughout the eastern Mediterranean; secondly the far-reaching organization of life on a household basis, through which even Caesarism itself had been built up; and thirdly the unofficial associations which provided small-scale community life under religious auspices for trade or other interest groups.[65]

Though Judge does not acknowledge the debt, it is hard to miss here a dependence on the Aristotelian understanding of "man" as a threefold being—political (ζῷον πολιτικόν), familial (ζῷον οἰκονο–μικόν), and communal/associational (ζῷον κοινωνικόν).[66] In Aristotle human existence is defined in terms of community or relationship, κοινωνία. The abstract goal of community (κοινωνία) is worked out within the competing venues of republic (πολιτεία) and

[63]Adolf Deissmann, *Light from the Ancient East: The New Testament Illustrated by Recently Discovered Texts of the Graeco-Roman World*, trans. Lionel Strachan (London: Hodder and Stoughton, 1910).

[64]E.A. Judge, *Social Patterns*, p. iii.

[65]E.A. Judge, "The Social Identity of the First Christians: A Question of Method in Religious History," *Journal of Religious History* 11 (1980): 201-217, p. 202.

[66]See Finley, *Economy*, p. 152.

household (οἰκονομία). If in the πόλις human community attains its highest and most inclusive expression,[67] in the οἶκος it is experienced in a primeval and more fundamental form.[68]

Judge accounts for much of the dynamic of first century social life by an appeal to inter-institutional competition. Whereas the traditional Greek family structure was patriarchal, the democratic ideal, championing the citizen's autonomy, had sought in part to mitigate domestic despotism.[69] Athenian democracy had institutionalized various measures against nepotism: the filling of offices through the drawing of lots rather than through election; the retention of even day-to-day decisions in the popular assembly; the subsidization of citizen participation; the holding of taxation to minimal levels. But the democratic ideal was always mitigated by money and blood; that is, by reliance on the benevolence of the wealthy and by the intrusion into the political arena of family ties. The former of these factors can be seen as a function of the sentiment that the taxation of citizens was odious except in emergencies.

> Essential public works were therefore undertaken at the personal
> charges of the wealthy, the competition in honour being relied upon to
> keep the system working.[70]

Dependence on the good graces of the wealthy was in fact dependence on wealthy household heads; this brings family loyalty into play in the life of the body politic:

> Wealthy proprietors commanded the support of their economic dependents, such as the labourers who worked on their land or in their businesses, even though not held in slavery. Provided one had the means to gratify the needs of one's dependents there were practically

---

[67]Aristotle *Politics* 1252a4-7. δῆλον ὡς πᾶσαι μὲν ἀγαθοῦ τινος στοχάζονται, μάλιστα δὲ καὶ τοῦ κυριωτάτου πάντων ἡ πασῶν κυριωτάτη καὶ πάσας περιέχουσα τὰς ἄλλας· αὕτη δ᾽ ἐστὶν ἡ καλουμένη πόλις καὶ ἡ κοινωνία ἡ πολιτική. ("It is therefore evident that, while all partnerships aim at some good, the partnership that is the most supreme of all and includes all the others does so most of all, and aims at the most supreme of all goods: and this is the partnership entitled the state, the political association." English citations of Aristotle follow the Loeb translation.)

[68]Aristotle *Nichomachean Ethics* 1162a15ff. ...ἄνθρωπος γὰρ τῇ φύσει συνδυαστικὸν μᾶλλον ἢ πολιτικόν, ὅσῳ πρότερον καὶ ἀναγκαιότερον οἰκία πόλεως.... ("...since man is by nature a pairing creature even more than he is a political creature, inasmuch as the family is an earlier and more fundamental institution than the state....").

[69]Judge, *Social Patterns*, pp. 30-31.

no limits to household groupings of this sort. Family connections could be exploited for the pooling of resources, with the result that even in a democracy political affairs were frequently dominated by aristocratic coalitions whose real power was derived from their social following.[71]

Democratic ideals were precarious enough in the Greek experience; in the periods of the Roman Republic and Principate they very nearly perished. Augustus' maintenance of the fiction of republican constitutional legitimacy for the Principate in the face of his actual rule through the personal patronage of his troops and his role as *Pater Patria* over an ever extending family is a familiar phenomenon. It is, however, but the most visible expression of the way patrons exploiting personal followings for political ends had transformed democratic institutions into outlets for their own paternalism.[72] Judge argues that in the early imperial period household and republic both so fostered paternalism that where the democratic ideal thrived, it did so in unofficial, voluntary associations, or κοινωνίαι.

The defining of the right of spontaneous association had been a critical step in breaking the original family domination of Greek society.[73] The inability of the republic and the household to meet the needs of most members of the Hellenistic cities for an experience of community (κοινωνία in the abstract sense) spawned a plethora of unofficial groups. Judge understands these unofficial associations (κοινωνίαι), usually organized on the basis of occupation for the sake of mutual aid and conviviality, to have had a particularly democratic function in the Roman period. In the first place, their memberships did not derive in the main from those aristocratic circles which were preoccupied with public, political life. Rather, the associations flourished among circles that lacked access to official means of expression. And, by virtue of the fact that their charters were consistently patterned after republican constitutions, they could be conceived of as mini-republics within their host cities. This accounts for the fact that associations were often recognized as alternate bases of social power and were therefore suspected of being sources of political unrest. In the second place, their membership was voluntaristic and egalitarian in principle, as opposed to household membership and the possession of citizenship which

---

[70]Judge, *Social Patterns*, pp. 18-19.

[71]Judge, *Social Patterns*, p. 31.

[72]Judge, *Social Patterns*, pp. 38-39.

[73]Judge, *Social Patterns*, p. 40.

were based predominantly on birth. However, the voluntarism and egalitarianism of the associations knew circumscriptions similar to those experienced by the municipal republics. For unofficial associations were no less dependent on the generosity of their own rich than were the cities after which they were patterned. Just as municipal life thrived on competition among its elite members for the honor attendant upon the bestowing of benefits, so an association's life was based on the vying of its wealthier members with one another for the privilege of shouldering the costly obligations of office.

It should be clear that Judge's preference for a schematization of Roman society in terms of institutional differentiation (republic, household, and association) rather than social stratification (upper, middle, and lower class) cannot be taken for naivete about the presence or importance of inequality in the social order. His contention is that the grouping of people according to what the modern world recognizes to have been their common class interests disguises the nature of the inequality experienced by first century people themselves. Key to a proper understanding of the structure of Roman society, he asserts, is a relational mode originating in the household organization but spilling over into the political arena.

> The (Roman) republic recognized not only the sweeping powers the Roman *pater familias* enjoyed over his personal family, bond and free alike, but also the rights and duties imposed by the relationship of *clientela*. Freedmen, who had formerly been members of a household through slavery, retained their link with it, and in some respects their obligation, as its clients. Others also freely associated themselves with it for their mutual benefit. But clientship once accepted was binding. Loyalty to the household interest was expected, though the authority of the patron was grounded in his trustworthiness, which guaranteed that the material and social needs of the client's family were met.[74]

By creating vertical bonds of interest, this pervasive client structure frustrated the erection of horizontal connections of economic interest (class). Competition was experienced horizontally rather than vertically, as aristocrats competed with one another for clients, and members of lower orders competed with one another on behalf of their patrons.

Without denying the presence of economic differentiation, Judge finds it more useful to analyze society in terms of this dynamic between benefactors and their dependents and then in terms of

---

[74]Judge, *Social Patterns*, p. 31.

three institutions that vary in the degree to which they bear the marks of the client structure (the household predominantly, the republic increasingly, and the association less overtly). Rationale for doing so lies not simply in the fact that such a conceptualization allows for the description of social affinity more along the lines it would have been felt—e.g., between household heads and their dependents rather than between heads of separate households, or between dependents of different households—than a scheme of class stratification would have. Perhaps more significantly, if ironically, such a conceptualization allows the dimension of verticality to come even more into relief than a scheme of class stratification.

2. *The Social Provenance of Early Christianity*

For Judge, attention to the venue-specific nature of stratification and to the function of benefactions in the shaping of relationships serves as backdrop to a critique of attempts to explain Christianity as a movement of lower class origins.

As long as the Roman literary sources are taken as normative, he asserts, Christianity cannot help but appear to be a movement of the socially dispossessed. For to the first century literati, themselves sponsored by and reflective of the Roman senatorial and equestrian world, outside these orders there were only the poor. From the point of view of this vocal, but minuscule, segment of the population of the Roman Empire, there were but two classes of people: the aristocracy (themselves) and the masses.[75] As Judge notes, to show that Christian groups did not draw upon the upper orders of the Roman ranking system is a correct but pointless observation.[76] It is true that Rome's elite make only cameo appearances on the stage of the New Testament,[77] but that is not to say the leading parts go to country bumpkins. In point of fact, when the social world of the New Testament writers is measured by the bounds of the Hellenistic republics of the Eastern Mediterranean basin—which is the region in which the churches flourish—a picture emerges of a movement that grows precisely where it is able to win the protection and sponsorship of people who are well-situated. He marshals data at several levels to argue that these early Christian communities not only draw a significant portion of their

---

[75]See MacMullen, *Relations*, pp. 97, 187, n. 18.

[76]Judge, *Social Patterns*, p. 52.

[77]Judge, *Social Patterns*, pp. 52-53.

membership from cities' leading citizens but rely on the hospitality, leadership, and resources of their wealthy and respectable patrons.

Though he realizes the limitations of prosopography in the reconstruction of a social history of the movement, Judge nonetheless appeals to Paul's own elevated background as an index of the way the movement depends on the leadership of people of stature and substance.[78] Judge points to the combination of the apostle's classical Jewish education and his standing in republican society (as citizen of both Tarsus and Rome). This unusually well balanced set of social qualifications makes it a matter of little surprise when he is found to "move freely in the best circles," surrounded by a significant retinue,[79] in the manner of a sophistic teacher.[80]

Paul's constant sensitivity to the humiliatiqns he suffers (1 Corinthians 4:13) and his offering of his own life as a lesson in humility (1 Corinthians 4:16; 11:1) receive their poignancy from the social snobbery to which he feels himself entitled and which Luke portrays him as freely showing (Acts 21:39; 22:28—Judge might well have mentioned Philippians 3:4-6). Further, Judge claims that Paul's decision to support himself through manual labor has more to do with the establishment of a point of honor than with any actual need for income (1 Corinthians 9:24; 2 Corinthians 11:8; 12:13; Acts 20:33-35).[81]

He calls attention to the importance of wealthy household heads to the Pauline mission. According to Judge, the household becomes an institution vital to the mission when it becomes apparent that Paul's attempt to minister as a rabbi out of the Hellenistic Jewish synagogues is doomed—when it becomes clear that his principle of a gospel for the Jew first and then the Greek is going to have to be more a theological ideal than a practical reality.[82] He argues that the

---

[78]Judge, *Social Patterns*, pp. 57-58.

[79]Judge, "Scholastic II," pp. 131-134; he numbers at approximately forty the known persons who at one time or another populate Paul's "international touring company."

[80]Judge, "Scholastic II," pp. 125-126.

[81]Judge, *Social Patterns*, p. 58.

[82]Judge, "Scholastic II," pp. 126-128. Judge draws his scenario chiefly from Acts. The first missionary journey is made under the sponsorship of the church at Syrian Antioch, and uses local synagogues as its base. Although he gains popular support, the mission runs into difficulty when Jewish leaders are able to marshal local notabilities against him. Because he takes the synagogue as his platform and relies on his status as a rabbi, he establishes no independent standing in the communities. Therefore when the Jews reject him, the urban elites are persuaded to act against him. For his part, Paul allows himself to be

constant traveling evidenced in the Pauline mission, involving the sending of delegations and individuals, presupposes wealthy hosts and sponsors: "They all belong together as persons of substance, members of a cultivated social elite...'devout and honourable' citizens of the Hellenistic states."[83] Judge emphasizes the fact that it is private individuals not churches as organizations that maintain his tours.[84] Small wonder, he claims, that Paul's letters contain lengthy passages insisting on the maintenance of household order, while they have little to say about the conduct of the church's government or worship.[85]

Because the Corinthian situation is generally considered to be paradigmatic of the lower class origins of New Testament Christianity, Judge's remarks about the composition of this group are particularly striking. It is significant for our interest in the make-up of the Pastoral communities that Judge believes the data to belie the usual view of the poverty of the Corinthians. The group is socially pretentious, riddled with snobbery and divisions: "debates, envyings, wraths, strifes, backbitings, whisperings, swellings, tumults" (2 Corinthians 12:20).[86] They have been courted not only by the mercurial Paul, but also by the impressive Alexandrian theologian, Apollos, and others. In addition, the group has been entertained by a number of generous patrons: Stephanas, who earns a reputation as a benefactor of the Christians (1 Corinthians 1:16; 16:15); Phoebe, the διάκονος τῆς ἐκκλησίας and προστάτις of many,

---

victimized without appealing to his special status as a Roman citizen. The second missionary journey marks a significant shift in strategy. He establishes platforms in the homes of the very urban elites who had previously been rallied against him. Now when the Jews reject him he still has a communal base of support. Judge points to the conversion of Lydia and her household and the subsequent acceptance of the hospitality she offers as the pivotal point. From this point, Paul's mission takes on the patronage of eminent persons, under whose auspices he preaches. Also at this point Paul begins to protect the mission by adding to his posture as a Jewish rabbi an appeal to his status as a Roman citizen and therefore as one of the social elite of the Hellenistic states.

[83]Judge, "Scholastic II," pp. 128-130. In his sketch of Paul's sponsors, Judge relies less on Acts and more on the letters, chiefly Romans 16 and 1 Corinthians, passim.

[84]Judge, "Scholastic II," p. 128.

[85]Judge, "Scholastic II," p. 131.

[86]Judge, *Social Patterns*, pp. 47, 59, citing their factious supporting of rival leaders (1 Corinthians 1:12); their lawsuits against one another in the public courts (6:7); the poisoning of their common meal by selfishness (11:21); the splitting of the group by social discrimination (12:23); their reluctance to support one another financially (16:1).

64   *Wealth and Beneficence in the Pastorals*

including the apostle himself (Romans 16:1,2); Gaius, who was Paul's own host at the writing of the epistle to the Romans (Romans 16:23); and Erastus, the church member who was also οἰκονόμος τῆς πόλεως (Romans 16:23).[87] Says Judge:

> Far from suggesting anything else, the overworked exclamation "not many wise..., not many mighty, not many noble, are called" (1 Corinthians 1:26) plainly admits this situation.[88]

At face value the exclamation merely implies the group did not contain many intellectuals, politicians, or persons of gentle birth; but it simultaneously appears to assume that the group did at least draw upon this minority to some extent. The passage, however,

> is hardly intended as a factual statement. Properly evaluated as a piece of impassioned rhetoric, it leaves no doubt that in their own opinion, and presumably also in that of their contemporaries, they were anything but a collection of unintelligent nonentities. Paul in fact states this later. "Now ye are full, now ye are rich, ye have reigned as kings without us....We are fools..., but ye are wise...; we are weak, but ye are strong; ye are honourable, but we are despised" (1 Corinthians 4: 8,10).[89]

His purpose is to disabuse them of the idea that their status in Christ has anything to do with the position they enjoy on other grounds. Paul's deeply ironic apostolic self-humiliation should be a lesson to them precisely because it is an appeal to join him in the renunciation of that pride of place which being wise, mighty, and noble naturally bring. Judge generalizes from the Corinthian situation:

> Far from being a socially depressed group, then, if the Corinthians are at all typical, the Christians were dominated by a socially pretentious section of the population of the big cities. Beyond that they seem to have drawn on a broad constituency, probably representing the household dependents of the leading members.... The interests brought together in this way probably marked the Christians off from the other unofficial associations, which were generally socially and economically as homogeneous as possible. Certainly the phenomenon led to constant differences among the Christians themselves, and helps to explain the persistent stress on not using membership in an association of equals to justify breaking down the conventional hierarchy of the household (e.g., 1 Cor. 7:20-24). The interest of the owner and

---

[87]Judge, "Scholastic II," pp. 128-130.
[88]Judge, *Social Patterns*, p. 59.
[89]Judge, *Social Patterns*, p. 59.

patron class is obvious in this. It was they who sponsored Christianity to their dependents.[90]

In sum, he asserts that the Christian communities directly reflect the diverse social constituencies of their cities, and do so not only in terms of who is in the community, but also in the dynamic of relationships within the community. In particular, he posits the relationship between patrons and dependents, or between benefactors and beneficiaries, as being as important to the rise of Christianity in the Hellenistic cities as it is constitutive of political and social life within the cities themselves. He is careful to avoid the language of upper, middle, or lower class, and is content instead to argue that the movement was dominated "from above." If the socially well-placed persons upon whom the movement was dependent cannot be named among the Roman elite, this is not to exclude them from local, provincial elites. Further, some conflicts within the early Christian movement can be traced to a tension built into its diverse social make-up; for the movement is an association (κοινωνία) of equals that is simultaneously accepting of the conventional hierarchy of the household (οἰκονομία).

Though he does note that the household becomes a theological motif in 1 Timothy (along with Ephesians),[91] Judge has little to say about the Pastoral epistles.[92] Of some note, though, is the fact that he takes the bishop list (1 Timothy 3:2-7) and the instructions to the rich (1 Timothy 6:17-19) as warnings against pressing his conclusions about the social provenance of early Christians. Social eminence is not listed as a qualification for office, nor does the insistence upon the duties of the rich seem particularly sympathetic to them. But, he maintains, these later possible qualifications do not destroy the general impression

> that in the most distinguished period of his mission Paul depended heavily upon the hospitality and sponsorship of a select circle of patrons. They provided him with his platform.[93]

---

[90] Judge, *Social Patterns*, p. 60.

[91] Judge, "Scholastic II," p. 131, citing 1 Timothy 3:15 and Ephesians 2:19.

[92] A classicist rather than a New Testament specialist, he simply accepts, for the sake of argument, all the canonical letters claiming Pauline authorship, as well as their conventional datings. He does maintain that his main points would be unaffected if inauthenticity were to be shown for some ("Scholastic II," p. 137, n. 17).

[93] Judge, "Scholastic II," p. 131.

We shall be interested in exploring whether data from the Pastorals require such a caveat to the overall portrait, or whether, to the contrary, they offer confirmation of it.

3. Reaction to and Use of Judge

a. Use of Acts

Against Judge, Robin Scroggs warns that the historical unreliability of the Acts disqualifies them for use in reconstructing the Pauline ministry.[94] Malherbe consistently maintains that it is especially with regard to the social make-up of the Pauline movement that Luke's account, which has "a recognized tendency to describe Christianity as 'middle class,'" not be used.[95]

Of Judge's sketch of Paul the sophist, Meeks says, it "is bold and impressionistic, based more on the account in Acts than on evidence from the letters, and ignores critical questions about both kinds of sources."[96] Meeks would rather see more attention be paid to the pictures the letters themselves present of "a less grand and public mission."[97] At the same time, he grants that there is agreement between Acts and the letters in giving an impression that: "The families and houses of certain individuals seem to have been starting points, and connections of work and trade seem to have been important."[98] Still, Meeks credits Judge with "imbibing somewhat more of the skepticism that characterizes the discipline" as he has mastered specialized New Testament scholarship over time.[99]

In point of fact, the later Judge does appear to be more careful to separate the various strands of literature about the Pauline movement.[100] But twenty years after using Acts to unfold Paul's style of

---

[94]Robin Scroggs, "The Sociological Interpretation of the New Testament: The Present State of Research," *New Testament Studies* 26 (1980): 164-179, pp. 169-171.

[95]Abraham J. Malherbe, *Social Aspects*, p. 30; idem, "'Not in a Corner': Early Christian Apologetic in Acts 26:26" *The Second Century* 5:4 (1985/1986): 193-210, p. 196; idem, *Paul and the Thessalonians: The Philosophic Tradition of Pastoral Care* (Philadelphia: Fortress Press, 1987), pp. 16-17.

[96]Meeks, *Urban Christians*, p. 82; cf. p. 223, nn. 46-48, 51.

[97]Meeks, *Urban Christians*, p. 28.

[98]Meeks, *Urban Christians*, p. 28.

[99]Meeks, *Urban Christians*, p. 204, n. 122.

[100]See, for instance, his "Moral Terms in the Eulogistic Tradition," in *New Documents Illustrating Early Christianity: A Review of the Greek Inscriptions and Papyri Published in 1977*, ed., G.H.R. Horsley (N. Ryde, Australia: Macquarie

ministry, Judge appears to be unreconstructed in his defense of Luke's accuracy in his "record of the legal, administrative and social background of the Hellenistic and of the superimposed Roman world."[101] All the same, Judge continues, the view he champions— that of a significantly higher social level for the Pauline churches— could be argued from the evidence of the Pauline letters alone and does not depend upon the Acts material being trustworthy.[102]

b. Corinth as Paradigm

In a series of essays published in the mid-70s and translated by John Schütz in the early 80s, Gerd Theissen has demonstrated that the main contours of Judge's description can be borne out from the letters themselves—or at least from the Corinthian correspondence. His analysis is much more detailed and methodologically self-conscious, but the case he makes is at significant points like Judge's. Marshalling evidence from across a range of indices—prosopography,[103] mention of households,[104] services rendered,[105] travel,[106] divisions within the church[107]—Theissen concludes that Paul's

---

University, 1982), pp. 105-106. Here Judge recognizes that terms from the Hellenistic eulogistic tradition (e.g., εὐ– and φιλ– compounds—see ch. III, below) are far more likely to show up in the Acts and in the Pastorals than in the Pauline homologoumena.

[101]Judge, "Social Identity," p. 208, here quoting J.J. Nicholls' review (*Journal of Religious History* 1 [1964]: 92-95) of A.N. Sherwin-White's *Roman Society and Roman Law in the New Testament*.

[102]Judge, "Social Identity," p. 208.

[103]Theissen, *Social Setting*, pp. 69-119; especially noteworthy is his thorough exploration of the identity of Erastus, οἰκονόμος τῆς πόλεως (perhaps *quaestor*, eventually to become *aedile*); see also Meeks, *Urban Christians*, pp. 55-63.

[104]Theissen, *Social Setting*, pp. 83-87, arguing that οἶκοι like those of Crispus (Acts 18:8) and Stephanas (1 Corinthians 1:16; cf. 16:15ff.) probably include slaves.

[105]Theissen, *Social Setting*, pp. 87-91.

[106]Theissen, *Social Setting*, pp. 91-92.

[107]Theissen, *Social Setting*, pp. 96-99. He maintains that the groupings which emerge around the Lord's Supper betray a dichotomization between rich and poor (1 Corinthians 11, see pp. 96, 145-174), as do the dispute over the eating of meat (1 Corinthians 8, 10, see pp. 121-143), Paul's refusal to accept support (1 Corinthians 9:1ff; 2 Corinthians 10-13, see pp. 27-67, 96-97), litigation among Christians (1 Corinthians 6:1-11), and even the debate over "wisdom" (arguing in this case, and most precariously, from history-of-religions observations about proclivities for "saving knowledge" among more educated classes; with pp. 97-98 compare pp. 198-199, n. 30, on attempts at understanding the social location of later Gnosticism).

68   *Wealth and Beneficence in the Pastorals*

Christianity was neither a proletarian nor an upper class movement. "On the contrary, what is characteristic for its social structure is the fact that it encompassed various strata—and thus various interests, customs, and assumptions."[108]

With respect to 1 Corinthians 1:26-29, he says:

> It can only be concluded that the phrase "not many" doesn't mean very much. In 1 Cor. 1:26ff. Paul does not wish to contest the significance of those congregational members from the upper classes but simply objects to their all-too-well-developed consciousness of their own status. Naturally, he is right. These representatives of the upper classes were a minority within the congregation, but apparently a dominant minority. At the very least, several members of the Corinthian congregation who appear to be very active may be counted in their group.[109]

With Judge, he concludes that what set the Christians apart was their bringing together within the same fellowship people who were bound to see life differently. He appears to be less inclined than Judge to assume that people of lower status in the church are there simply as members of the retinue or household of people of high status.[110] Thus he stresses more vigorously perhaps the fact that the churches represented a cross-section of society than is the impres-

---

[108]Theissen, *Social Setting*, p. 106.

[109]Theissen, *Social Setting*, p. 73. Note also the articles by W. Wuellner ("The Sociological Implications of 1 Corinthians 1:26-28 Reconsidered," *Studia Evangelica*, 4, vol. 112 of *Texte und Untersuchungen* [Berlin, 1973]:666-672; and "Ursprung und Verwendung der σοφος-, δυνατος-, εὐγενης- Formel in 1 Kor. 1, 26," in *Donum Gentilicium: New Testament Studies in Honour of David Daube*, ed. E. Bammel et al. [Oxford, at the Clarendon Press, 1978], pp. 165-184), who, though quite unlike Theissen, argues that these verses make no sociological statement, nonetheless registers his opinion that whether the Corinthians "did, or did not, belong to low social and cultural circles is as hard to prove for Corinth as for any other Pauline community. I would rather suspect that, inferences drawn from archaeological sources notwithstanding, the Corinthian Christians came by and large from fairly well-to-do bourgeois circles with a fair percentage also from upper class people as well as the very poor. But to use 1 Cor. 1:26-29 as the most important text in the whole New Testament for allegations of Christianity's proletarian origins is indefensible and no longer tenable simply and chiefly on grammatical grounds" ("Sociological Implications," p. 672). His grammatical argument is that the ὅτι of 1:26 is interrogative and sets up a question that should be answered in the affirmative: "Look at your calling—are not many of you...?".

[110]Theissen, *Social Setting*, p. 98, noting that 1 Corinthians 7:8ff indicates some Christians live in the homes of pagans and that the Christian congregation is therefore not simply the union of several households.

sion one derives from Judge. The latter is anxious to press home his contention that it was the socially powerful minority who—as sponsors and disputants—set the tone of the church. So successful is Judge that he draws from Scroggs the charge that by allowing the presence of a wealthy minority to change, in effect, the social location of the community as a whole, he engages in elitism.[111] Judge's response is that, while the process Paul et al., initiated was by the fourth century to result in a type of common culture more socially pervasive that Hellenism had been:

> The important point is that the movement, in social class terms, is downward rather than upward. The number of those who think and argue about ethical questions is being expanded, but this does not come from below. It is the work of highly articulate people with social influence. [112]

This is merely to repeat what Theissen has already granted: that the movers and the shakers in the Corinthian church—alongside whom Paul himself, apart from his apostolic self-humiliation, must be named—did not come from the ranks of the "low born" and the social "nobodies." This also, despite the fact that Theissen postures himself as mediating the proletarian position of Deissmann and the elitist view of Judge.[113] Schütz's observation is a sage one:

> E.A. Judge has canvassed the evidence for early Christians in such diverse locations as Jerusalem, Antioch, and Corinth, concluding that they represent a diverse mixture with clear contributions from those who are relatively well off. His judgment about Corinth could even be taken as the text which Theissen...(in his essays on Corinth)...unfolds in greater detail: "Far from being a socially depressed group, then, if the Corinthians are at all typical, the Christians were dominated by a socially pretentious section of the population of the big cities. Beyond that, they seem to have drawn on a broad constituency, probably representing the household dependents of the leading members."[114]

c. A New Consensus?

With the publication in 1977 of the first edition of his *Social Aspects of Early Christianity*, Malherbe put the ideas (though not

---

[111]Scroggs, *Interpretation*, p. 171.
[112]Scroggs, *Interpretation*, p. 171.
[113]Theissen, *Social Setting*, p. 69.
[114]From Schütz's introduction to Theissen, *Social Setting*, p. 5, and citing Judge, *Social Patterns*, p. 60.

uncritically)[115] of Judge and Theissen before an American reader-ship. Though his own interests have moved in the direction of gaining a clearer vision of first century Christianity's relation to philosophical schools,[116] he states his agreement with Judge and Theissen that upper strata people were a dominant minority in the church at Corinth.[117] He even suggests that "a new consensus" may be emerging that the social status of first century Christians may have been higher than previously thought (e.g., by Deissmann et al.). And it is a consensus that he defends in the second edition against Gager who appears to attribute to the Judge (and Malherbe) position the claim that the majority of Christians were from the upper strata. In a manner that anticipates Scroggs' objection, Gager asserts:

> No one, for instance, denies that *some* believers were educated and stood relatively high in the social hierarchy of their local towns and cities. But what ought to concern us is not the few but the majority and thus the character of the movement as a whole.[118]

Malherbe follows Judge's lead in insisting that there is no access to "the character of the movement as a whole" apart from

> those persons from the relatively higher social strata who wrote the documents which constitute our primary access to the communities, and who figured importantly in the communities themselves.[119]

The work of R.F. Hock, a student of Malherbe, forces a significant caveat to Judge's work. Focusing on Paul's tentmaking, Hock asserts that Paul consciously chooses not to adopt the professional philosopher's position under the protection of patrons. Instead, he chooses to support himself through his work, and that not as a hold-over from his rabbinical background, but as one of a number of strategies available to philosopher-teachers who desire to impress

[115]Malherbe, *Social Aspects*, pp. 45, 56, 73 n. 27, 75, 76, 80 n. 41, 118-119.

[116]See, for example, his articles "Cynics," and "Epictetus," in *Interpreter's Dictionary of the Bible*, Supplementary Volume, pp. 201-203, 271; the volume of Cynic epistles published under his oversight, *The Cynic Epistles: A Study Edition*, Society of Biblical Literature Sources for Biblical Study, no. 12 (Missoula, MT: Scholars Press, 1977); *Moral Exhortation, A Greco-Roman Sourcebook* (Philadelphia: The Westminster Press, 1986); and *Paul and the Thessalonians*.

[117]Malherbe, *Social Aspects*, pp. 29ff, 72.

[118]John G. Gager, "Shall We Marry Our Enemies?: Sociology and the New Testament," *Interpretation* 36 (1982): 256-265, p. 262.

[119]Malherbe, *Social Aspects*, 2nd ed., p. 121.

upon their students the pattern of life appropriate to their social station.[120] In one sense, Hock stands Judge on his head by arguing that it is the teachers with whom Paul is in dispute, rather than Paul himself, who accept the hospitality and patronage of wealthy household heads.[121] In another sense, Hock's challenge to Judge's sophistic, salon-model for Paul's teaching venue in the interest of a Cynic-like, workplace-model supports the overall picture of a congregation that feels the weight of its wealthy. As Hock says:

> To those of wealth and power, the appearance (σχῆμα) of the artisan was that befitting a slave (δουλοπρεπές).
> It is no wonder then that Paul thought it necessary to defend his practice of supporting himself by his work at a trade (1 Cor. 9:1-27) and that the dominant theme of this defense was whether he was free or slavish (vv. 1,19). To Corinthians who, relative to Paul, appeared to be rich, wise, powerful, and respected (cf. 4:8,10), their lowly apostle had seemed to have enslaved himself with his plying a trade (cf. 9:19).[122]

Indeed, Judge expresses gratitude for Hock's corrections, averring that the "new consensus" is hardly put in jeopardy by them, for:

> The status opportunities Paul declined remain the measure of his potential professional standing, and of the expectation of his supporters for him. The extent of his renunciation helps to explain Paul's intense consciousness of debasement. He was stepping firmly down in the world.[123]

In his study on the Thessalonian correspondence, Malherbe portrays a congregation of a more modest social background. Carefully distinguishing Christian self-sufficiency and brotherly love from Cynic meddlesomeness on the one hand and from Epicurean utilitarianism on the other, Paul articulates a work ethic apposite, Malherbe contends, to a lower class congregation. The quiet pursuit of labor with one's hands without interference in other people's business is a style of life that would be deemed appropriate to someone with an artisan's social status.[124]

---

[120]Ronald F. Hock, *The Social Context of Ministry: Tentmaking and Apostleship* (Philadelphia: Fortress Press, 1980).

[121]Hock, *Social Context*, esp., pp. 37, 65.

[122]Hock, *Social Context*, p. 60, and note the discussion in Theissen, *Social Setting*, pp. 27-67.

[123]Judge, "Social Identity," p. 214.

[124]1 Thessalonians 4:11-12; see Malherbe, *Paul and the Thessalonians*, p. 106.

Nonetheless, Malherbe carefully notes what a comedown his own manual labor among the Thessalonians is for Paul, who is not himself from the working class:

> Paul's decision to engage in manual labor was a sacrifice, for he did not belong to the working class. The reference to his work in this context (1 Thessalonians 2:9) therefore reveals another understanding of his manual labor: it demonstrated how Paul was prepared to give up his social status in order to identify with manual laborers.[125]

The brevity of the Thessalonian correspondence (especially if critical scruples do not permit appeal to 2 Thessalonians)[126] makes conclusions about the social level of Thessalonian Christians risky. It is difficult to contest Malherbe's reading, for he is quite right when he notes that 1 Thessalonians gives no evidence of social stratification in the community—then again, we may never have learned about it in Corinth either if it had not become such an acute problem and (at least in part) occasioned such an extensive correspondence. The possibilities are at least twofold: 1) it may be that one church is richer and the other poorer—that is certainly the way Paul portrays things to the Corinthians when he appeals to the generosity of the impoverished Macedonians as a reason why the Corinthians should be especially generous (2 Corinthians 8:1-2), and it could account for Paul's manual labor apparently being perfectly acceptable in Thessalonica but such an offense in Corinth. Alternatively, or perhaps even additionally: 2) it may be that the brevity of 1 Thessalonians masks a social make-up that is every bit as textured as Corinth's, with the other side of the tale being told in Acts.[127]

---

[125]Malherbe, *Paul and the Thessalonians*, pp. 55-56; he further notes that Paul's attitude toward his labor is reflected by the fact that he lists it in a series of hardships (1 Corinthians 4:12) and that he regards it as servile (1 Corinthians 9:19) and an act of abasement (2 Corinthians 11:7).

[126]And, according to Hock (*Social Context*, pp. 11-12, 17)—upon whom Malherbe is dependent for Paul's view of labor—it is important not to appeal to 2 Thessalonians precisely because of its high and therefore deutero-Pauline view of labor (esp. 3:10).

[127]Framing a suitable rapprochement between the epistles and the Acts would seem to be an especially worthy enterprise when it comes to the material on Thessalonica. For as Malherbe notes, Luke goes out of his way to show local luminaries in this church (Acts 17:4, prominent women; 17:5-9, a generous host named Jason), and makes Paul's ministry there victim to a conspiracy between marketplace good-for-nothings and Jews jealous of Paul's success among the well-to-do (17:5). In the end, the pictures may be complementary, for if

d. The Church and Analogous Institutions

Judge's depiction of the social landscape of early Christianity as being dominated by the social facts of republic (πολιτεία), household (οἰκονομία), and association (κοινωνία) has proven to be fruitful. Though Meeks corrects Judge for making too much of the academic and too little of the cultic side of Paul's congregations, he credits him for calling upon known institutions as bases for comparison. And while his own comparison of Paul's churches with analogous institutions departs from Judge's in excluding the republic while adding the synagogue and the philosophical school, he comes back to the two that are most basic to Judge as well: the household and the association.[128]

Meeks also notes that Judge calls attention to the pervasive but seldom-mentioned importance of *amicitia* and *clientela* in Roman society. But the texture of relationships as conditioned by cultural

---

Malherbe's analysis about the fine line Paul has to walk in distinguishing the way of Christ from the schools of the Cynics, the Stoics, and the Epicureans is valid, I cannot help but think Paul is presupposing no small amount of sophistication from *someone* in his readership. What Malherbe does not address in this study, as opposed to his earlier *Social Aspects* (pp. 35-59), is the relevance of literary and educational level to overall social level. What literary and social level must be presupposed if this group of "manual laborers" is supposed to be able to follow the subtleties of Paul's social ethics?

This is not even to mention the broader sociological implications (most of which are still to be developed) of studies of the rhetorical dimension of Paul's letters—see especially the work of G. Kennedy (*New Testament Interpretation through Rhetorical Criticism* [Chapel Hill, NC: The University of North Carolina Press, 1984]) and H.D. Betz (*Der Apostel Paulus und die sokratische Tradition: Eine exegetische Untersuchung zu seiner "Apologie" 2 Korinther 10-13* [Tübingen: J.C.B. Mohr (Paul Siebeck), 1972]; idem, *Galatians: A Commentary on Paul's Letter to the Churches of Galatia* [Philadelphia: Fortress Press, 1979]). Meeks also notes that at least the leaders of the Pauline circle apparently were acquainted with major topics current in Hellenistic moral discourse and with some aspects of the style of that discourse (*Urban Christians*, p. 83).

[128]See Meeks, *Urban Christians*, pp. 75-84. He lays out Judge's thesis that Paul's communities were not cultic but "scholastic" in nature, pursuing an "intellectual mission" in ways that often resembled a "debating society." After examining the extent to which the Pythagorean and Epicurean schools resembled Pauline communities, he concludes they did so just to the extent they took the form of modified households or voluntary associations. It is useful to know, he allows, that there was a strong scholarly, academic, and rhetorical element in the activities of the Pauline groups, but we cannot make those elements constitutive of the movement. Judge far too quickly rejects the cultic association as an analogy for Paul's groups (see Meeks' chapter on ritual, pp. 140-163).

notions of obligation, reciprocity, and the like, appears to be a field of study as yet relatively unexcavated.[129] One should think that it would be increasingly desirable to move beyond structural descriptions of institutions that parallel Christian communities and attempt to engage the inner workings and "feel" of venues within which structured relationships occur.

e. Conclusions

At the heart of Judge's analysis lies the observation that Pauline Christianity as a whole marks an ecological shift from rural Palestine to the urban Mediterranean basin.[130] If it is still impossible to locate early Christians among Rome's elite in the early days of the Pauline movement, at least it should be impossible to leave them languishing among the Empire's dispossessed either. The hint lies in the title to Meeks' study of the social world of the seven acknowledged letters: *The First Urban Christians*. If by "bourgeoisie" is meant that wide spectrum of urban inhabitants of the Eastern Mediterranean basin which falls somewhere between the social extremes, it ought to be recognized that this group provides the constituency of Paul's churches all along. In this mundane and virtually meaningless sense, from day one the Pauline movement is a "bourgeois" phenomenon.

More to the point, however, is the contention that the Pauline movement as a whole contains within itself the acute stratification that in general marks municipal society, and this by virtue of the dominating—if minoritarian—representation of people well-placed in that society. This is true even before the Pastoral epistles are brought into the equation. To the extent that the so-called "new consensus" is valid—and I happen to find it persuasive—serious difficulties are posed for maintaining that the distinctives of the Pastorals have to be accounted for on the basis of a post-Pauline rise

---

[129]Significant exceptions to this statement are: J. Paul Sampley, *Pauline Partnership in Christ: Christian Community and Commitment in Light of Roman Law* (Philadelphia: Fortress Press, 1980); Peter Marshall, *Enmity in Corinth: Social Conventions in Paul's Relations with the Corinthians* (Tübingen: J.C.B. Mohr [Paul Siebeck], 1987); and the use to which Victor P. Furnish puts Marshall's study in his own *II Corinthians: Translated with Introduction, Notes, and Commentary*, Anchor Bible, vol. 32A (Garden City, NY: Doubleday and Co., 1984).

[130]See Judge, *Social Patterns*, pp. 7-17; the important essay by Sainte Croix, "Early Christian Attitudes to Property and Slavery," *Studies in Church History*, vol. 12, *Church, Society and Politics*, ed. Derek Baker (Oxford: Basil Blackwood, 1975), pp. 1-38; *Class Struggle*, pp. 425-441; and Theissen *Social Setting*, pp. 27-67.

into the "middle classes." Not that it means very much, but Pauline Christianity is already there from its inception. In the next section, we attempt to come to grips with what is distinctive about the social contours of Pastoral Christianity.

I share, finally, Judge's sense that some conflicts within early Christian communities may have resulted from competing understandings of social reality; it will be my argument that, at least in part, such is the case in the Pastoral epistles, and that it had to do with the rights and responsibilities of the very patrons or benefactors on whom Judge says the Pauline movement was so dependent. In fact, it so happens that a significant motif for describing the structure of social life in the Pastorals is that of the household. One of the studies we shall take up at length is based upon this insight. Another takes as its point of departure a comparison between the church and Hellenistic associations (κοινωνίαι).

D. PASTORAL CHRISTIANITY: THE PRESENCE OF THE RICH AND THE SHAPE OF THE COMMUNITY

Because my own understanding of the Pastorals' social make-up and dynamic has been worked out in conversation with these two recent studies, they shall serve as our point of entry into the letters themselves.

1. L. William Countryman

The centerpiece of L. William Countryman's study of rich people in the early church is a comparison between Clement of Alexandria and Cyprian of Carthage.[131] However, as part of his preliminary survey of canonical and early patristic literature he takes note of the Pastoral epistles and makes some intriguing suggestions about their social composition and about conflicts rooted in that make-up. Three aspects of his comments about the Pastorals are of significance to us.

a. The Danger of the Rich to the Church

In the first place he believes the letters evidence concern for the present and potential danger of the rich Christian to the church. He

---

[131]L. William Countryman, *The Rich Christian in the Church of the Early Empire: Contradictions and Accommodations* (New York and Toronto: The Edwin Mellen Press, 1980).

calls attention to the two passages that had been Spicq's central focus: the women of 1 Timothy 2:9 and the rich people of 1 Timothy 6:17-19.[132] The reason the women come under discussion early in the epistle is that they are considered to be a disruptive force in the church's worship. The highlighting of their "braided hair, gold, pearls, and costly attire" betrays the grounds of their ability to exert an inordinate amount of influence: their ostentatious wealth.[133] That the subject of the threat of the wealthy remains prominent in the author's mind is signaled by the fact that the exhortation to the rich (6:17-19) stands in emphatic position, just before the final salutation. Having dealt with the problem of insubordination and its attendant heresies, the author of 1 Timothy gives as his final word the proper role of rich Christians in the church: to support the church generously. It is their office not to compete with properly constituted authorities, but to give alms.[134]

b. The Church as Association (κοινωνία)

Second, Countryman appeals to an analogy between the church and the Roman or Greek club (κοινωνία) in order to account for the ability of the wealthy Christian to mount a threat to the leadership of the church. Like associations, the church was a voluntary society organized for purposes of worship and fellowship. And though the church was working out a distinctive pattern of leadership, it shared enough with the associations to have been influenced by them in its expectations of newcomers.[135] Like wealthy club members, for instance, rich Christians would expect (and be expected) to act as benefactors by opening their homes to the church in hospitality, and by donating generously of their wealth and time. However, once he accepts the analogy, Countryman focuses on several negative points of comparison. For example, unlike their non-church contemporaries, rich Christians would not be able to specify the use of their

---

[132]Spicq, *Pastorales*, pp. 293 n. 3, 424-425; and cf. I.C.2., pp. 25ff, above. Heinz Kreissig ("Zur sozialen Zusammensetzung der frühchristlichen Gemeinden im ersten Jahrhundert u.Z.," *Eirene* 6 [1967]: 91-100) highlights these two passages in his attempt to portray early Christianity as being a non-proletarian movement.

[133]Countryman, *Rich Christian*, p. 153.

[134]Countryman, *Rich Christian*, p. 154.

[135]Countryman relies on Robert L. Wilken, "Collegia, Philosophical Schools, and Theology," in *Early Church History: The Roman Empire as the Setting of Primitive Christianity*, ed. Stephen Benko and John J. O'Rourke (London: Oliphants, 1971), pp. 268-291.

gifts, nor would they almost automatically become leaders of the church by virtue of their beneficence, nor could they expect the sort of honors their benefactions would ordinarily return—e.g., honorific titles (like *patronus* or εὐεργέτης), birthday celebrations in their honor, crowns, inscriptions, statues.[136]

c. Buttressing the Leadership, Co-opting the Rich

Thus, in the third place, Countryman suggests the Pastoral epistles are written to buttress the position of apostolic emissaries whose authority—because it is spiritual and extra-local—is being challenged by wealthy, local Christians who are asserting their natural expectations of being afforded honors and influence commensurate with their gifts.[137] Analogous to the situation in the Pastorals is that in 1 Clement, where socially powerful newcomers have challenged the institutional order.[138] The strategy is twofold: 1) to head off the attack frontally by specifying who is to be honored in the church: the ministry (1 Timothy 5:17);[139] and 2) paradoxically, to show the local elites how they can in fact eventually gain the influence they desire: by conforming to the citizenship ideal of the Hellenistic πόλις.

> In the Pastorals, the intent was clearly to co-opt such men into the clergy. The proper candidate for bishop is a *paterfamilias*, a householder whose conduct is well-known to be hospitable, sober and restrained and who has shown the ability to keep a family under control (1 Timothy 3:2-7; Titus 1:5-9). When such men were ordained, the local elite and the clergy would become identical.[140]

And in light of the similar requirements for deacons (1 Timothy 3:12f) he says: "all ranks of ministers are expected to display the virtues appropriate to prosperous householders; they are to be drawn from among the elite of the church."[141]

---

[136]Countryman, *Rich Christian*, pp. 164-165.

[137]Countryman, *Rich Christian*, pp. 152-153.

[138]See Countryman, *Rich Christian*, pp. 154-157 for the comparison with 1 Clement. He is taking the νέοι of 1 Clement 3:3 as "new to the faith" rather than literally "young."

[139]Countryman, *Rich Christian*, p. 174, n. 1.

[140]Countryman, *Rich Christian*, p. 167.

[141]Countryman, *Rich Christian*, p. 181, n. 42.

2. David C. Verner

a. The Church as Household (οἰκονομία)

While Countryman appeals to the club-life of antiquity to illu-
mine the social dynamic and structure of this community, David C.
Verner appeals to the classical household. His point of departure is
the Pastorals' own central motif, the household of God. In this, he
honors 1 Timothy's telic statement, that the purpose for the writing
of this epistle and perhaps the Pastorals as a corpus is to promote
right behavior in the household of God (γράφω … ἵνα εἰδῇς πῶς δεῖ
ἐν οἴκῳ θεοῦ ἀναστρέφεσθαι, 3:14f). Specifically, he understands
the *Haustafeln* of the Pastorals to be a schematic adaptation and
development of the classical topos: περὶ τῆς οἰκονομίας.

1) Development of the Haustafeln

The context for his interest in the household topos is the sticky
issue of the literary genesis of the *Haustafeln*. In fact, his monograph
is valuable for its contribution to this discussion if for nothing
else.[142]

Weidinger, a student of Dibelius, had seen the *Haustafeln* as
being superficially Christianized versions of Stoic duty lists, which
themselves were dependent on an unwritten, traditional code of
laws from ancient Greece.[143]

James Crouch accepted the rootedness of the *Haustafeln* in the
ἄγραφοι νόμοι of the popular Greek and Roman world as reflected
in the Stoic duty lists.[144] But he noticed an important difference
between the biblical *Haustafeln* and the Stoic duty lists. The duty
lists spoke to the way individuals were to conduct their affairs,
especially with their inferiors. But the *Haustafeln* addressed the way
groups of people (especially wives, children, and slaves) were to
relate to other groups (husbands, parents, and masters). He
accounted for the transition by hypothesizing the mediation of
Hellenistic Judaism; the contribution of Jews who had adapted the
Greek duty lists was to introduce a strong note of reciprocity into
the duties and to lump wives, children and slaves together in a

---

[142]Verner, *Household of God*, pp. 13-25, 83-125.

[143]K. Weidinger, *Die Haustafeln: Ein Stück urchristlicher Paränese* (UNT 14:
Leipzig, 1928).

[144]James E. Crouch, *The Origin and Intention of the Colossian Haustafel*
(Göttingen: Vandenhoeck and Ruprecht, 1972).

consistent fashion. The latter feature led Crouch to focus on the patterned form of the *Haustafeln*; consequently his characteristic designation for them is a "schema." Further, he rejected Dibelius' contention that the introduction of the *Haustafeln* into early Christian paraenesis had been a function of waning eschatological expectation. Rather, it was a conservative response to a widespread brand of Christian enthusiasm that defied established social convention, especially in the case of wives and slaves. One implication of Crouch's account of the origin of the *Haustafeln* was to downplay the importance of the household itself to the schema.

David Balch realized the Greek and Roman world offered another candidate for prototype of the Christian *Haustafeln*, one that had the dual advantage of being group-oriented from the outset as well as being able to take the household setting with utmost seriousness.[145] This was the topos on household management (περὶ τῆς οἰκονομίας), appearing as early as Plato and Aristotle and playing an important part in philosophical and moralistic discourse at least through the fourth century of the common era.[146]

The topos ordinarily addressed four dimensions of household life: the master/slave relationship (δεσποτική), the husband/wife relationship (γαμική), the parent/child relationship (τεκνοποιητική), and the art of getting wealth (χρηματιστική). Furthermore, the topos repeatedly occurred in discussions concerning the state (πόλις, πολιτεία), often reflecting the conviction that since the οἶκος was the foundation of the πόλις, the proper management of households was a matter of fundamental political and social significance.[147] Because of the tie between οἶκος and πόλις, Balch found, the topos on household management tended to appear either as *propaganda* on behalf of political establishments to encourage good citizenship or as *apology* by minority groups, especially religious minority groups, who were suspected of undermining the estab-

---

[145]David L. Balch, *Let Wives Be Submissive: The Domestic Code in 1 Peter* (Chico, CA: Scholars Press, 1981).

[146]Verner, *Household of God*, p. 20; see also Balch, *Let Wives,* pp. 33-62; Aristotle *Politics* 1253b1-14, says Balch, is the most important parallel to the New Testament codes; for an important avenue of Aristotle's influence on social and ethical thinking in the early Roman Empire, see the *Epitome* of his thought written by Caesar Augustus' friend, the Stoic Areius Didymus; Balch translates a portion of it (pp. 41-42) and conveniently includes cross-references to Aristotle.

[147]Note Judge's discussion of the interrelation between οἶκος and πόλις, *Social Patterns*, pp. 30-39; and see II.B.1., pp. 38f, above.

lished political order.[148] In the case of 1 Peter (the focus of Balch's study), the topos is put to an apologetic use because Christians have been alleged by outsiders to be promoting deviant behavior in households.[149] Balch differed from Crouch in stressing the topos (content) over the schema (form), as well as in positing the source of tension to have been external to the community.

2) Verner's Reconstruction for the Pastorals

In his literary analysis of the *Haustafeln* of the Pastorals, Verner weaves together strands from Crouch and Balch into an account of how one of the most developed of the Christian *Haustafeln* came about.[150] With the latter he favors viewing the classical household topos as being the material antecedent. With both he agrees that the form of this paraenesis is not so stereotyped and general as to preclude its use to address live issues in a coherent and deliberate fashion. And though he does note that part of what is at stake is the estimation of outsiders, he agrees with Crouch that the occasion for the use of the *Haustafeln* has more to do with conflicts within the community. But unlike Crouch he believes the stress on domestic life is not accidental; within the bounds of the developing Christian schema, the author is shaping the traditional topos in such a way as to assert the legitimacy of the hierarchical social structure of the church in the face of a rebellion against the domestic values that buttress this hierarchy.

The distinctive argument of the Pastorals, in Verner's reconstruction, is that the church should be so patterned after the household as to require a transferral of governing principles directly from domestic into ecclesiastical life. And the distinctive role of the Pastorals in the history of the development of the *Haustafeln* is to extend the material logic of the ἄρχειν/ἄρχεσθαι relations beyond the administration of discrete family units. A new form is created— Verner calls it a station code schema—in which the logic of the household topos is applied to various relationships within the community—e.g., between older men and younger men, and between the rich and the rest of the community—the most straightforward of which is Titus 2:1-10 and the most extensive, 1 Timothy 2-6.[151]

---

[148]Balch, *Let Wives*, pp. 63-80.

[149]Balch, *Let Wives*, pp. 81-116.

[150]Verner, *Household of God*, pp. 83-107.

[151]Verner, *Household of God*, pp. 90-91.

3) The Role of the Household Management Motifs, and the Primacy of γαμική

The motifs of the household topos emerge in the Pastorals with varying emphasis. Apposite, for example, to the normal appearance of the household management topos in the context of the discussion of the larger πολιτεία is the appearance of instructions to pray for governmental authorities and to be submissive to them as well (1 Timothy 2:1ff and Titus 3:1).[152]

Though it may be alluded to in the instructions to the rich, Verner contends, the art of getting wealth is not directly discussed in the Pastorals. Despite the fact that the instructions to the rich in 1 Timothy 6:17-19 may be an adaptation of the motif, "the negative evaluation of wealth...runs directly counter to what one would expect based on, for example, Aristotle's discussion of property and wealth in *Politics* (1256a.1ff)."[153]

Relations between parents and children receive more focus: the qualification that a church officer have believing children; the need for the church properly to manage and instruct younger men and women; and the responsibility of younger family members to care for their elders (1 Timothy 3:4,12; Titus 1:6; 2:1-8; 1 Timothy 5:1-2,4,8,16). Relations between masters and slaves also come up for direct discussion (1 Timothy 6:1-2; Titus 2:9).[154]

But the motif that receives by far the most attention, and is therefore most likely to be the center of controversy, is that concerning relations between husband and wife, or, as expanded into the life of the church, between men and women (especially 1 Timothy 2:11-12). The Pastorals vigorously affirm matronly virtues, particularly those of submission and motherhood (on the emphasis on silence for women, see Aristotle *Politics* 1260a30: "Silence (σιγή) gives grace to a woman"). In fact, Verner argues that a perceived need to reestablish proper rule in the home and between the sexes (γαμική) is the driving force behind these letters: the "false teachers" are having their greatest impact among women and are "upsetting households" (2 Timothy 3:6-7; Titus 1:11); women themselves are teaching (1 Timothy 2:11-15); "false" teaching involves a prohibition of marriage (1 Timothy 4:3), which if the evidence from

---

[152]Verner, *Household of God*, p. 92.
[153]Verner, *Household of God*, p. 92.
[154]Verner, *Household of God*, p. 91.

the Acts of Paul and Thecla is any indication,[155] amounts to a rebellion against the traditionally subordinate role of women in the household and in society; marriageable women are in fact rejecting marriage, to the chagrin of the author (1 Timothy 5:11-15). Thus, Verner's analysis turns on the conclusion that the decisive and the most controverted form of stratification in the Pastorals is that of gender.[156]

b. Other Indices of Stratification

Besides clues from the *Haustafeln*/station code material, other indices of stratification are present. Verner acknowledges the difficulty of finding criteria by which to measure the social station of the Pastoral Christians according to contemporary standards. He notes something we have seen before: those who would have been acknowledged as being upper class (senators, equestrians, and decurians) were a tiny segment of the empire's population, and everyone else would have been considered lower class. Because he accepts a second century dating for the Pastorals, his noting of the official distinction in this century between *honestiores* and *humiliores* is significant. He would appear to number most of the Pastoral Christians among the latter, noting at the same time that this group exhibited great social diversity.[157] This is not remarkable. What is of note is that he all but places the church's leadership in the order

---

[155]This apocryphal narrative generates from Asia Minor in the mid-second century, but probably preserves older traditions—text in *Acta apostolorum apocrypha* 1: 235-269; translation in Edgar Hennecke, *New Testament Apocrypha*, vol. 2, *Writings Related to the Apostles; Apocalypses and Related Subjects*, ed. Wilhelm Schneemelcher, trans. ed. R. McL. Wilson (Philadelphia: Fortress Press, 1965), pp. 353-364. In it "Paul" preaches against marriage on the grounds that one must abstain from sexual intercourse in order to participate in the resurrection (ch. 11). In simultaneous obedience to Paul's preaching and rebellion against the traditionally subordinate role of women, Thecla refuses to marry her betrothed. Condemned to death for her insubordination, she miraculously escapes and sets off to find Paul and follow him (ch. 20). In the process she symbolically appropriates maleness by donning men's clothing (ch. 40) and by declaring her wish to cut her hair, though from the latter she is restrained by the apostle (ch. 25). Paul, who plays much the supporting role in this narrative, finally commissions her to teach (ch. 40), and this only after she baptizes herself during a confrontation with wild beasts in a public arena (ch. 34). See Verner, *Household of God*, pp. 177-178; Wayne Meeks' "The Image of the Androgyne: Some Uses of a Symbol in Earliest Christianity," *History of Religions* 13 (1974), p. 196; and the instructive parallels drawn by D.R. MacDonald, *Legend*.

[156]See esp. Verner, *Household of God*, pp. 175-180.

[157]Verner, *Household of God*, p. 53.

of the decurionate, though probably because of his attention to gender-based rather than economic or political stratification, he is not clear on this location.

1) Household Heads as Officers

A critical piece of evidence indicating that church officers are from the higher strata of their cities is the requirement that deacons govern both their children and their own households well (τέκνων καλῶς προϊστάμενοι καὶ τῶν ἰδίων οἴκων, 1 Timothy 3:12). Unless the special mention of καὶ τῶν ἰδίων is superfluous, the phrasing indicates that not only wives and children are considered to be a part of the household, but slaves as well.[158] Housing accommodating more than a nuclear family would have been available only to the wealthy.[159] Slaves themselves were expensive to buy and maintain, with slaveholders probably making up no more than twenty-five percent of any of the Empire's large urban centers.[160] Thus, he asserts, the Pastorals' assumption that officers in 1 Timothy 3:12 (and by extension other passages in which officers are assumed to be household heads) would be slave owners "in itself locates these householders in the higher social strata of the Asian cities."[161]

---

[158]Verner, *Household of God*, p. 133. See also Theissen, *Social Setting*, pp. 83-87; and above, II.C.3.b., p. 67. In addition, Bartchy, *Slavery*, pp. 59-60, and Kreissig, "Zur sozialen Zusammensetzung."

[159]Verner, *Household of God*, pp. 57-60, summarizes work based on archaeological evidence from residential housing in Ostia outside Rome (James E. Packer, "Housing and Population in Imperial Ostia and Rome," JRS 57 [1967]: 80-95; and *The Insulae of Imperial Ostia*, Memoirs of the American Academy of Rome 31 [1971]) and in Ephesus (A.G. McKay, *Houses, Villas and Palaces in the Roman World* [Ithaca: Cornell University Press, 1975]).

[160]Verner, *Household of God*, p. 61. It was common to value slaves (unskilled males), according to Duncan-Jones (*Quantitative Studies*, p. 348), at 2,000 sesterces—or, calculates Keith Hopkins, as much as would support an average peasant family for four years (*Conquerors and Slaves: Sociological Studies in Roman History*, [New York: Cambridge University Press, 1978], 1:110), or, following MacMullen's reckoning, better than a year's salary for the highest paid of rank and file Roman soldiers (*Relations*, p. 94—cf., Verner, *Household of God*, p. 61). And skilled slaves could cost significantly more—note the wide range in Appendix 10, "Prices of Slaves in Rome and Italy," in Duncan-Jones, pp. 348ff. Thomas Wiedemann includes several helpful documents in his collection of texts on slavery (*Slavery*, pp. 104-105, 109-110, 126-127).

[161]Verner, *Household of God*, p. 133.

2) *Church Office as Parallel with Civic Office*

This high social station supplies the nuanced sense in which the office of overseer is a καλὸν ἔργον: a charitable deed performed on behalf of someone less fortunate than oneself. It will be recalled that Spicq referred to the bishopric as a *noblesse oblige.* Such an understanding of the responsibility not only fits the way the language of "good works" functions in the Jesus tradition; it also fits "the general concept of public office that one commonly finds in the Hellenistic municipalities, namely, that office holding is a public service to be undertaken by the (comparatively) well-to-do."[162] This social station and this concept of office also account for the fact that the deacon who serves well is promised the attainment of a καλὸν βαθμόν, that is, a "noble rank" or "high standing."[163] Present is "an outlook in which office is viewed as community service undertaken by the well-to-do, whose prestige is thereby enhanced."[164]

---

[162]Verner, *Household of God,* p. 151, in partial dependence on Jeremias, *Timotheus,* p. 40.

[163]Verner, *Household of God,* p. 155. Commentators note other possible contexts of meaning. Clement of Alexandria uses βαθμόν to refer to "gnosis" as one stage in the soul's journey into heaven (*Stromata* 2.45.4, Stählin); the Corpus Hermeticum uses it similarly (13.9). So intended, the term here would refer to a promise of spiritual progress, or a closer relationship with God which deacons may attain through their service (note a similar idea in Hermas *Mandate* 4.4.2, of the person who foregoes marriage after losing a mate, and thus "gains for himself more exceeding honour and great glory with the Lord" [περισσοτέραν ἑαυτῷ τιμὴν καὶ μεγάλην δόξαν περιποιεῖται προς τὸν κύριον]). In later ecclesiastical writings, the term βαθμόν comes to be used of actual rank in the church (*Apost. Const.* 8.22). If the term is so meant here, the idea would be that those who pass the test as deacons would be eligible for the higher rank of overseer—a phrase in Hadrian's *Sentences* is sometimes cited as a parallel: ἐὰν καλὸς στρατιώτης γενῇ, τρίτῃ βαθμῷ δυνήσῃ εἰς πραιτώριον μεταβῆναι, "if you are a good soldier, on the third promotion you will be able to change over to the Praetorium." The former interpretation strikes many as being unnecessarily esoteric for the Pastorals (e.g., Fee, p. 52) or at least too abrupt for this context (e.g., Kelly, p. 85). The latter (adopted, for example, by Lock and Barrett) presupposes an ordering between or among the offices that cannot otherwise be substantiated in the Pastorals. Though other commentators do not see the connection with civic virtue that Verner does, many do agree that the author of the Pastorals is referring more straightforwardly to "high standing," "good reputation," or "heightened prestige" that will result from service in the church (e.g., Dibelius, Spicq, Kelly, Fee). Indeed, this understanding does answer nicely to the outlook of *noblesse oblige* that the encouragement to aspirants for the episcopate introduces in 3:1.

[164]Verner, *Household of God,* pp. 155-156.

His summary comments about the church's leadership are worth quoting at some length:

> It thus appears that the governing group in the church of the Pastorals was something of an aristocracy in relation to the general membership. In this respect this church exhibits the same social structure which Judge and Theissen have found in the first generation Pauline churches, where the leading figures in the churches appear to have been well-to-do householders who brought their dependents into the church with them.
>
> ...The author appears to speak for his church in regarding office in the church as socially prestigious in the same way that citizens of Greek cities and members of associations regarded office holding (1 Timothy 3:1,13). One undertook office as a socially prominent member of one's community in order to fulfill one's civic duties. The social rewards were increased recognition and further enhanced social standing. *Thus, although the leaders of the church may not have been on the same social level as the members of their municipal aristocracy, they shared the same aristocratic social aspirations within a smaller sphere.*[165]

3) Wealthy Women

He similarly places wealthy women. At one point he argues that it is not the wealth of the women in 1 Timothy 2 that is a problem in the community, since the denunciation of wealthy women's dress was a common Hellenistic topos.[166] The problem is that by assuming the role of teachers—especially teachers of ethical exhortation—they are committing insubordination, violating their τάγμα.[167] At another point, however, he says the women "who wore elaborate hair styles, expensive jewelry and fine clothes must have belonged either to the social stratum of the municipal aristocracies, or to that of the aspirants to these aristocracies."[168] Verner does not explain what sort of distinction he has in mind between members of the local aristocracy and aspirants to it. In a departure from the imprecise way in which he normally uses the term, perhaps he intends here to limit the phrase "local aristocracy" to those of the curial order, for which there was a property qualification (standard was 100,000 sesterces—i.e., one-tenth the

---

[165]Verner, *Household of God,* pp. 159-160, emphasis mine.
[166]Juvenal, *Sat.* 6.492; Petronius, *Sat.* 67.
[167]Verner, *Household of God,* pp. 168-169.
[168]Verner, *Household of God,* p. 180.

minimum of a Roman senator),[169] and from which the members of
local councils were elected. "Aspirants," then, would apparently be
those not quite, but potentially qualifying for membership in this
ordo. One recalls Rostovtzeff's characterization of the plutocratic
"upper bourgeoisie" which drew from those just beneath themselves. MacMullen notes that among the kind of people who were
likely to earn (or buy) their way into the curial order of a large
provincial city were retiring military officers, whose savings and
mustering out bonuses could put them among such cities' wealth-
iest.[170] He also cites Callistratus to the effect that "those who deal in
goods and sell them, though they may be scourged by the *aediles*,
must not be scorned as low persons. Indeed, it is not forbidden for
people of this sort to seek the decurionate or some magistracy in
their city; for they are not dishonored" (*Digest* 50.2.12).[171]

4) Attitude Toward Slave Owners and the Rich

Other indications that the community enjoys the presence of the
socially advantaged are the attitudes taken toward slave owners and
the wealthy. He points out that Christian slave owners are protected from the potentially leveling effect of being thought of as
"brothers" by their slaves. Instead, slaves are to continue according
them the status due benefactors (1 Timothy 6:2).[172] And he maintains that while the entrepreneurial, would-be rich are emphatically
condemned (1 Timothy 6:6-10), those who are already rich are
granted tacit approval (1 Timothy 6:17-19).[173] While the former are
given a lesson in the necessity of αὐτάρκεια, the latter are encouraged to a liberality and generosity which would make their wealth
serviceable to the community and win them a reward in the life to
come. In fact, though Verner does not quite spell it out, it would
appear that there are more than casual links between three prominent groups in this community: the leadership (1 Timothy 3:1-13;
Titus 1:5-9), Christian slave owners (1 Timothy 6:2), and the rich in
this world (1 Timothy 6:17-19).

---

[169]MacMullen, *Relations*, p. 90; Duncan-Jones, *Quantitative*, pp. 243, 304.
[170]MacMullen, *Relations*, p. 108.
[171]Cited in MacMullen, *Relations*, p. 99.
[172]This passage will occupy us at length below, III.B.3., pp. 140ff. For now, see Verner, *Household of God*, pp. 140-145.
[173]On this distinction, see Verner, *Household of God*, pp. 174-175, and below, II.D.3.b.2), pp. 93ff.

5) Function of the Letters: To Conserve an Aristocratic Order in the Name of Aristocratic Values

Although Verner is careful to point out that high social position is never advanced as a prerequisite for office, always appearing simply as its assumption, there is also a prescriptive dimension to the use of the household image. For the function of the epistles, in defining the church as a hierarchically ordered household, is, first, to solidify the leadership positions of wealthy, slave owning family heads over the church, and second, to freeze the social stations of everyone else, especially women, slaves, and the would-be rich. The church as Verner's author would envision it is one in which contemporary values of prosperity and propriety reign. These are conservative, aristocratic social values associated with the leadership circles in the municipalities of the Hellenistic-Roman world.[174]

3. Evaluation of the Data

The Pastorals do appear to presuppose the presence, in fact, the significant presence of rich people. How weighty this presence is—particularly whether it signals the emergence of Spicq's "Christian bourgeoisie"—is still to be seen.

a. Linguistic Milieu: The Eulogistic Tradition

Broader considerations of the linguistic milieu of these epistles support Verner's claim that they advance values associated with the leadership circles of the Hellenistic-Roman cities. Early in our analysis we noted Dibelius' contention that a prime mark of the *bürgerlich* nature of the Pastorals is the fact that their ethical language comes from the world of the honorific inscriptions and the Hellenistic moralists.[175] This is a point worth underlining. For, according to C. Panagopoulos, when taken together the honorific inscriptions and the moralists

> paint a social and moral portrait of a certain historic type of individual, that comprising the dominant class in the Greek cities of the empire, which has been referred to for a long time since Rostovtzeff as a "bourgeoisie of the cities," but which is more exactly to be designated as a class of "leading citizens" (*notables*), according to recent remarks of M.I. Finley, since they derive from their landed property the mate-

---

[174]Verner, *Household of God*, pp. 182-183.

[175]Dibelius/Conzelmann, *The Pastoral Epistles*, pp. 39-40, and see above, I.C.1.a., pp. 12ff.

rial of their wealth, their power, and even, one may say, of their moral values.[176]

From the inscriptions, Panagopoulos argues, may be derived a set of rubrics which form a lexical grid corresponding to the leading citizens' idea of the type of humanity appropriate to themselves and the image they wanted to perpetuate.[177] The inscriptions are especially valuable because of their great number, their distribution throughout the Greek-speaking world, the particular and concrete circumstances under which they were written, and their public, non-idiosyncratic nature.[178] They thus provide a homogeneous corpus for studying the values important to the municipal aristocracies (Rostovtzeff's bourgeoisie). Panagopoulos himself uses the inscriptional rubrics as a background against which to read Plutarch's *Moralia*.[179] And Danker's collection of benefactor documents—mostly honorific inscriptions—should be seen as an attempt to give specificity to a semantic field vital to understanding certain New Testament motifs—especially, he notes, motifs surfacing in the Pastoral epistles.[180]

Contemporary moralists complement the inscriptional evidence not only by expanding the data base, but by allowing a darker side to come into view. By their very nature honorific inscriptions

---

[176]C. Panagopoulos, "Vocabulaire et mentalité dans les *Moralia* de Plutarque," *Dialogues d'histoire ancienne* 5 (1977): 197-235, p. 197.

[177]Panagopoulos, "Vocabulaire," p. 199. Following are the rubrics with which Panagopoulos works: 1) Good citizenship (εὐβουλία); 2) Noble birth (εὐγένεια); 3) The praise of wealth but not of the love of money (εὐεργεσία, not φιλαργυρία); 4) Love of glory (φιλοδοξία or φιλοτιμία); 5) Good morals (ἔθος); 6) Family spirit (φιλοστοργία); 7) Meekness (πραότης); 8) Courage (ἀνδρεία); 9) Justice (δικαιοσύνη); 10) Intellectual qualities (παιδεία); and 11) Excellence (ἄριστος, ἄμεμπτος, ἀνέγκλητος, ἀνεπίληπτος, ἐξαιρέτως, διαφερόντως, ἀπροσίτως).

[178]Panagopoulos, "Vocabulaire," p. 198.

[179]Koester tells us that Plutarch (along with Dio Chrysostom and Lucian of Samosata) is one of those popular philosophers who must be distinguished from the philosophers of the marketplace by virtue of their comprehensive education, erudition, literary activity, advocacy of the Greek educational tradition, championing of propriety and morality in the name of philosophy, and their attempt primarily "to influence the comparatively broad middle class of the cities" (*Introduction* 1:358, with discussion of Plutarch, pp. 359-361). We have already noted that Koester cites the circulation of Pastoral Christianity within this sort of a middle class as an indication of its late date (*Introduction* 2:305).

[180]See Danker, *Benefactor*, pp. 28-29 on the value of the inscriptions as a data base for New Testament study due to their archival and public nature.

praise. Moralists often warn, even excoriate. They themselves are often leading citizens of their cities; indeed, Rostovtzeff makes of Plutarch and Dio principal spokesmen for the bourgeoisie of the early second century.[181] And they pass along to us invaluable (sometimes unconscious) insights into the failures of the system. We have already had occasion to mention Dio's ugly confrontation with citizens who think one of their benefactors has bilked them (*Oration* 46).[182] Dio's encouragement to the angry crowd to approach someone else in the city who has qualified for but not yet served in a municipal post answers nicely to other indications that the celebrated flight of the curial class in the second and third centuries had roots in the first.[183] In fact, his later Bithynian speeches show how embroiled in litigation and discord a leading citizen could get, as Dio's own resolve to complete a portico promised to his hometown is contested.[184]

Plutarch, too, demonstrates the gap between the social ideals of the inscriptions and the reality behind them. "The masses," he says, "are more hostile to a rich man who does not give them a share of his private possessions than to a poor man who steals from the public funds" (*Moralia* 822A).[185] And benefactors who insist on making expenditures toward things "useful and moderate"—like public buildings—rather than toward the wild exhibitions the populace so often demands, may very well find themselves being criticized for doing such menial things as overseeing the measuring of tiles and the delivery of stones (*Moralia* 811B-C).[186] So great is the pressure on people of means to spend on public benefactions that Plutarch claims to know of people who bankrupt themselves by foolishly borrowing to finance their gifts, "so that it is not reputation or power, but rather shame and contempt (μὴ δόξαν...μηδ' ἰσχὺν ἀλλὰ μᾶλλον αἰσχύνην καὶ καταφρόνησιν), which they acquire by such expenditures" (*Moralia* 822DE).

He denounces a poverty of spirit among the wealthy that has led to a sort of commercialism polluting the classical ideal of φιλοτιμία,

[181]Rostovtzeff, *Roman Empire*, pp. 125f, 589f, n. 32.

[182]See above, II.B.2.b., p. 49.

[183]Peter Garnsey, "Aspects of the Decline of the Urban Aristocracy in the Empire," *Aufstieg und Niedergang der römischen Welt* 2.1 (1974): 229-252.

[184]*Orations* 40-51 are addresses Dio delivers in the context of local political life. See the discussion on Dio's benefactions in Jones, *Dio*, pp. 104-114.

[185]See Hands, *Charities*, p. 41. (English citations of Plutarch follow the Loeb translation.)

[186]Jones, *Dio*, p. 112, Rostovtzeff, *Roman Empire*, p. 590, n. 32.

and leading in his day to the mere "purchase of reputation by great expenditures" (*Moralia* 822A).[187] The masses (ὄχλοι or οἱ πολλοί) gladly "grant an ephemeral and uncertain reputation" (ἐφήμερόν τινα καὶ ἀβέβαιον δόξαν) when they have been given "theatrical performances...distributions of money...gladiatorial shows...(which) are like harlots' flatteries, since the masses always smile upon him who gives to them and does them favours." But once the initial wave of applause washes over them, benefactors so honored "suddenly give a sigh, as their appetite for glory subsides, leaving behind mere love of money" (ὑπονοστεῖ ἡ φιλοδοξία εἰς τὴν φιλαρ-γυρίαν, 556D). Among the wealthy what appears to be a healthy sort of ambition, "love of honor" (φιλοτιμία), often masks sheer "love of gain" (φιλοκέρδεια, 819F), "love of wealth" (φιλοπλουτία, 819E, 793E, and the essay on the subject, 523C-528B), or "love of money" (φιλοχρηματία, 819E; or φιλαργυρία, 556D, 523E).

Even so, the moralists largely confirm the ideal portrayed in the inscriptions. And the places at which Plutarch, for instance, over-laps the Pastorals provide strong hints that similar audiences are in view. Formally, the Pastorals share with the language of public eulogies for leading citizens a taste for compounds with φιλ– and the use of the ἀ– privative.[188]

Particularly striking is the use of attributes of meekness and gentleness (πραότης, ἐπιεικής) in Plutarch: 1) as a prime virtue to be learned from public life (*Moralia* 468EF); and 2) as the best means by which a city's leading citizens can win the docility (ἡσυχία καὶ πραότης) of the lower classes (*Moralia* 144E, 78B, 823F).[189] It will be recalled that it is in the Pastorals that a special premium is placed on the meekness and gentleness of the leaders (1 Timothy 3:3, ἐπιεικής; 1 Timothy 6:11, πραϋπαθία; 2 Timothy 2:25, πραΰτης) with a view to

---

[187]Panagopoulos, "Vocabulaire," pp. 205-209.

[188]Observed by Judge, "Moral Terms," p. 106. A passage in Plutarch illustra-tive of the piling up of φιλ– compounds is *Moralia* 793E, where he uses ἡ φιλοτιμία, τὸ φιλόπρωτον, τὸ φίλαρχον, τὸ φιλόπλουτον, τὸ φιλήδονον. Examples of the Pastorals' penchant for this feature (not necessarily paralleled in Plutarch) are φιλάγαθος, ἀφιλάγαθος (Titus 1:8; 2 Timothy 3:3; cf. *Moralia* 141AB); φίλανδρος (Titus 2:4); φιλανθρωπία (Titus 3:4; cf. *Moralia* 796E); φιλαργυρία, φιλάργυρος, ἀφιλάργυρος (1 Timothy 3:3; cf. *Moralia* 556D, 523E); φίλαυτος (2 Timothy 3:2; cf. *Moralia* 471D); φιλήδονος (2 Timothy 3:4; cf. *Moralia* 793E); φιλόθεος (2 Timothy 3:4); φιλόξενος (1 Timothy 3:2; Titus 1:8); φιλότεκνον (Titus 2:4).

[189]Panagopoulos, "Vocabulaire," p. 218.

encouraging gentleness and meekness within the community at large (Titus 3:2, ἐπιεικής καὶ πραΰτης).[190]

The eulogistic setting also sheds light on the seemingly mundane terms that appear as qualifications for office in the Pastorals: ἀνέγκλητος, ἀνεπίλημπτος (1 Timothy 3:2; Titus 1:6-7). As Panagopoulos notes, such terms stem from the ideal of moral excellence (ἀρετή) and signify little in themselves, only that a person fully answers to the criteria called for by a task. The terms are rather more significant in the frequency of their occurrence in eulogistic contexts, marking "the self-satisfaction which the dominant class enjoys."[191] The point is that the language that distinguishes the Pastorals within the New Testament is precisely that which the inscriptions and moralists employ to shape the civic virtue of urban notables. It is not unlikely that this fact is an accurate reflection of the epistles' audience.

b. Use of the Household Topos

Beyond considerations of the broader linguistic milieu, the way the household topos is used in the Pastorals suggests the dominating presence of rich people. Despite Verner's caveats that the connection to the broader πόλις is absent and that the theme of money-making is all but missing, his thesis that behind the Christian *Haustafeln* stands the classical teaching about household administration is plausible. This is not necessarily to suggest that our author has read Aristotle or the Roman Stoics among whom the ideas circulated. For, as can be illustrated in Philo, the topos had already found its way into ethical reflection among Jews.[192] The

---

[190]See the note by E.A. Judge ("πραΰτης," *New Documents Illustrating Early Christianity: A Review of the Greek Inscriptions and Papyri published in 1979*, ed. G.H.R. Horsley [N. Ryde, Australia: Macquarie University, 1987], pp.169-170) on the convergence in the New Testament of the classical tradition of gentleness and the Old Testament tradition of humility.

[191]Panagopoulos, "Vocabulaire," p. 231.

[192]Philo *Decalogue* 165-167: "In the fifth commandment on honouring parents we have a suggestion of many necessary laws drawn up to deal with the relations of old to young, rulers to subjects, benefactors to benefitted, slaves to masters. For parents belong to the superior class of the above mentioned parts, that which comprises seniors, rulers, benefactors and masters, while children occupy the lower position with juniors, subjects, receivers of benefits and slaves. And there are many other instructions given, to the young on courtesy to the old, to the old on taking care of the young, to subjects on obeying their rulers, to rulers on promoting the welfare of their subjects, to recipients of benefits on requiting them with gratitude, to those who have given of their own

ideas and concerns of the topos seem to have had wide enough currency to allow us to assume that they comprised part of the intellectual environment of Mediterranean municipalities—ideas therefore with which the urban church would almost have had to come to terms. The supposition of its use in the Pastorals does give *prima facie* validity to the thesis that the primary contemporary model for church life is the household—at least for our author. At the same time, the very fact that the rules of the household are having to be explicitly extended to apply to ecclesiological life—and this in the face of contrary understandings about the shape of the church's life—suggests there is a conflict over models. Countryman's thesis that the church is like a κοινωνία could well correspond to the perception of the opponents.

Less clear is why Verner feels his caveat about money-making to be necessary. In that the Pastorals include no discussion of the proper way to make a living as in Aristotle *Politics* (1256a1ff), Verner is right: χρηματιστική is not there. Verner does acknowledge that the advice to the rich may take the place of the money-making motif, but leaves it at that. By contrast, Countryman cites the penultimate position of this pericope in 1 Timothy and tries to make the problem of the rich Christian the primary focus of the Pastorals. I am unable to give this positioning such a decisive role by itself. But these letters do show a considerable amount of interest in the wealth both of individuals within the household of God and of the household of God itself—and this interest is not confined to 1 Timothy 6:17-19. Whether this interest manifests an intentional and functional equivalent to the χρηματιστική motif is perhaps impossible to say.[193] Nonetheless it would be unfortunate to overlook the

---

initiative on not seeking to get repayment as though it were a debt, to servants on rendering an affectionate loyalty to their masters, to masters on showing the gentleness and kindness by which inequality is equalized." See also *Special Laws* 2.225-227, 3.169-171; *On Joseph* 38-39; *Cain* 181—all cited in Balch, *Let Wives*, pp. 52-54. Note Harrison's suggestion (*Paulines*, pp. 14, 135-136) and Mott's extensive argument ("Benefactor," passim) that the writer of the Pastorals has been influenced by Philo.

[193]It should be noted, in the first place, that this part of the topos is the most flexible and expendable (Balch, *Let Wives*, pp. 35-37, 45), in the second, that literary dependence is not the issue, and third, that to whatever extent the Pastorals are dependent on the topos they are already adapting it to a group that is not strictly speaking a family. If the Pastorals, in dependence on the traditional topos, take up the question of the place of wealth in the church's households and in the church-as-household itself, nothing demands that they do it in a conventional way.

extent to which learning "how to behave in the household of God" (1 Timothy 3:15) involves managing the church's financial resources and learning how to minister to the congregation's wealthier members.

1) The Haustafeln *and the Rich*

The form of the instructions to the rich in 1 Timothy 6:17-19 conforms exactly to the *Haustafeln* schema that Verner outlines.[194] Because the norm is to apply the pattern (address, imperative, amplification, and reason) to family relationships, it is striking to find the form being stretched to speak to relationships that are not, strictly speaking, familial. The function of such instructions would appear to be to place the rich qua rich structurally in the conceptualization of the church as family of God. Given the importance of the wealthy person in the life of the πόλις and the κοινωνία, the adaptation of the *Haustafeln* to cover a non-household relationship suggests that fitting the rich into this structure is being experienced as problematic.

2) The Unity of 1 Timothy 6:3-21: On Godliness and Gain

The key to what is difficult about fitting the wealthy into the structure of the house of God lies in the literary and thematic unity of 1 Timothy 6:3-21. For despite the fact that Dibelius sees only loose connections between the various elements of this passage,[195] a

---

[194]Verner, *Household of God,* Chart 2, p. 93, and Chart 4, pp. 96-97. It will be recalled that Verner traces the development in the church of the *Haustafeln*—rules addressed to family members (husbands/wives, parents/children, masters/slaves) and following the more or less set pattern: address, imperative, amplification, reason—beyond familial boundaries to include nonfamilial groups within the community. He refers to the use of the *Haustafeln* form in this extended sense within the church as the station code schema. In the passage on the rich, the addressees are the rich, the imperative is not to be haughty, the amplifications run from the middle of v. 17 (not to set their hope on the uncertainty of riches) through the end of v. 18, and the reason is supplied in v. 19 (storing up a treasure for the future).

[195]According to Dibelius/Conzelmann (*The Pastoral Epistles,* p. 83), 1 Timothy 6:2b-16 "can be divided into three parts: the refutation of heretics (6:3-5), a sequence of sayings which are attached to the catchwords 'business' (πορισμός) and 'religion' (εὐσέβεια) (6:6-10), and a concluding paraenesis to Timothy (6:11-16)." The warning against greed (6:6-10) "is only superficially connected with the polemic against heresy in 6:3-5" (p. 84). The section 6:11-16 "appears to be an intrusion between vss 10 and 17" (p. 87). Nor do 6:17-19 seem to find a place

case can be made for its unity of concern.[196] The coherence of the
larger passage is important because this pericope provides the
broader context for the instructions to the rich; its unity is thus of
import for an evaluation of Countryman's thesis that part of the tension in the Pastorals is between Timothy and the local elites.

The ethical lists warn prospective officers of the church against
avarice and love of money (1 Timothy 3:3,8; Titus 1:7). The last
chapter of 1 Timothy takes up this theme at some length, mounting
a two-dimensional admonition to the apostolic delegate: 1) spare
yourself and the church the destruction that comes from the love of
money; and 2) be aware of the true source of your wealth. Of no
small importance in the mysterious matter of the false teaching the
Pastorals combat is the participial explanation of what makes the
troublers of the church depraved-minded and truth-bereft; νομιζόν–
των πορισμὸν εἶναι τὴν εὐσέβειαν: "for they imagine that godliness
is a means of gain" (1 Timothy 6:5).[197]

This could be written off as sheer rhetorical flourish,[198] did not
the writer stay with just *this* issue in his charge to Timothy[199] at
verse 11. The point should not be missed that the proverbial[200] "we
brought nothing into this world..." (verse 7), "if we have food and
clothing..." (verse 8), and "for the love of money is the root of all
evils..." (verse 10) all culminate in the command to the apostolic delegate: σὺ δέ, ὦ ἄνθρωπε θεοῦ, ταῦτα φεῦγε: "But as for *you*, man of
God, flee *these things!*"

In striking ways, in fact, the two main sections of this passage,
6:3-10 and 6:11-21, stand as reverse images of each other. A lack of
sound words and teaching in accordance with godliness which char-

in their context; rather, they show that "lack of logical coherence" which is
"characteristic of parenetic texts" (p. 91).

[196]Jukka Thurén, "Die Struktur der Schlußparänese 1. Tim. 6,3-21," *Theologische Zeitschrift* 26 (1970): 241-253.

[197]With Spicq and the RSV, and against Dibelius, the NIV, and the NASB, the
participle is adverbial instead of attributive, since it lacks the καὶ which would
have made it parallel to the two previous attributive participles. Rather, it provides the grounds for describing the false teachers as corrupt of mind and bereft
of truth.

[198]E.g., by Robert J. Karris, "The Background and Significance of the Polemic
of the Pastoral Epistles," *Journal of Biblical Studies* 92 (1973): 552.

[199]I shall freely refer to the apostolic delegate (Countryman's term) by the
name given to him in the texts—i.e., Timothy—without prejudice to his historic-
ity.

[200]Note the contemporary parallels to these sayings in Dibelius/
Conzelmann, *The Pastoral Epistles*, pp. 84-86.

acterizes the false teachers (6:3) is to be answered by Timothy's pursuit of (among other things) godliness and by his noble battle on behalf of the faith (6:11b,12).[201] The self-destructive pursuit of false wealth (mere money—6:9-10) is to be countered by the truly enriching and life-bestowing practice of liberality and generosity (6:18-19). At the same time, the use of the economic term παραθήκη as a summary of Timothy's positive duties (6:20) binds his own good confession (see the development of the "deposit" motif in 2 Timothy) with the financial responsibilities he is to pass on to the rich. Thuren summarizes: "As the heretics sin through the false-teaching of avarice, so Timothy and the faithful serve God through a pure confession and through liberality."[202] And just as Timothy is rewarded with the "taking hold of eternal life" (ἐπιλαβοῦ τῆς αἰωνίου ζωῆς, 6:12), so the wealthy may anticipate the "taking hold of that life which is real" (ἵνα ἐπιλάβωνται τῆς ὄντως ζωῆς, 6:19).

An additional connection between the two halves of this chapter comes into view with the setting aside of Verner's assumption that οἱ βουλόμενοι πλουτεῖν (6:9) and οἱ πλούσιοι ἐν τῷ νῦν αἰῶνι (6:17) are two different groups: the would-be rich and the already rich.[203] The assumption that two groups are in view does have a sort of *prima facie* persuasiveness about it. Yet, I find myself balking at it on two levels: 1) grammatical, and 2) contextual.

First, if οἱ βουλόμενοι πλουτεῖν were aimed at those who are not yet rich, one would expect the infinitive to be in the punctiliar tense, in accordance with βούλεσθαι's preference for a complementary infinitive in the aorist,[204] especially since πλουτεῖν itself generally

[201]Reading τῆς πίστεως of v. 12 as: a) *faith quae creditur*, and b) genitive of advantage; though see Zerwick's opinion (*Grammatical Analysis*, ad loc.) that the genitive is subjective: "the fight which faith wages."

[202]Thurén, "Struktur," p. 243; see the treatment of the parallelism, pp. 242-244.

[203]Verner, *Household of God*, pp. 174-175; see also Brox, *Pastoralbriefe*, p. 219.

[204]F. Blass and A. Debrunner, *A Greek Grammar of the New Testament and Other Early Christian Literature*, trans. and rev. by Robert W. Funk (Chicago and London: The University of Chicago Press, 1961), §338(2), (hereafter cited as BDF). The fact that, as in our passage, in the other three appearances of βούλεσθαι in the Pastorals the infinitive is in the linear tense is not relevant, as each of these carries the force of a decree—e.g., "I decree that men should pray in every place..." (1 Timothy 2:8). Spicq (*Pastorales*, p. 372) claims this use of βούλεσθαι is expressive of an "apostolic mandate," in imitation of Hellenistic chancellery style—examples in C. Bradford Welles, *Royal Correspondence in the Hellenistic Period: A Study in Greek Epigraphy* (London: Yale University Press,

means "become rich" in the punctiliar tense.[205] Since πλουτεῖν is in the linear tense, the phrase reads more naturally as "those who are determined to maintain their wealth" than as "those who are determined to become wealthy." An instructive parallel is Aristotle *Nichomachean Ethics* 1120b16, where he expresses sympathy for liberal people who have difficulty πλουτεῖν (staying rich) because they are better at giving away what they have than at acquiring more.

More important than a minor grammatical point, secondly, is the question of which reading of the phrase makes more sense in this context. That 6:9 is no less addressed to the already rich than is 6:17 appears the more likely reading when due weight is given to what we have noted above: where the denunciation of φιλαργυρία (the burden of 6:9-10) occurs elsewhere in the Pastorals it does so in the officer lists—lists aimed at wealthy household heads.

This is consonant with Plutarch's bemoaning the degeneration of wealthy people's quest for glory into a crass purchase of fame: when φιλοτιμία masks φιλαργυρία. One kind of φιλαργυρια is miserliness (*Moralia* 524A-527A); it will not spend and is unwilling to share (ζῆν...ἀμεταδότως, *Moralia* 525C). This is a false, privatized form of φιλοτιμία the antidote of which is attention (ἐπιμέλεια , see 2C-F) to one's obligations to the public (811C). Due note should be taken of the Pastorals' instruction to the "rich in this world": be εὐμεταδότος, "generous" (1 Timothy 6:18). As in Plutarch, becoming εὐμεταδότος is a wealthy person's antidote for a miserly strain of φιλαργυρία.

Another kind of φιλαργυρία is prodigality (527A-528C), an overwillingness to spend on benefactions which do not benefit but actually harm those who receive them, and which also bring to oneself an illusory and destructive sort of glory (527D; cf. 822A,C). Plutarch would have the prodigally rich, first, learn "self mastery" (σωφροσύνη, 527F-528B), which includes learning to live moderately (523E-F); note 1 Timothy's parallel interest in setting αὐταρκεία rather than πορισμός alongside εὐσέβεια (6:6-8). Second, Plutarch

---

1934; reprint ed., Chicago: Ares Publishers Inc., 1974), Nos. 44.9; and 12.12, as opposed to 12.8,22.

[205]Note that Bauer (W. Bauer, W. Arndt, F. Gingrich, *A Greek-English Lexicon of the New Testament and Other Early Christian Literature,* 2nd ed. rev. and aug. by F. Gingrich and F. Danker [Chicago and London: The University of Chicago Press, 1957, 1979]—hereafter cited as BAGD) lists the meaning for πλουτεῖν as "be rich" in the present tense and "become rich" in the aorist. See Ben Sirach 27:1 for the latter sense: ὁ ζητῶν πληθῦναι (aorist active infinitive of the synonym πληθύνω) = "the one who seeks to get rich."

would have the prodigal spend: 1) without an eye to getting a return, and 2) on things that promote εὐσέβεια (822B).

It is difficult not to be reminded of the Pastorals' warning that the gain εὐσέβεια brings is εὐσέβεια itself. For 1 Timothy 6:9-10 may very well have in view a prodigal love of money in this context—that is, one that delights in using money to gain acclaim, power, and status through spending which promotes what our author considers to be a sham εὐσέβεια. If this is the case, the author's assertion that to "long for" (ὀρέγεσθαι) money[206] (or better, money's effect in providing clout in the community) is to fall from the faith and grievously wound oneself (6:10) is nicely answered by his earlier maintaining that "longing for" (ὀρέγεσθαι) the bishopric (a venue of community service) is a noble thing (3:1).

Love of money, in a word, is preeminently a vice of those who have money to love. And our author's intent would not appear to be, *pace* Verner, to legitimize the position of the already wealthy by keeping the would-be wealthy in their place. Rather, he lays out an alternative for the same people—those who have the kind of resources that can be either a boon or a bane to themselves and their community. Those who long to use their wealth in the service of others and who will promote sound doctrine aspire to a noble work. But those who see their money as piety's reward and as an entitlement to leadership in the church—especially if they are careless in their doctrine—are headed for trouble.

Though the evidential base is not solid enough to put the conclusion beyond question, there is support for Countryman's thesis that the apostolic delegate's antagonists have arisen from among the wealthy in the church. Note, additionally, the warning about being hasty in the laying on of hands (5:22) and about making neophytes into overseers lest their getting "puffed up" about it cause them to fall into the devil's condemnation (3:6). It so happens that part of the description of the avaricious, false teachers in chapter six is that they are "puffed up" (verse 4), and the danger of avarice is that it causes one to fall into temptation and a snare (verse 9).[207]

Further, despite the best efforts of commentators to describe the opponents' teaching in the Pastorals, there is scant evidence of a

---

[206]The –αργυρια of φιλαργυρία is the antecedent of ἧς and therefore the object of the participle ὀρεγόμενοι.

[207]1 Timothy 3:7 also uses the image of a snare (of the devil) to depict the fate of the person who is made an officer but does not enjoy a respectable reputation with people outside the church.

theological system behind the opponents' teaching.[208] The hints of an over-realized eschatology (2 Timothy 2:18), of myths and antitheses and genealogies (1 Timothy 1:4; 4:7; 6:20; Titus 1:14), of independence from the domestic order (1 Timothy 4:3; 5:11-15; Titus 1:11), and of dietary asceticism (1 Timothy 4:3-4; 5:23) are certainly tantalizing to the interpreter. But they were not necessarily any more than tantalizing to their original auditors either—"speculations" that "tickle the ear" (1 Timothy 1:4; 2 Timothy 4:3).

More plausible than the thesis of the rise of a coherent and compelling form of heresy is that of the emergence of some people who have been invested with an authority that, at least in the estimation of our author, their spiritual maturity and theological discernment do not warrant. These are people who by virtue of wealth and stature would naturally come into the ascendency of an association. Because they and others would see in their material prosperity the proof of their piety (6:9) and thus of their authority to teach (or perhaps to choose their own teachers), and despite the fact that the genuineness or depth of their faith has not had time to be tested, they have gained positions of considerable influence in the church. If it is indeed the case that it is more the social status of the opponents than their ideas that has gained them an audience, this would at least account for the fact that our author—despite his stated intent (1 Timothy 1:3-4) and as wide of the mark as their ideas may indeed be—actually addresses the situation with an eye more to the restoration of order than to the refutation of heresy.

If this scenario is correct, why the need to warn Timothy himself against the wedding of godliness to material success? And how do the positive instructions to Timothy in verses 11b-16 answer the problem?

From evidence in both 1 and 2 Timothy, it appears that the apostolic delegate has come under some sort of attack. His youthfulness has been cited as evidence of his lack of fitness for leadership (1 Timothy 4:12a), leading to the apostle's urging that he not neglect the gift that is within him by virtue of the laying on of the hands of

---

[208]Dibelius/Conzelmann (*The Pastoral Epistles*, pp. 65-67) describe it as an early Jewish form of gnosticism; Spicq (*Pastorales*, pp. 85-119) draws attention to parallels with Qumran teaching, and identifies the heretics as Jewish-Christian practitioners of "haggadic midrashim"; Brox (*Pastoralbriefe*, pp. 31-42) draws lines of connection with the Colossian heresy and with the gnostic *Gospel of Thomas*, noting a docetic hint at 1 Timothy 2:5; von Campenhausen ("Polykarp") sees Marcionism in the background; Koester (*Introduction*, 1:304) believes all heresies in general are in view, but none in particular.

the presbytery (4:14). He is reminded in 2 Timothy that he has not received a Spirit of timidity, but rather of power, love, and sound thinking (1:7). Instead of caving in to his detractors, he ought to be rekindling his gift (1:6) and getting on with his work (4:5).

Along with Countryman, I do not find it difficult to imagine that a younger man whose claim to authority is extra-local and who shares the cultural milieu of his detractors could himself be persuaded that those with wealth and local standing deserve not only to be heard, but to shape the community of faith.[209]

Timothy is told, to the contrary, to flee the notion that there is any connection between these individuals' godliness and their prosperity (6:6-11a). Rather, their claim to automatic status in the church is one that has to be challenged. Additionally, Timothy is reminded about the source of his own true wealth (6:11b-16, 20-21).

To appreciate the force of this reminder, we turn to an earlier section of 1 Timothy (4:1-5:2) in which the author moves (as he also does in chapter 6) from a description of the false teachers to first person singular instructions to his apostolic delegate about how in his own person he should answer the challenge. If the parallel with 4:1-5:2 is instructive, the intent in chapter six is both to bolster Timothy's confidence and to show him how he may be an example to those too easily impressed with material prosperity.

That previous section (4:1-5:2) also hinges on the profitability of εὐσέβεια. There, piety's value is asserted over against bodily training (4:7b-8). While the words γυμνάζειν and γυμνασία cast the earlier discussion in terms of an athletic image, it is likely that the issue is that of a brand of asceticism being pushed by the false teachers: the forbidding of marriage and the enjoining of abstinence from foods (4:3).[210] Following the word to Timothy about the superiority of training in piety to physical rigor stands an instruction for the apostolic delegate to be an example in speech and conduct. The exercises that follow appear to be antidotes to the sham piety forwarded by the rival teachers—examples of precisely the kind of piety that *is* profitable: love, faith, purity, public reading of Scripture, encouragement, teaching, concern for personal growth (4:14-16), relationships with people appropriate to their station (5:1-2).

---

[209]Countryman, *Rich Christian*, p. 153. Critical concerns, of course, push beyond the pale the material in Acts about the historical Timothy's origins from among the more aristocratic Greek-speaking elements of the Roman colony Lystra—Spicq, *Pastorales*, p. 48, and n. 4, pp. 48-49. It can, however, be noted that the Acts material is corroborative on this point.

[210]Brox, *Pastoralbriefe*, pp. 170ff; Jeremias, "Timotheus," pp. 32-33.

Though the instructions to Timothy in 4:6ff take their cue from the false asceticism that is passing for a disciplined life while the instructions in 6:11ff follow from an avarice that is passing for godliness, the logical flow of the latter section is of a piece with that of the former. The man of God's profit, his πορισμός, lies in δικαιοσύνη, εὐσέβεια, πίστις, ἀγάπη, ὑπομονή, πραϋπαθία, in the noble fight of faith, in eternal life, in the good confession (6:11-12). These things, not money, are worth pursuing, and, more importantly, are the source of status in the church. While he can take nothing from this world (6:7), the man of God can keep God's command spotless and free from reproach in this world until the manifestation of the Lord Jesus (6:14). And while the "good confession" calls for contentment and faithfulness in the face of persecution rather than the enjoying of the good life this side of Jesus' ἐπιφάνεια (a persistent theme in 2 Timothy), the exalted language about God with which the charge closes is a reminder of just how valuable is the παραθήκη (i.e., entrustment with the ministry of the gospel) which has been placed in the hands of the steward of the house of God (6:20; cf., 3:15,16; Titus 1:7). If not by standards the avaricious will acknowledge, nonetheless by the only standards that matter, the man of God has resources that should put him in no small standing in the church.

After first saying what he considers to be necessary to dispel the notion that naked wealth confers the right to lead (6:6-10), the apostle turns to his delegate to remind him how as a person his own wealth and standing lie in εὐσέβεια μετὰ αὐταρκείας and in the παραθήκη which has been entrusted to him (6:11-16; cf. verses 6,20). Finally, he returns to the wealthy and outlines attitudes and behaviors that would bespeak εὐσέβεια μετὰ αὐταρκείας on their part: freedom from haughtiness instead of swollen-headed conceit, hope in God rather than trust in wealth's deceitfulness, a generous and liberal spirit rather than an appetite for gain (6:17-19).

c. The Economic Dimension of the Gender Conflicts

Modern scholarship has begun to find important material in the Pastorals for the reconstruction of the early church's treatment of women. Verner's is one of a number of recent studies maintaining that gender underlies the crisis which has occasioned the Pastorals. As indicated above, he notices that of the four themes of the household topos, it is γαμική that is dominant in the Pastorals. He also appeals to the fact that the false teachers are having success particularly among women (2 Timothy 3:6-7) and are "upsetting households" (Titus 1:11). Further, not only does the false teaching expressly forbid marriage (1 Timothy 4:3), some marriageable women are in fact foregoing domestic life (1 Timothy 5:11ff). The widows passage (1 Timothy 5:3-16) has also drawn considerable attention; and the argument has been advanced that not only does an official order of widows exist, it has become a haven for unmarried women (whether technically widows or not) who are attempting to live independent of domestic structures.[211] And while the plight particularly of the younger women of the Pastorals has long been compared with that of Thecla, recently a case has been made that the traditions preserved in the Acts of Paul and Thecla are old enough to permit us to believe that the Pastorals are written specifically to rescue Paul from the emancipated portrait of him in those traditions.[212]

Gender stratification is indeed pivotal to an understanding of the Pastorals. Although women were not regarded as a separate rank within the Roman *ordines*, their legal rights were different from those of men; the Hellenistic-Roman age saw some blurring of the legal distinctions, accompanied by no small discussion over the social status of women relative to men.[213] Sainte Croix argues that the male-female dynamic in the ancient world is best analyzed in class categories, since nothing is more fundamentally a function of the relation to the means of production than the reproductive role:

> The *production* which is the basis of human life obviously includes, as its most essential constituent part, the *reproduction* of the human

---

[211]Bassler, "Widows' Tale."

[212]MacDonald, *Legend.*

[213]Meeks, "Androgyne," pp. 167-180; Balch, *Let Wives*, passim, but especially pp. 139-149; Verner, *Household of God*, pp. 27-47, 64-81. Imperial law saw the attenuation of the absolute power of the *patria potesta*; marriages became increasingly a transaction between a woman and a man rather than between a woman's guardian and her future mate; women were gaining more property rights, especially pertaining to divorce and inheritance. In the women of the Diadochoi, the Hellenistic age knew women of considerable political power; Tacitus' account of the lives of the Caesars is testament to the power of women (albeit through behind-the-scenes intrigue) to shape imperial government; Jews, too, came to celebrate the political exploits of female heroes like Esther and Judith. Although it appears to have been realized in a practical way only among the Epicureans, philosophical schools (especially Stoics and Cynics) increasingly championed egalitarianism. Meeks summarizes the situation for early imperial society: "...the age brought in all places a heightened awareness of the differentiation of male and female. The traditional social roles were no

species. And for anyone who, admitting this, believes (as I do) that
Marx was right in seeing position in the whole system of production
(necessarily including *re*production) as the principal factor in deciding
class position, the question immediately arises: must we not allow a
special *class* role to that half of the human race which, as a result of the
earliest and most fundamental of all divisions of labour, specialises in
reproduction, the greater part of which is biologically its monop-
oly?[214]

The virulence with which some writers of the age assert the traditional domestic role of women in the face of winds of change[215]
lends weight to Sainte Croix's contention that one of the most basic
of class conflicts is that over gender. Our own documents, in fact,
see in the rising of women to teach in the assembly a threat to an
order that is primordial and fundamental to human existence (1
Timothy 2:11-15). Especially because the traditional household
topos which the Pastorals are employing has "rulership" as its over-
arching rubric (τὸ ἄρχειν καὶ τὸ ἄρχεσθαι, Aristotle *Politics*
1254a22ff), inquiry into these epistles in terms of an extension of
relational class categories (see Ossowski above) to include man and
woman could be fruitful.

My concern, however, is with the way wealth conditions even
this issue. In fact, I believe Verner overstates the matter when he
makes gender stratification *the* issue in the Pastorals. For even
where gender holds center stage, money is at farthest remove a supporting actor. To be sure, the Pastorals would object in principle to
any sort of woman teaching and leading the assembly, seeing this as
a violation of the τάγμα assigned to her by virtue of creation and fall
(1 Timothy 2:12-15). However, it is not just any sort of woman who
has committed the breach of τάγμα in 1 Timothy 2:9. As all the
authors on whom we are dependent observe, these are rich women.
Countryman is correct in pointing to the high social station implicit

longer taken for granted but debated, consciously violated by some, vigorously
defended by others" (p. 179).

[214]Sainte Croix, *Class Struggle*, pp. 98-99 (emphasis his).

[215]E.g., Juvenal *Satire* 6; Philo's conservatism is especially striking in view of
the assimilationist tendencies of the Jewish community in Alexandria. He,
according to Meeks, "associates with woman an extraordinary number of pejo-
rative expressions: weak, easily deceived, cause of sin, lifeless, diseased,
enslaved, unmanly, nerveless, mean, slavish, sluggish, and many others"
("Androgyne," p. 176). Philo's use of the *Haustafeln* material is most radical:
woman is to δουλεύειν her husband— i.e., "serve as a slave"—and procreation
is the sole legitimate purpose of marriage or sexual intercourse (*Hyp.* 7.3—see
Meeks, "Androgyne," p. 177).

in their ostentatious attire as providing the basis of their ability to assume the role of authoritative teachers.

Wealth is also more an issue in the widows passage than might be apparent at first blush. In the first place, there is the matter of rendering honor (τιμᾶν) to those who are "really" widows (αἱ ὄντως χῆραι, 1 Timothy 5:3). The linguistic parallel with 5:17-18, where what may well be the paying of elders is expressed with the cognate noun τιμή, should not be pressed too quickly into the service of the notion that the entirety of 5:3-16 is referring to an office of widow. For 6:1 uses the same noun (τιμή) in a clearly non-economic sense: in reference to the "honor" that slaves owe their masters. Rather, the meaning of "render honor" in 5:3 lies in 5:16's reference to the duty of the church to "support" (ἐπαρκεῖν) widows who have neither family nor benefactress (πιστή, 5:16).[216]

Bracketing the entire widows section, 1 Timothy 5:3-8,16 are actually best read as speaking to the problem of the *destitute* widow, the death of whose husband has left her with insufficient resources to be self-supporting. She is "poor" (πτωχός = "beggarly") in the classically Greek sense (though the word is not used).[217] Hebrew religion had seen such women as special objects of God's love and demanded community support for them, as did early Christianity.[218] What is noteworthy about the Pastorals' approach is, first, that this is the only place where truly destitute people surface in the epistles. Further, the Pastorals insist that the support of destitute widows be handled first by immediate family members or by women of means.[219] Where familial or otherwise private and vol-

---

[216]The parallels between 5:3-4 and 5:16 are several: 1) conditional clauses identical in construction; 2) references to "true" widows; 3) widows having offspring who ought to help them is paralleled in reverse by a believing woman (πιστή) having widows she can help; 4) the church's final responsibility is variously τιμᾶν and ἐπαρκεῖν. The parallels at opposite ends of this pericope do not, *pace* Bassler ("Widows' Tale," p. 33), imply that the entire passage is talking about one kind of widow.

[217]See Hauck, "πένης," TDNT 6:37-40, and idem, "πτωχός in the Greek World," TDNT 6:886-887.

[218]Deuteronomy 14:29; Job 31:16; Psalm 146:9; Isaiah 1:17,23; Luke 2:36-38; Acts 6:1; James 1:27.

[219]Following Verner, p. 139, in seeing the πιστή of 5:16 as a woman of means. If Anna the widowed prophetess who lives in the temple precincts provides a paradigm for the destitute widow of 1 Timothy 5:3-5 (Luke 2:36-38), Tabitha/Dorcas the Jewish-Christian woman who has supported widows by her charity (NB: she extends rather than receives ἔργα ἀγαθὰ καὶ ἐλεημοσύναι) is paradigmatic of 1 Timothy 5:16's faithful woman (Acts calls Tabitha a μαθή–τρια) who is in a position to support widows. On Tabitha, see Ernst Haenchen,

untary support cannot be found, the church's wealth is to be made available.

The point is to notice the dynamic between the wealth of households themselves and the wealth of the household of God: there is a boundary between household and church which the application to the church of the image of the household of God is not to blur. In the placing of its resources at the service of the truly destitute, the church is not to function so much as a family that it unnecessarily assumes the responsibility of actual families.

This leads to the "enrolled" widows of 5:9-15. Various grounds may be offered for seeing a reference in these verses not merely to a second group of widows, but to an office not unlike that of bishop or deacon as well. The view that this section (5:9-15) is not likely to be referring to the same type of widow as 5:3-8,16 arises principally from problems with reading the passage as though it were talking about one group. First, different criteria for inclusion emerge in verses 3-8 and 9-15: verses 3-8,16 stress the "true widows'" need and their devotion to prayer, while verses 9-15 present standards of age and past behavior for "enrollment." Second, if both sections refer to the same group, one would have to assume that the church refuses assistance to any widow, regardless of need, if she is younger than sixty;[220] moreover, a young widow who follows the advice to remarry automatically disqualifies herself from relief should she be widowed a second time.[221]

That this second group may comprise an official order, even an office as such, is suggested by two considerations. In the first place, just as deacons are to be tested (δοκιμάζεσθαι) then admitted, so these widows appear to be required to take an oath and either be "enrolled," perhaps even "voted in" (καταλέγεσθαι, 5:9), or "rejected," perhaps "voted down" (παραιτεῖσθαι, 5:11)[222] —all of which, it has been argued, appears to be more elaborate a procedure than is necessary to establish eligibility for the relief envisioned in 5:3-8,16.[223] In the second place, not only are the requirements for "enrollment" more rigorous than those for "honor/support," they

---

The Acts of the Apostles: A Commentary, trans. Bernard Noble and Gerald Shinn (Philadelphia: The Westminster Press, 1971), pp. 338-339.

[220]See Bassler, "Widows' Tale," p. 34. Verner accepts this reading and accepts the consequences as well. Kelly accepts the reading but brushes aside the difficulty (*Pastoral Epistles*, p. 116), as does Fee (*Timothy and Titus*, p. 80).

[221]Bassler, "Widows' Tale," p. 34.

[222]Stählin, "χήρα," TDNT 9:456f.

[223]Verner, *Household of God*, p. 163.

answer closely to the officer lists of 1 Timothy 3 and Titus 1. Thus, while office-holding men are expected to be μιᾶς γυναικὸς ἄνδρες, enrolled widows are to have been ἑνὸς ἀνδρὸς γυναί.[224] Proper care of children is required of both (cf. 1 Timothy 5:10 with 1 Timothy 3:4; Titus 1:6). So is the virtue of hospitality (cf. 1 Timothy 5:10 with 1 Timothy 3:2; Titus 1:8). The lives of both bishops and enrolled widows are to be nobly attested (δεῖ δὲ καὶ μαρτυρίαν καλὴν ἔχειν ἀπὸ τῶν ἔξωθεν, 1 Timothy 3:7; ἐν ἔργοις καλοῖς μαρτυρουμένη, 1 Timothy 5:10). And while the bishop is not to be a neophyte, the enrolled widow is not to be less than sixty years of age.

Because the qualifications for becoming an "enrolled widow" have to do with character rather than duties it is impossible to be certain that an office is in view in verses 9-15. But the supposition is an attractive one, especially if the parallel between the officer lists and the enrolled widows list extends to social level as well—i.e., if it is not just that 5:9-15 contemplates an office in the church, but envisions the filling of that office by women from the same type of households as the overseer and deacon passage in chapter 3.

Under the assumption that the "true widows" are different from the "enrolled widows," the verses dealing with the latter group are most plausibly read as dealing with an office being opened up precisely to patronesses of the church in consideration of their beneficence to the church. The verses dealing with the former would speak to the problem of the unwillingness of families to care for their own destitute widows (verses 3-8), as well as to the service patronesses who can afford to support widows themselves will provide to the church by doing so (verse 16). Meanwhile, verses 9-15 indicate the official recognition the widowed woman of means is to be afforded for her service.

---

[224]Verner understands these phrases to require that officers and enrolled widows literally have been married only once (i.e., no remarriage after a partner's decease)—see also Spicq, pp. 402f, 430f; Kelly, pp. 75-76. But Verner presses his conclusion (arguable enough in itself) into the creation of a major crisis for young widows who are being urged, through remarriage (5:14), to disqualify themselves from ever becoming "enrolled" widows (pp. 131, 165). He does this in the face of his own realization that so to read the phrases is to place the author into the same camp as his ascetic enemies (4:3; p. 131). More sober is the judgment of other interpreters that the considerations which determine the meaning of μιᾶς γυναικὸς ἄνδρες and ἑνὸς ἀνδρὸς γυναί are: a) the prevalence of divorce and marital unfaithfulness in the Roman Empire; and b) the teaching of Jesus proscribing divorce and remarriage on any grounds save adultery (Lock, pp. 36-38, 60; Jeremias, p. 24; Fee, pp. 43-44).

In short, while the official teaching office is being fenced off from the prosperous and socially powerful woman (2:11-15), provisions are being made for her to exert her considerable influence in the church: first within the home itself, then on behalf of the needy, oppressed, and desolate (5:10,16). It may or may not be coincidental that the one office (besides that of widow) that does appear to be open to women is the diaconate (3:11),[225] an office that evolved into one concerned with practical matters and subordinate to that (or those) of presbyter/overseer.[226]

d. Honoring Elders

Of some relevance to the social portrait of Pastoral Christianity is the stipulation that elders who govern well be deemed worthy of "double honor" (1 Timothy 5:17). If, as is generally agreed, this is a reference to financial remuneration for church leaders, it must somehow affect the characterization of the leadership as coming exclusively from the upper echelons of municipal society. Malherbe puts his finger on the issue when he points out that if the offices are one and we assume from 1 Timothy 3 that the ἐπίσκοποι/ πρεσβύ–τεροι are "financially well-off and generous, 1 Timothy 5:17f. might be read as contrary evidence, for there the elder is the recipient of material reward, not the provider for the church."[227]

Two related questions come immediately to the fore: first, are "overseer" (ἐπίσκοπος, 1 Timothy 3:2 and Titus 1:7) and "elder" (πρεσβύτερος, 1 Timothy 5:17 and Titus 1:5) terms for holders of the same office?[228] And second, does "double honor" (διπλῆ τιμή) refer to financial remuneration as is generally conceded?[229]

---

[225]Spicq, *Pastorales*, p. 456f; Lock, *Pastoral Epistles*, p. 41; Jeremias, "Timotheus und Titus," p. 20f; Brox, *Pastoralbriefe*, pp. 154-155; Fee, *Timothy and Titus*, pp. 50-51; Schwarz, *Bürgerliches Christentum?*, pp. 43-44. Verner (*Household of God*, pp. 100, 132-133) dissents.

[226]See Ignatius *Magnesians* 6.1-2; Schoedel, *Ignatius*, pp. 46, 107, 141-142.

[227]Malherbe, *Social Aspects*, p. 99.

[228]For identity of office, note the following considerations: in Titus 1:5ff ἐπίσκοπος appears to be used interchangeably with πρεσβύτερος (as is also the case in Acts 20:17,28); a two-office configuration (ἐπίσκοπος/πρεσβύτερος and διάκονος) as opposed to a three-office configuration (ἐπίσκοπος and πρεσβύτερος and διάκονος) is consistent with what little is said about office in the Pauline churches—see Philippians 1:1. Against identity of office: the three-office configuration is attested for churches influenced by Paul at least as early as Ignatius (e.g., *Magnesians* 6.1-2), certainly not too late to be considered relevant to the Pastorals' ecclesiology; the Pastorals always use ἐπίσκοπος in the singular and πρεσβύτερος in the plural, suggesting at least the possibility that

Three explanations suggest themselves with some plausibility:
1) The offices are one, the officeholders are indeed wealthy
householders, and the language of 1 Timothy 5:17-18 is ironic. Well-
off people who aspire to office neither need nor want remuneration
for their services.[230] The images of a muzzled ox and of a laborer
and his wages would not be attractive to a wealthy person, who
would see wage labor as little more than slavery.[231] In fact, municipal and associational offices usually came at a cost to officeholders
themselves. Though our author is not talking about extending to
wealthy people financial remuneration which they would neither
need nor want, he uses working class language from the Scriptures
and from the Jesus tradition to make the point that though the
community does *not* owe its benefactors standard expressions of
honor, it does owe them *something.* Verse 19 may be of some help:
the purpose of the passage is not so much to state a positive reward
for office, but to prevent frivolous charges against officers who serve
the community well. The respect they deserve ought at least to gain
them this.
2) The offices are one, and 1 Timothy 5:17-18 simply indicates
that not all overseers/elders are wealthy. Just as some may do more
"presiding" and some more "teaching and laboring in the word," so
some are financial providers for the church, and some must live on
the good graces of the church. If this is indeed the case, these verses

there was a single overseer presiding over a council of elders (the πρεσβυτέριον
of 1 Timothy 4:14); nor does Titus ever make explicit an identification of the two
terms; moreover, 1 Timothy separates them, treating ἐπίσκοπος in chapter 3
and πρεσβύτερος in chapter 5.

[229]E.g., Dibelius/Conzelmann, *Pastoral Epistles*, p. 78; Kelly, *Pastoral Epistles*,
p. 125; Fee, *Timothy and Titus*, p. 89; Brox, *Pastoralbriefe*, p. 149; Schwarz,
Bürgerliches Christentum?, p. 38.

[230]W. Michaelis asserts that διπλῆ τιμή refers only to honor or respect, arguing that 3:4,12 imply officers keep their professions and therefore do not need
financial compensation (*Pastoralbriefe und Gefangenschaftsbriefe. Zur Echtheitsfrage der Pastoralbriefe*, NF 1,6 [Gütersloh: Bertelsmann, 1930], pp. 61-63; and
idem, *Das Ältestenamt der christlichen Gemeinde im Lichte der Heiligen Schrift*
[Berlin, 1953], pp. 112-119). While the verses cited do appear to refer to wealthy
household heads, it is not at all clear that these individuals hold down "professions." Unfortunately, he excises v. 18 as a gloss because it does not fit his
position. And, as Bornkamm points out, διπλῆ τιμή can refer to an honorarium
without having to imply support for full-time work ("πρέσβυς," TDNT 6.666-
667—see also J. Schneider, "τιμή," TDNT 8.176-177).

[231]Finley, *Economy*, pp. 40-42, in dependence upon Aristotle *Rhetoric* 1367a32;
Aristophanes *Plutus* 552-554; Cicero *De officiis* 1.150-151.

do require a caveat to the portrait of the leadership of the church as originating monolithically from the upper social strata.

3) There are separate offices of overseer and elder, and one of the differences between them is economic in nature: whether alone or in concert with others who also go by the title, an overseer is a wealthy patron who must also happen to be able to teach (3:2), while elders may be drawn from among the nonwealthy and may expect the financial support of the community.

Short of more study of the matter, I cannot firmly decide for any one of the options, though it does appear that the first option has against it the obstacle of assuming quite a subtle reading of the text. The second and third reduce themselves at some point to a difference in terminology, resulting in a picture of a leadership structure that itself reflects the social stratification of the community at large. If it is the case that there is but one office, with some officeholders needing financial support and others not, it at least becomes clear that the leaders of the church do not come exclusively from the rich in the church. At the same time, if "overseers" and "elders" are distinct groups (as they have indeed become by Ignatius), wealth *could* be one of the differentiating factors: an overseer would be a wealthy patron, while an elder would be (or could be) a paid functionary. Either way, the leadership is not as homogeneously well-off as Verner contends.

e. Conclusions

The Roman system of orders (the Pastorals mention only slaves) and gradational appeals to class language provide us with few clues as to the social level of any of the Pastoral Christians. The data do not even allow a firm decision as to whether the more wealthy members of the congregation are of the curial order, the official local aristocracy.

However, there are clear indications that the church does have its own aristocracy. Status is differentially distributed. And the conflicts that have emerged within the community betray the interests of people who would presumably compare well with their non-Christian counterparts, the kind of people Rostovtzeff has referred to, perhaps misleadingly and certainly anachronistically, as a "bourgeoisie." The tenor of the epistles in general reflects their social world, addressing their place in the household of God.

As distinctive as these social contours appear to be, however, it has to be acknowledged that the homologoumena yield their own evidence of the importance even to the early Pauline ministry of just this sort of people. That being the case, it is unclear how the presence—even dominating presence—of wealthy people in the Pastorals could be used (*pace* Dibelius) as an indication that the movement has undergone a rise in social class between the homologoumena and these letters.

We return to this matter in the conclusions to the dissertation as a whole, after we have had opportunity to take up two additional matters. In Chapter III we ask to what extent the Pastorals' approach to recognizable cultural ideals about the citizen of means fits the Hellenistic-Roman municipal social setting. And in Chapter IV we ask how the Pastorals' style of ethics and how their mode of integrating ethics and eschatology stack up against the acknowledged letters, taking up specifically the different approaches to wealth in Paul and in the Pastorals.

CHAPTER III

Beneficence in the Pastoral Epistles:
A Culturally Accommodative Ethic?

A. BENEFICENCE AND *BÜRGERLICH* LIFE

What comes to expression in the Pastorals' view of wealth, according to Dibelius, is an attitude of "prudent moderation." On the one hand, these epistles warn against the danger of riches, counseling contentment instead of love for money (1 Timothy 6:6-10). On the other hand, they take for granted a certain amount of property ownership in the congregation (1 Timothy 6:17-19; 5:16).[1] This taste for a position between the extremes is supposed to be part of what marks the epistles as *bürgerlich*. The appearance of this *via media* in an early Christian writer does not, of course, need to be attributed to direct dependence on Aristotle's "mean" (μεσότης),[2] since the virtue of "neither too much nor too little" was already quite at home in the Jewish wisdom tradition.[3] But the sort of association Aristotle idealizes between people of middling prosperity (τὸ μέσον) and the ability to live moderately is partly what Dibelius' depiction of this version of Christianity as being "middle class" is intended to convey. If there is reason to question the adequacy of this conceptualization as social description, there are also grounds for wondering whether the ethical genius of the epistles is exhausted by the bare observation that they urge a lifestyle somewhere between avarice and austerity.

Our investigation of the social provenance of the Pastorals suggests that one of the reasons the envisioning of this community of Christians as "middle class" is problematic is that at least with respect to some of the members—the movers and shakers, at that—the designation aims too low. A more textured picture of this urban

---

[1]Dibelius/Conzelmann, *The Pastoral Epistles*, p. 40. See discussion there, and summary above, I.C.1.a., pp. 12ff, for other respects in which the Pastorals' ethics are those of prudent moderation.

[2]See esp. *Nichomachean Ethics*, passim.

[3]E.g., πλουτὸν δὲ καὶ πενίαν μή μοι δῷς, Proverbs 30:8.

group of Christians takes into account an internal stratification atop which prosperous and powerful people sit. The quest for what is *bürgerlich* about the ethics of the epistles follows a similar track. It is not adequate to observe—as correct as the observation may be—that the approach to wealth is one which excludes the extremes.

What has to be asked is: does the Pastorals' ethic of wealth evidence an accommodation to *bürgerlich* life—that is, of urban life in the Hellenistic-Roman social world? Dibelius himself has suggested that these letters participate in a program of *Bildungschristentum*, a rapprochement between Christian thought and cultural ideals about life as it ought to be for the educated citizen of means. Is it indeed possible to recognize behind the instructions to the rich a picture of "the ideal *Bürger*,"[4] a redefining of Christian existence in the light of antiquity's ideal of the citizen (*Bürger*) of the polis?

Our specific line of approach to whether the Pastorals are in this sense *bürgerlich*[5] will take us through an inquiry into the system of incentives and reciprocities used in this social world to bind the wealthy to their communities. If the letters are aware of such an ideal, do they accommodate it? critique it? attempt to transform it?

Accordingly, it will be necessary in this chapter to do two things: 1) to sketch out features of the way wealth was thought of and put to work by rich people in Greek and Roman urban life—this sketch will comprise my standard for asking about the *Bürgerlichkeit* of the Pastorals' approach to wealth; and 2) to ask pertinent texts in the Pastorals how they were expected to impact their audience.

1. Aristotle on Wealth, Beneficence, and Honor

Once again, behind the ethicist who strives everywhere for the mean there is in Aristotle an observant student of society. And he is of no small help in outlining the parameters of municipal social expectation still operative in the first century. Aristotle defines property ownership as the right of alienation (i.e., the right to give away or to sell a piece of property). This implies, he adds, that wealth consists in the putting to work and in the use of goods rather than in their mere possession: καὶ γὰρ ἡ ἐνέργειά ἐστι τῶν τοιούτων καὶ ἡ χρῆσις πλοῦτος (*Art of Rhetoric* 1361a28).[6] Aristotle understands that the root of contemporary social life lies in the putting to work of wealth in the form of beneficence, the doing of good (ἡ

---

[4]See above, I.C.1.b., p. 19.

[5]See the terminological note above, I.D., pp. 29f, n. 107.

[6]Both Hands (*Charities*, p. 34) and Danker (*Benefactor*, p. 369, n. 24) notice this passage.

εὐεργεσία).⁷ The return on wealth used in this manner is honor (ἡ τιμή, 1361a33ff).⁸ The subtle interplay between benefactor and beneficiary comes to expression in his description of the benefactor's "gift" (τὸ δῶρον) as simultaneously an embodiment of the money or the object that its recipient desires and the "honor" that its giver loves.⁹

Aristotle observes that the increasing democratization of city-state life has brought with it the formation of symbiotic relationships between wealthy people who strive for honor and poorer people who aim at benefits. He touches on this dynamic in that portion of his *Nichomachean Ethics* devoted to "Friendship," (φιλία, Book 8). The sense of reciprocity and affection which constitutes friendship most naturally flourishes between equals. But all relationships can know a friendship appropriate to them, depending on the nature of a particular relationship's constitution (monarchic, aristocratic, or timocratic—*Nichomachean Ethics* 1160a31ff). Accordingly, private friendships can exist between rich and poor—associations of mutual advantage to which each side contributes what it has to offer and receives what it needs (1159b12):

> Both parties should receive a larger share from the friendship, but not a larger share of the same thing: the superior should receive the larger share of honour, the needy one the larger share of profit, for honour is the due reward of virtue and beneficence (τῆς μὲν γὰρ ἀρετῆς καὶ τῆς εὐεργεσίας ἡ τιμὴ γέρας), while need obtains the aid it requires in pecuniary gain. The same principle is seen to obtain in public life (ἐν ταῖς πολιτείαις).... Requital in accordance with desert restores equal-

---

⁷He offers a rather broad description of what beneficence can entail: ἡ εὐεργεσία can relate to matters of personal security (εἰς σωτηρίαν), or anything for that matter having to do with the maintenance of existence (καὶ ὅσα αἴτια τοῦ εἶναι); it can consist in the bestowal of wealth itself, or any other good thing that is difficult to come by (*Rhetoric* 1361a35-39).

⁸He is more explicit about the forms honor can take: sacrifices, memorials in verse and prose, privileges, grants of land, front seats, public burial, state maintenance, and among the barbarians, prostration and giving place, and all gifts which are highly prized in each country (*Rhetoric* 1361a39-43).

⁹καὶ γὰρ τὸ δῶρόν ἐστι κτήματος δόσις καὶ τιμῆς σημεῖον, διὸ καὶ οἱ φιλοχρήματοι καὶ οἱ φιλότιμοι ἐφίενται αὐτῶν· ἀμφοτέροις γὰρ ἔχει ὧν δέονται· καὶ γὰρ κτῆμά ἐστιν, οὗ ἐφίενται οἱ φιλοχρήματοι, καὶ τιμὴν ἔχει, οὗ οἱ φιλότιμοι (*Rhetoric* 1361a43-1361b3). It is worth noting, even if in passing, that Aristotle fully expects the needy to be "lovers of money" and the wealthy to be "lovers of honor"; it is against this backdrop that Plutarch's railing against those who have the opportunity to pursue greater honor but go after more money instead can be appreciated (*Moralia* 523C-528B, 819E-825F).

ity and is the preservative of friendship (τὸ κατ' ἀξίαν γὰρ ἐπανισοῖ καὶ σῴζει τὴν φιλίαν, 1163b1-6,12,13).

Applied in public life, the principle means that the poor contribute their political and social allegiance,[10] symbolized in the various concrete τιμαί they present to their benefactors. And the rich limit their consumption and accumulation by spending their wealth on their cities and by donating their time to the holding of unpaid municipal offices.[11] As long as there is a perceived reciprocity (though not identity) of benefit, the symbiosis produces a special brand of equality between the two dissimilar groups and can even be called φιλία.

This is the ideological underpinning of the clientele system Judge describes as characterizing Roman social life,[12] as well as for the system of values governing municipal elites' behavior which MacMullen summarizes as φιλοτιμία.[13] Already in Aristotle, the establishment of this kind of "friendship"—i.e., mutual interest—between rich and poor is vital to municipal life. For he recognizes that where the wealthy fail to experience the rewards as commensurate with the expenditure, the symbiosis, at least from their point of view, falls apart. This possibility he expresses as a transformation of φιλία into λειτουργία, variously translated as "liturgy," "forced public service," "charity" (*Nichomachean Ethics* 1163a29). It is also possible to trace the transformation of urban life throughout antiquity in terms of whether in a given time and place wealthy people feel gladly bound to their communities by φιλία or begrudgingly obligated to them by λειτουργίαι.[14] For all the historical and geo-

---

[10]Hands, *Charities*, p. 35. One is reminded of the symbiotic relationship between rich and poor in Hermas *Similitude* 2.

[11]*Nichomachean Ethics*, 1163b5-13; and see Hands, *Charities*, pp. 36-38.

[12]Judge, *Social Patterns*, pp. 18-35, and see above, II.C.1., pp. 57ff. Note the comments of R. Oster on "the ease with which Graeco-Roman urban dwellers accepted the compatibility of the two notions of benevolent actions and structural authority. In fact, much of the political theory of Jewish, Greek and Roman cultures was based on the concept of benevolent *imperium*.... While authority and leadership in urban celebrations secured one's reputation and prominence, this authority required one's care and patronage of the city, usually expressed financially." ("Holy Days in Honour of Artemis," in *New Documents Illustrating Early Christianity: A Review of the Greek Inscriptions and Papyri published in 1979.* ed., G.H.R. Horsley [North Ryde, Australia: Macquarie University, 1987], p. 82.)

[13]MacMullen, *Relations*, p. 125, and see above, II.B.3., p. 54.

[14]See Hands, *Charities*, pp. 26-48, with Marcel Mauss, *The Gift: Forms and Functions of Exchange in Archaic Societies*, trans. Ian Cunnison (New York: W.W.

graphical fluctuation, there is one assumption that remains constant: εὐεργεσία deserves τιμή, financial burdens should be adequately compensated by honor.

2. *Menander on Securing the Future through Friendship*

Menander's *Dyskolos* (first performed in Athens in 316 B.C.) portrays the formation of just such a symbiosis between a wealthy family and a poor one. In doing so, it draws our attention more directly to the interest of the wealthy family in securing its fortune through the use of its wealth to gain friends. Danker has astutely observed that despite a gap of several centuries, this play helps us sharpen our appreciation of the social and intellectual climate reflected in the New Testament.[15] This is especially apparent in the *Dyskolos'* attitude toward wealth.

The play's main character is one Sostratos, a rich city boy who, under Pan's spell, falls in love with the daughter of a rural misanthropist, Knemon.[16] Sostratos' intentions are at first thought to be ignoble by the daughter's half brother, Gorgias. So Gorgias warns Sostratos not to be lured into evil by his affluence. Though he himself is poor, Gorgias assumes the equation between right living and prosperity. He asserts that there is a boundary or turning point between the rich and the poor:

Norton & Co., 1925, 1967) as important background; additionally, note Richard P. Saller, *Personal Patronage under the Early Empire* (Cambridge, at the University Press, 1982); and Peter Garnsey and Richard P. Saller, *The Roman Empire: Economy, Society, and Culture* (Berkeley and Los Angeles: University of California Press, 1987), pp. 148-159.

[15]Frederick W. Danker, "Menander and the New Testament," *New Testament Studies* 10 (1964): 365-368.

[16]Menander carefully crafts his play in such a way as to turn on a multifaceted distinction between rich and poor, urban and rural. When Pan describes the boy's father in his opening speech he refers to him as very rich (μαλ' εὔπορος), and when the father finally comes on stage at the end of the fourth act, one of the characters gasps: "By Zeus, a wealthy man!" (πλούσιός γ' ἀνήρ). The people who farm the land themselves see themselves as πένης, the working poor. But to the leisured, urban rich man who has others work his land for him, these people are πτωχοί, that is, he would not appear to distinguish them from the beggars he would encounter in the street of the city. One social distinction on which the story turns is between being ἀστικός (a city dweller, urban) and being ἄγροικος (a country dweller, rustic). This division of people into urban and rural is arguably the most fundamental social bifurcation in the ancient world (See MacMullen, *Relations*, pp. 1-87).

The successful man's
Worldly prosperity continues just so long
As he can buttress his good fortune (ἡ τύχη) by
Avoiding any crimes. However, if
He's lured to evil by his affluence,
His fortune switches then, I think, into decline.
If, on the other hand, the less successful,
Despite their poverty, keep clear of evil,
Shouldering their destiny with honor (φέρωσι
    δ' εὐγενῶς τὸν δαίμον'), and
Achieving in the end a credit balance, they'll
Expect their stock to improve (274-283).[17]

His advice follows:

You may be very rich, but don't you bank on it (μητ'
...πίστευε τούτῳ),
Don't trample, either, on us down-and-outs (μήτε
τῶν πτωχῶν πάλιν ἡμῶν καταφρόνει)! Always
Show onlookers that you deserve a durable
Prosperity (285-287)!

The footing which riches provide is not a sure one, and the apparent security that comes from wealth should not embolden those who have it to abuse their inferiors. As young as he is, Sostratos is convincing enough about his intentions not only to allay Gorgias' fears, but to win him as an ally in his campaign to win the girl's hand from her reluctant father.

After finally proving his mettle (with no small help from Gorgias), Sostratos attempts to persuade his wealthy father, Kallippides, to provide one of his daughters to be a wife for Gorgias in return for the hand of Knemon's daughter. To Kallippides' protest that he has no intention of taking on "two paupers-in-law at one go" (νύμφην γὰρ ἅμα καὶ νυμφίον πτωχούς, 795), Sostratos responds with a short discourse: "on money...an unstable substance" (περὶ χρημάτων... ἀβεβαίου[18] πράγματος, 797-812).

If wealth can in fact be kept forever, he lectures his father, it should be guarded and not shared (μεταδίδοσθαι) with anyone. However, if one's title to riches is not absolute, if riches are instead

---

[17]The translation is that of W.G. Arnott in the Loeb Classical Library edition. See p. x, where he explains his (by Loeb standards) unusually colloquial translation as an attempt to capture Menander's style.

[18]There is a word play here, for Kallippides has just granted permission for his son to marry beneath his station since "when you're young, it adds stability (βέβαιος) to marriage if it's love that prompts the bridegroom."

on loan from fortune, then one should not begrudge them to others. It is in this sense that wealth is ἀβέβαιος, for fortune may at any time take it all away and give it to someone who does not deserve it. Therefore, as long as one has control over a measure of wealth, continues Sostratos, he should use it generously: he should aid everyone, and by his acts enrich all whom he can. Such conduct never dies (τοῦτο γὰρ ἀθάνατόν ἐστι, 808-809). And what accounts for the immortality of such a style of life?

> If you by chance
> Should ever stumble, it will yield to you a like
> Repayment. Better far than hidden wealth
> Kept buried is a visible true friend (πολλῷ δὲ κρεῖττόν
> ἐστιν ἐμφανὴς φίλος ἢ πλοῦτος ἀφανής, ὃν σὺ
> κατορύξας ἔχεις, 809-812).[19]

Kallippides' reply is that he certainly does not plan to be buried with his wealth. Therefore, if his son wants to seal a friendship with a man whom he has proven (βούλει περιποιήσασθαί τινα φίλον δοκιμάσας, 815), he is welcome to share his inheritance: πόριζε... δίδου, μεταδίδου (817-818). Kallipides allows the bonding of his family to Knemon's at no small expense: he accepts a dowry half the comic norm for his son's bride, and at the same time he offers a dowry half again the comic norm for Gorgias' bride.[20] But the audience is to understand that an advantageous deal has been struck, for Kallipides has made a solid provision for his family line. Not only will his son's marrying a wife whom he will always cherish[21] promote the stability of the family; perhaps even more significantly, Sostratos has been ensured the lifelong service of a mature friend, one noble of character if not lineage.

Other texts from Hellenistic moralists confirm the opinion among thoughtful people that the best way to secure one's posterity is not through the accumulation of wealth, but through the bestowing of benefactions on others in order to create reciprocal bonds of service, or friendship. In a passage most reminiscent of Menander, Cicero calls foolish the person who has everything money can buy,

---

[19]Note Arnott's explanation that "Menander plays here on the distinction in Athenian law between 'hidden' (ἀφανής) and 'visible' (ἐμφανής) property. 'Visible' property was one's openly acknowledged possessions, assessable for taxation; 'hidden' property included such things as debts owed to the person concerned, claims, and—because easily concealed—cash."

[20]See Arnott's note at line 740.

[21]Cf. 308-309 where Sostratos promises πίστιν ἐπιθεὶς διατελεῖν στέργων.

but fails to add friends, "the finest equipment that life can offer" (*On Friendship*, 54-55). In one of the first century pseudepigraphical Socratic letters, "Socrates" defends his decision not to provide a legacy for his children.[22] Contrary to him "who has no understanding, but trusts in gold and silver" (χρυσίῳ δὲ πιστεύοντα καὶ ἀργυρίῳ), and who therefore never attains right thinking and virtue, Socrates has provided his children with a truly lasting inheritance:

> I will not leave gold for my sons, but rather something which is more valuable than gold, namely good friends (*Cynic Epistles* 234.20; 236.19-20).

Martial's couplet puts it perhaps most succinctly:

> What's given to friends is outside fortune's grasp:
> Your gifts will prove the only wealth to last (5.42.7-8).

3. Dio Chrysostom on the Moral Worth of the Wealthy

One of the things that makes Dio Chrysostom such a valuable source of knowledge about the New Testament social world is that he was at one and the same time a teacher of philosophy and a leading and active citizen of a provincial city, Prusa of Bithynia. Having been forced by Domitian into exile early in his career, Dio speaks of the plight of the privileged with some authority: the prosperous man derives a large income from loans, and has a good deal of land; not only does he enjoy good health, but has children and a wife living; and he enjoys some position of power and high office without war, rebellion, or open dangers (*Oration* 27.8). But a man in such circumstances is vulnerable to calamity (τι πταῖσμα): he may become poor after having been rich (πένης ἐκ πλουσίου) or weak and powerless after having been influential (ἀσθενὴς καὶ ἀδύνατος ἐκ δυναμένου); or he may see fortune (ἡ τύχη) take his wife or loved ones. Dio's counsel is to find security in that resignation which only (Stoic) philosophy can provide.

While Dio's picture of the vulnerability of the rich is generally recognizable,[23] his counsel to take refuge in philosophy is less mainstream—and it is so as much for its individualism as for its

---

[22]Deferring to Malherbe's (*Cynic Epistles*, p. 27) dating of the seven letters attributed to Socrates in his *Cynic Epistles* to the first century or perhaps even earlier.

[23]See Hands, *Charities*, pp. 78-79 and refs., for the special susceptibility of the prosperous to the vagaries of fortune.

intellectualism. His teaching on wealth is in fact governed by Stoic reserve, and in places betrays Cynic contempt. And it is just for this reason all the more interesting; for side-by-side with this stated inner distance from wealth's importance stands a career spent in a persistent pursuit of municipal virtue: the struggle to bring honor to himself and his family by bringing glory to his beloved Prusa. In this regard study of the speeches dealing with local politics and Dio's relations with Trajan on behalf of his hometown are especially rewarding.[24] The lingering conflict over the portico he attempts to build as a gift to the city is suggestive of the difficulties many would-be benefactors must have experienced in bringing their plans to fruition.[25]

Also of interest in Dio is the residence in the same mind of the idealization of poverty (see especially the *Euboean* discourse, *Oration* 7) and an assumption of the worth of the wealthy and socially powerful. In this latter regard, Dio shows himself to share the most widespread of assumptions in the ancient world: being at the top of the social pyramid of wealth is an absolute good, a sign of virtue, while being at the bottom is an unmitigated disaster, a sign of moral deficiency.[26] Recall the similar point made by the poor man Gorgias in Menander's *Dyskolos*.

Dio illustrates the point in his use of an apothegm from Hesiod. The latter (fl. ca. 700 B.C.) had opined that virtue and fame attended wealth (πλούτῳ δ' ἀρετὴ καὶ κῦδος ὀπηδεῖ, *Works and Days* 313). Before a personal exile which is to bring him into sympathetic contact with Cynic teaching, Dio is able to declare that the converse of Hesiod's dictum is also true: "wealth likewise and of necessity accompanies virtue" (ἀλλὰ καὶ πλοῦτος ἀρετῇ συνέπεται ἐξ ἀνάγκης, *Oration* 12.11). Yet even after he has returned from his wanderings to take up a position of responsibility in his hometown, the respect Dio has acquired for the philosophical (read: impoverished) lifestyle does not prevent him from warning members of the δῆμος who suspect city officials of misappropriating funds that they

---

[24]C.P. Jones, *Dio*, esp. pp. 95-131, is helpful in this regard; and *Orations* 40-51 are of particular interest.

[25]On Dio's portico see *Oration* 40.5; 45.12-14; 47; cf., also Pliny, *Epistles* 81-82. See, again, Panagopoulos ("Vocabulaire") on Plutarch.

[26]See Finley, *Ancient Economy*, pp. 35-38 for attitudes on wealth. Not that there were no dissenting voices. But precisely what gave the dissenting voices their edge was the reality of the situation they critiqued. Such voices are those of Socrates, Plato, the Stoics (e.g., Musonius Rufus 6.54.32-35, in Cora E. Lutz, "Musonius Rufus: 'The Roman Socrates,'" *Yale Classical Studies* 10 [1947]: 3-147), and the Cynics (Malherbe, *Cynic Epistles*, passim).

should be wary of criticizing their rich and powerful betters (οἱ βελτίους ὑμῶν, *Oration* 48.9):

> For if the better men among you are base, what should one assume regarding the others?...These men are generous; they have often made contributions to you out of their own resources....Is it not you who often praise us all day long, calling some of us nobles, some Olympians, some saviors, some foster-parents?...Will you not cease your turbulence and recognize that you have fellow citizens of refinement and a city that can be prosperous?

The *bürgerlich* universe is a world of verticality, recalling MacMullen's assessment, a world in which "the sense of high and low press heavily on the consciousness of both."[27] The formal orders are attempts to express, if imperfectly, these proportions, as is the "lexicon of snobbery" culled by MacMullen.[28] What we see in acute form in Dio is this verticality pressing itself on the consciousness of the privileged by means of an ideology unafraid of drawing the moral inference from the fact of prosperity.

4. *The Inscriptions and the Quest for Lasting Glory*

In public life it is the honorific inscriptions that show the lengths to which wealthy people might go to exchange their volatile currency for something lasting. Concern for durability is most obvious in the stone used to record for all posterity the largess of benefactors.[29] But that concern also surfaces in a plethora of strategies designed to wrest some form of immortality from fortune's hands.[30] The frequent language of self-immortalization through the bestowal

---

[27]MacMullen, *Relations*, p. 94.

[28]MacMullen, *Relations*, Appendix B, pp. 138-141.

[29]Antiochos I of Commagene (fl. mid-first century B.C.) may hold pride of place in his zeal to make sure posterity is not deprived a record of his benefactions. When he erects a mausoleum to stand as a shrine to his own piety and auspicious reign, not only does he set the inscription of his aretalogical autobiography in stone that would be "unassailable to the ravages of time," he has two copies of it set in the ground, one to the east and one to the west of the monument. The text is available at OGI 383; Bernhard Laum, *Stiftung in der griechischen und römischen Antike*, 2 vols. (Leipzig, 1917), No. 210; and Allen Wikgren, E.C. Colwell, and Ralph Marcus, *Hellenistic Greek Texts* (Chicago and London: The University of Chicago Press, 1947), pp. 137ff; translations appear in Danker, *Benefactor*, No. 41 (with commentary) and F.C. Grant (ed.), *Hellenistic Religions: The Age of Syncretism*, The Library of Liberal Arts (Indianapolis: Bobbs-Merrill Educational Publishing, 1953), pp. 20ff.

[30]Much of this discussion is dependent on Hands, *Charities*, pp. 55-61.

of gifts on others is poignant from the sheer fact of its use by people whose religious ideas offer, in the main, scant hope for anything like a literal immortality.[31]

One of the most fortunate features of Danker's collection of inscriptions and documents is the prominence he gives to municipal magnates—members of Rostovtzeff's *bourgeoisie*—who emulate on a smaller scale the virtues of benevolence that are on display on a grand scale in the lives of the gods and the kings and caesars.[32] Among these local lights, Menas (fl. ca. 133-120 B.C.) of the Thracian city Sestos[33] enjoys a career that is exceptionally illustrative of the benefactor ideal.

If the inscriptionist is to be believed, this is a man who from his earliest youth has sought to present himself as useful to his city, and has spared no expense nor avoided any danger in doing so. During his career he has served as ambassador (lines 10-26a), priest (26b-30a), gymnasiarch (30b-43a), supervisor of coinage and administrator of various offices and liturgies (43b-53a), and gymnasiarch a second time (53b-86a). While we learn nothing about the source of the doubtless significant resources behind these expenditures, we are told exactly what motivates them:

> he constantly wishes through his own zeal to supply something useful to the people and thereby, through the thanksgiving (εὐχαριστία)[34] that constantly redounds to him from the multitude, to acquire for

---

[31]MacMullen, *Paganism*, pp. 53-56, and judicious caveats in Meeks, *Urban Christians*, pp. 181-182, with notes on pp. 241-242.

[32]We note with interest the thesis proposed by M.P. Charlesworth ("Some Observations on Ruler-Cult, Especially in Rome," *Harvard Theological Review* 28 [1935]: 5-44) and A.D. Nock ("The Cult of Heroes," *Harvard Theological Review* 37 [1944]: 141-174; idem, "Deification and Julian," *Journal of Roman Studies* 47 [1957]: 115-123; idem, "Notes on Ruler-Cult, I-IV," *Journal of Hellenic Studies* 48 [1928]: 21-43; idem, "Soter and Euergetes," in *The Joy of Study*, F.C. Grant Festschrift, ed. S. Johnson [New York: Macmillan, 1951], pp. 127-148), and subsequently developed by Mott ("Benefactor," esp. pp. 146-178) that the ruler cults were a matter of rendering appropriate thanks to individuals who had conferred the highest of benefactions upon their fellow humans: ruling in "godlike" fashion. Exactly what their immortality and divinization consisted in need not detain us. Our concern is with the kind of immortality that might have been expected by people whose status and therefore aspirations were more circumscribed.

[33]Danker, *Benefactor*, No. 17 (= Hands, *Charities*, Doc. 55 = OGIS 339).

[34]Danker (*Benefactor*, p. 96) invites a comparison between this hope that benevolent activity will increase thanksgiving and Paul's in 2 Corinthians 4:15. He might also have mentioned 2 Corinthians 8-9 as a whole.

himself and his family imperishable glory (δόξαν ἀείμνηστον περι–ποεῖν[35], lines 8-10).

Occasionally the desire to cheat death through investment in one's community is candidly (if hyperbolically) expressed, as in the case of the second century A.D. citizen of Gytheion (mainland Greece) who bequeaths his property to his city with "immortal prescriptions concerning my gracious gift" (τῆς ἐμῆς χάριτος καὶ δωρεᾶς ἀθάνατα προστάγματα, Laum, *Stiftung*, No. 9.11). It is his earnest hope that city officials will see to it that his gift supplies oil to Gytheion's citizens and guests forever (εἰς αἰῶνα) and that his philanthropic act may remain for the gymnasium and the city eternally (ἀΐδιος, lines 14,16). His goal?

> My idea is to achieve immortality (ἀθάνατος εἶναι) in making such a just and kindly disposal of my property and, in entrusting (πεπι–στευκῦα)[36] it to the city, I shall surely not fail in my aim (lines 56-58).

The wish that one's gifts—and through them one's self—would be remembered in perpetuity was often expressed.[37] However, the absence of the modern artifice of "legal personality" meant there were no guarantees a benefactor's long-term wishes would be carried out, for a legacy was merely a gift with an often unenforceable obligation attached.[38] But the difficulties did not stand in the way of many who were determined to live on through their benefactions.[39]

Benefactors might invest in their city's future by donating to its public works, rather than following the route to instant renown through providing "bread and circuses." Such far-sightedness was not always appreciated by its beneficiaries. A letter from Emperor Pius to the Ephesians (A.D. 145) illustrates both the point under discussion as well as the common linguistic milieu shared by the Pastorals and the discourse of municipal beneficence.[40] Pius

---

[35]Cf., the use of περιποιεῖσθαι at 1 Timothy 3:13; and note our further discussion of this inscription below, III.B.1.c., pp. 127ff; and III.B.3.b.4), pp. 152ff.

[36]See the entrustment theme in the Pastorals—e.g., 2 Timothy 1:12.

[37]E.g., Hands, *Charities*, Docs. 31 and 46.

[38]Hands, *Charities*, esp. Chapter II, "Charities and Legal Personality," pp. 17-25.

[39]Laum's *Stiftung* is the seminal work on legacies in antiquity.

[40]Danker, *Benefactor*, No. 8 (= Hands, *Charities*, Doc. 25 = SIG3 850). Plutarch, it will be recalled, complains of the lack of appreciation citizens could express for less glamorous benefactions (*Moralia* 811C), and warns benefactors against glitzy gifts (822F); see above, II.D.3.a., p. 89.

rebukes the Ephesians for being slow to show gratitude to a certain Vedius Antoninus who had undertaken to build a cultural center for the city. Pius praises him for not being like so many who display their love of honor (φιλοτιμία) by spending on "shows, distributions, and prizes for the games for the sake of immediate prestige" (τοῦ παραχρῆμα εὐδοκιμεῖν χάριν), but rather on "that by which he hopes[41] to make the city more imposing[42] in the future."[43] Other benefactors might attempt to ensure their memory by making it worth their beneficiaries' while to honor their wishes, stipulating that a portion of their estate be used to provide annual banquets and birthday celebrations in their honor in perpetuity, or, presumably, as long as the funds hold out.[44] Still others might stipulate that if their legacy is not being carried out according to set terms, it will revert to a new trustee and beneficiary.[45]

In point of fact, however, when the foundation inscriptions are left aside, it is clear that the Greco-Roman benefactor's reward is immediate, consisting largely in the "honor" or "glory" of being known as a giver. The specific rewards are but symbols of that status. What makes the enriching of others ἀθάνατος (immortal) is the inevitability of reciprocal acts by others. The security sought in Menander's *Dyskolos* is simply that of the family fortune in the next generation. The hope of "Socrates" is likewise that his children will be provided for after his decease. And the hope for immortality in the inscriptions is nothing more than the hope of living on in the memory of others—living on, that is, as one known for glorious giving.

Illustrative is the case of a certain Dionysius, founder of a private religious association at Philadelphia in Lydia in the second or first century B.C.[46] In response to a dream, Dionysius establishes a cult to Zeus and several savior gods in his own home, "giving access into his οἶκος to men and women, free people and slaves" (lines 5-

---

[41]ἐλπίζει, cf., 1 Timothy 6:17.

[42]σεμνοτέραν, cf., the use of σεμνός/σεμνότης in the Pastorals as a personal virtue; e.g., 1 Timothy 2:2; 3:4,8,11; Titus 2:2,7—elsewhere in the New Testament only at Philippians 4:8.

[43]πρὸς τὸ μέλλον, cf., 1 Timothy 6:19, εἰς τὸ μέλλον.

[44]E.g., Hands, *Charities*, Docs. 31, 34, 35, 36, 45, 73, 77 (= Dessau 6468, CIL 9.4789, Dessau 6638, 2927, MAMA 5.202, CIL 8.12422, *Not. Scav.* 1928.23).

[45]See the discussion in Laum, *Stiftung*, pp. 180ff; e.g., Hands, *Charities*, Docs. 40, 71, 77 (= Dessau 6530, Laum, No. 9, Dessau 6957).

[46]S.C. Barton and G.H.R. Horsley, "A Hellenistic Cult Group and the New Testament Churches," *Jahrbuch für Antike und Christentum* 24 (1981): 7-41, with text, translation, and full commentary.

6,15-16). Presumably also at the behest of the gods he has provided an inscription which specifies their ethical requirements; Dionysius hopes that the group's keeping of these ordinances will result in "health, a common salvation, and the finest reputation" (ἐφ' ὑγιείᾳ καὶ κοινῇ σωτηρίᾳ καὶ δόξῃ τῇ ἀρίστῃ, lines 1-2). While there is no mention of a return from the association for its host, Dionysius ends the inscription by praying that the gods "will be well disposed towards him and his family," and that they will "provide good recompenses, health, salvation, peace, safety on land and sea..."

The common theme in this selective survey of moralists and inscriptionists is that wealth which is merely accumulated is an unsure thing; "hidden wealth kept buried" cannot buy a secure future. Thus, as Aristotle had asserted, wealth must be put to work to benefit others, whether to the end of acquiring a personal clientele ("friends") or of putting a community (πόλις or κοινωνία) in one's debt. This willingness to spend could fairly be called the liquid capital of Hellenistic and Roman communities. For the rich themselves this willingness was simultaneously the surest path to social power, the best form of social security, and the most concrete opportunity for immortality one had.

Thus, it is not by virtue of whether our epistles adopt a *via media* with respect to wealth, but by whether they encourage such a transaction of benefits for honors between the community and its wealthy members that the *Bürgerlichkeit* of the Pastorals ought to be measured. Is there a noticeable correlation between wealth and the reception of honor(s) in these communities? Would a wealthy person coming into these churches confront familiar expectations on his or her resources? Could he or she expect rewards commensurate with expenditures?

B. *BÜRGERLICH* AND ANTI-*BÜRGERLICH* ELEMENTS IN THE PASTORALS' INSTRUCTIONS TO THE RICH

When the author of 1 Timothy speaks to a social world that is held together by these bonds of incentives and reciprocities—and is in this nuanced sense *bürgerlich*—he does so in a dialect both familiar and alien. A pivotal passage is 1 Timothy 6:17-19, the single place in those letters which bear Paul's name where the rich qua rich are addressed.[47] I have already indicated other elements of the significance of this pericope: a) it adheres formally to the *Haustafeln* schema even though its content is extra-familial; and b) in opposition to the view of some wealthy people in this community that their wealth is itself an index of their piety and therefore of their right to lead, this passage presents our author's views as to what attitudes and behaviors actually comprise the wealthy person's εὐσέβεια μετὰ αὐταρκείας. In addition, the passage offers several profitable points of comparison with the role of wealthy people in contemporary urban life. We consider first those elements of the passage which share contemporary values on wealth.

The station code addressing the wealthy is constructed around a command against haughtiness (on which, see the next section). The amplification of the imperative consists of three exhortations to rich people: first, not to trust in their riches (17c); second, to trust in God instead (17d); and third, to engage in good works (18) so that one might build a solid foundation for the future (19). As we have seen, Hellenistic sources often address the problem of the insecurity of wealth, the need to secure wealth through sound investments, and the nature of the return on investments in others. By taking up the terms of this discourse in a dialectical way, the Pastorals demonstrate that they simultaneously share and fail to share the most common of assumptions about wealth in this social world.

---

[47] For the sake of analysis, I shall adapt Verner's schematization of the pericope (see *Household of God*, pp. 96-97):

Address:
　　17a τοῖς πλουσίοις ἐν τῷ νῦν αἰῶνι
Imperative:
　　17b παράγγελλε μὴ ὑψηλοφρονεῖν
Amplification:
　　17c μηδὲ ἠλπικέναι ἐπὶ πλούτου ἀδηλότητι
　　17d ἀλλ' ἐπὶ θεῷ τῷ παρέχοντι ἡμῖν πάντα πλουσίως εἰς ἀπόλαυσιν
　　18a ἀγαθοεργεῖν
　　18b πλουτεῖν ἐν ἔργοις καλοῖς
　　18c εὐμεταδότους εἶναι, κοινωνικούς,
Reason:
　　19a ἀποθησαυρίζοντας ἑαυτοῖς θεμέλιον καλὸν εἰς τὸ μέλλον
　　19b ἵνα ἐπιλάβωνται τῆς ὄντως ζωῆς.

1. Bürgerlich *Elements*

a. *The Precariousness of Wealth*

First there is an acknowledgement of the precariousness of the position wealth provides: μηδὲ ἠλπικέναι ἐπὶ πλούτου ἀδηλότητι (6:17c). A solid future, maintains our author, cannot be grounded on such an ephemeral substance as money. While 1 Timothy's turn of phrase is unique,[48] the sentiment is not, for, as we have seen, protestations of the precariousness of wealth are very much a part of contemporary ethical discourse; and the ruins of cities across the Mediterranean basin are littered with monuments to the anxiousness of the prosperous to exchange their money for something more lasting.

b. *Wealth in Others*

This leads to another point of contact: the assumption that the power of wealth rests not in its accumulation but in its use in benefiting others. In 1 Timothy 6:17-19 this comes to the fore in verse 18b, where the wealthy believer is told to be rich in good deeds (πλουτεῖν ἐν ἔργοις καλοῖς). The impact of this injunction cannot be appreciated until it is realized that this is the fourth and final use of the πλου– root in this short passage. The three previous occurrences are designed to point away from the over-valuing of possessions in themselves. First, the rich are addressed as being merely "rich in this world" (17a), implying the worth of their possessions to be at best penultimate. Second, there is the warning not to set one's hopes on one's wealth, the grammatical construction placing the emphasis on wealth's undependability. Third, the use of the adverbial form in the description of God as one who lavishly (πλουσίως, verse 17d) provides benefactions takes the emphasis off the gifts themselves and places it on the divine Giver and the generosity with which He gives. The rich person's riches lie, finally in 18b, not in what one has for oneself, but in what he or she does for others, that is to say, in one's wealth of noble deeds. At least on the face of it, such a notion would not strike someone strange who believed, with Aristotle, that wealth's power lay in its being put to use to benefit others (*Rhetoric* 1361a28).[49]

---

[48]ἐπὶ πλούτου ἀδηλότητι = ἐπ' ἀδήλῳ πλούτῳ, BDF §165, genitive of quality.
[49]See above, III.A.1., p. 112.

c. Liberality and Generosity

The liberality and generosity (εὐμεταδότους εἶναι, κοινωνικούς, 6:18c) which 1 Timothy espouses as an expansion on "being rich in good deeds" would also be readily recognizable to wealthy residents of Greco-Roman cities. Spicq may overstate matters when he identifies the verbs of verse 18 with the aristocratic virtues of Aristotle's *Nichomachean Ethics*,[50] but he does have a point. "Liberality, magnificence, and greatness of soul"[51] were civic as well as private virtues; it is precisely they—in spirit if not in letter—which were visibly and publicly endorsed through the exhortations, inscriptions, and monuments that have survived. And the language of 1 Timothy 6:18 derives from that world.

We have already noted the use of the verb μεταδιδόναι in the *Dyskolos* to express the wealthy father's understanding that the only condition upon which wealth would not have to be "shared" with others would be if it could be kept forever. That being impossible, the wise thing for a young heir to do is to seal a relationship with a proven friend by sharing (again, μεταδιδόναι) his inheritance with him. Two of Danker's inscriptions use the term to laud the generosity of municipal notables who, in the course of carrying out priestly duties, pay for their cities' sacred meat and share it with their constituencies. As priest first of the "Great God," then of Sarapis, and finally of Dionysos, a certain Akornion of Dionysopolis[52] makes his ungrudging distributions as part of his "administering of processions and sacrifices splendidly, nobly, and magnificently,"[53] and as part of his "conducting himself admirably and generously[54] in connection with his expenditures." The beneficence of Menas of Sestos, whom we have already met, is so great that when he is gymnasiarch he not only shares (μεταδιδόναι) the sacrificial offerings with local participants, but makes his philanthropy common[55] to out-of-towners as well (17.73-74). The pedagogical worth of such generosity is amply illustrated in the following lines:

---

[50]Spicq, *Pastorales*, p. 577; see above, I.C.2., pp. 28f.

[51]ἐλευθεριότης (*Nichomachean Ethics* 1119b24ff), μεγαλοπρέπεια (1122a18ff), and μεγαλοψυχία (1123a34).

[52]Danker, *Benefactor*, No. 12 (= SIG3 762). Dionysopolis is near modern-day Sofia, and the inscription dates from about 48 B.C.

[53]λαμπρῶς, 12.11; καλῶς καὶ μεγαλομερῶς, 12.18.

[54]ἀνεστράφη καλῶς τε καὶ φιλαγάθως, 12.12-13; on this phrase, see below, III.B.1.d., pp. 129f.

[55]κοινὴν ποιούμενος τὴν φιλανθρωπίαν.

He not only shared (μεταδιδόναι) his sacrificial offerings with the young men, but through such love of glory as this he urged the young men on toward discipline and the endurance of hardship. Because of his example, the souls of the young men compete nobly for manliness and are directed in the development of their character toward the goal of virtue.[56]

What makes the generosity of an Akornion and a Menas particularly laudatory is its voluntary and ungrudging nature. Thus the piling up of adverbs: ἀφθόνως (12.9), μεγαλομερῶς (12.18; 17.68), λαμπρῶς (12.11), καλῶς (12.18), φιλαγάθως (12.12-13). It is not primarily the giving that is valued, but the willingness of the giver. When the author of the Pastorals encourages rich Christians to be εὐμετάδοτος, "well-disposed toward making distributions,"[57] there is little risk that his readers will find either the role or the disposition expected of them to be unfamiliar. As any group in a Greco-Roman *bürgerlich* setting, the church will be dependent upon both the resources and the generous spirit of its more prosperous members.

If εὐμετάδοτος expresses the expectation that the resources and the hearts of the wealthy will be oriented toward giving, the parallel term κοινωνικός points to the corporate or public nature of the giving. Time and again the couplet καὶ ἰδίᾳ καὶ κοινῇ ("individually and corporately," or "privately and publicly") appears.[58] The second member of the pair points to the benefactor's support of the group at large, in contrast to the aid extended to individual members. So much is this the case that the substantive τὸ κοινόν comes

---

[56]Lines 69-72. I offer my own translation to make the point clearer than it is in Danker's. The text reads: μεταδιδοὺς μὲν τοῖς νέοις τῶν καλλιερουμένων ὑφ' ἑαυτοῦ ἱερῶν, προτρεπόμενος δὲ διὰ τῆς τοιαύτης φιλοδοξίας πρὸς ἄσκησιν καὶ φιλοπονίαν τοὺς νέους, ἐξ ὧν αἱ τῶν νεωτέρων ψυχαὶ πρὸς ἀνδρείαν ἁμιλλώμεναι καλῶς ἄγονται τοῖς ἤθεσιν πρὸς ἀρετήν.

[57]Spicq aptly comments: "The compound εὐμετάδοτον (a biblical *hapax*) accents the importance of generosity, and demands of the rich person more than liberality: magnificence and magnanimity...or suggests the ease, the promptness, and the joy with which he makes his riches useful to others" (*Pastorales*, p. 577).

[58]E.g., OGIS 51.9-10; Welles, *Royal Correspondence*, 52.17-18; 63.4-5; Priene 65.6-8. Says Danker (*Benefactor*, p. 61) of the occurrence of the combination at No. 3.4 (= Jost Benedum, ZPE 25 [1977]: 272-274), "A stock phrase in descriptions of benefactors who not only accept assigned public responsibilities but exercise their own volition in private benefactions."

to stand for a group's pooled finances, its treasury.⁵⁹ Not far in the background is the axiom: κοινὰ τὰ φίλων ("Friends' goods are common goods").⁶⁰ When benefactors are lauded as being κοινωνικοί it is their "public-mindedness" that is in view, the employing of their resources in the service of the common good rather than of their private interests.

The coupling, then, of "being well-disposed toward making distributions and being oriented toward the common good" through the injunction τοῖς πλουσίοις ἐν τῷ αἰῶνι παράγγελλε... εὐμεταδό- τους εἶναι, κοινωνικούς (1 Timothy 6:17a,b,18c) is an explicit appeal to the wealthy to adopt a role within the community of Christians like that which they would be expected to play within nearly any political or social arrangement with which they would be familiar.

d. The Good and the Noble

The pairing, too, of the ἀγαθ– and the καλ– roots in 18a and 18b comes from a world of discourse that sees in the conjoining of the "good" and the "beautiful or noble" the embodiment of that which is most human. Indeed, while the potential benefactors of 1 Timothy are directed more to the doing of deeds (cf., the repeated ἐργ– root in 18a and 18b) than to the developing of character, these Christians would no doubt recognize their alter egos in those among their fellow citizens who are lauded in the inscriptions as οἱ καλοὶ καὶ ἀγαθοὶ τῶν ἀνδρῶν , or simply οἱ καλοκἀγαθοί.⁶¹

To return to the inscription on Akornion, Danker maintains that the extolling of him that ἀνεστράφη καλῶς τε καὶ φιλαγάθως (12.12- 13) is a variation of the stock epithet καλοκἀγαθός (12.43):

> Since service as a priest came under the rubric of public liturgy, and since it was common practice to describe a philanthropist as 'an exceptional gentleman' (see line 43), the adverbial construction as used in the inscription undoubtedly refers to Akornion's liberality rather than to his personal integrity.⁶²

---

⁵⁹H.G. Liddell, R. Scott, H.S. Jones, *A Greek-English Lexicon* (Oxford, at the Clarendon Press, 1968), κοινός,ή,όν, II.2.d.; e.g., Danker, *Benefactor*, No. 21.28 (= IG II2 1292).

⁶⁰Aristotle, *Nichomachean Ethics* 1159b31, *Politics* 1263a31; cf., the appropriation of the saying by (or on behalf of) the Cynics Crates and Diogenes (*Cynic Epistles* 26.10; 27.15-16; 104.6); see also the allusions in the book of Acts (2:44; 4:32).

⁶¹E.g., Danker, *Benefactor*, No. 17.87, 43.

⁶²Danker, *Benefactor*, p. 78.

This is a significant observation because of the use of the adjective φιλάγαθος in the list of requirements for an overseer in Titus (there in conjunction with hospitality, 1:8), as well as the use of ἀφιλάγαθος to express the absence of "lovers of the good," or the presence of "illiberal people" as an index of the harshness of the latter days in 2 Timothy (3:3). And though ἀνεστράφη is restored in the inscription, note should also be taken of the use of the verb ἀναστρέφειν in the theme verse of the Pastorals (1 Timothy 3:15), and of the cognate noun ἀναστροφή in the list of ways in which Timothy is to be an example to believers (1 Timothy 4:12).

This specification of the way wealthy believers are to express their Christian faith in terms of an ideal already familiar to its addressees is akin to the way Christian discipleship for all believers is treated in Titus 2:11-14. There, as Dibelius and Conzelmann note, the content of (though not the power enabling) the Christian life is precisely that of the Greek ideal: to live moderately, justly, and piously. In 1 Timothy 6:17-19 as well as in Titus 2:11-14, while the language is activistic and dynamic rather than aretalogical and static, the content of the ideal is not unrecognizable to the Greco-Roman *Bürger*.

2. *Anti*-bürgerlich *Elements*

a. *Against Haughtiness*

As is sometimes the case in the station codes, the substance of the imperative in 1 Timothy 6:17-19 is negative: "not to be haughty" (μὴ ὑψηλοφρονεῖν, 6:17b). Resuming as it does the cautionary mode of the first part of 1 Timothy 6, the denunciation of haughtiness among the early church's wealthy serves as a reminder that the teachings of that Jesus who had blessed the poor and cursed the rich (Luke 6:20,24) and who died an ignoble criminal's death did not produce a movement of people singlemindedly bent upon exalting the lowly and humbling the lofty. The fact that so much is said in early Christian literature about the danger of wealth and wealthy people is evidence enough that the movement as a whole was emerging in a social world within which wealth and the power it reflected mattered. Thus, while the command here in the Pastorals is in harmony with much in Jewish tradition,[63] the gospel tradition,[64] and the rest of the Pauline corpus,[65] it would be a mistake to

---

[63]E.g., 1 Samuel 2:7-8; Job 5:11-16; Isaiah 2:12-15; 40:4; Jeremiah 9:23.
[64]E.g., Luke 1:52.

overlook the extent to which it runs afoul of the fundamental reality of the social life of people in Greek and Roman urban life.

To be sure, Lock's judgment appears to be an overstatement: "As ταπεινοφρονεῖν was among the Greeks a term of reproach but in the Bible a virtue, so ὑψηλοφρονεῖν was a term of praise and becomes a reproach."[66] As a matter of fact, the verb ὑψηλοφρονεῖν appears in Greek writings for the first time in this verse,[67] and the two appearances of the cognate noun ὑψηλόφρων which LSJ lists are mixed, one negative and one positive.[68]

Nonetheless, the command against haughtiness stands against a social world that lends social power to wealth by conferring on its possessors a presumption of moral superiority. Whatever else our author will concede to them, he will not have wealthy Christians thinking of themselves, to cite Dio Chrysostom again, as οἱ βελτίους, "the better people" (*Oration* 48.9).[69] Nor would one expect him to sit by while the members of *this* household[70] call their leaders[71] "nobles, Olympians, saviours, and fosterparents" (*Oration* 48.10). To this extent at least, it would be wrong to suggest (*pace* Verner) that the Pastorals reflect contemporary respect for prosperity—that their values are in this respect *bürgerlich*.

b. Epiphany and Resurrection

Like the moralists and the inscription writers, the author of 1 Timothy writes with an eye to the rich person's need to plan for the future. Paths diverge dramatically though. For significant differences emerge with respect both to the *timing* and the *nature* of the return on the wealthy person's investment in others.

---

[65]E.g., Romans 11:20; 12:16; Philippians 2:1-11; Ephesians 4:1.

[66]Lock, *The Pastoral Epistles*, p. 74.

[67]Assuming it is not the original reading at Romans 11:20.

[68]Plato, *Republic* 550B, uses it concerning a young man who is caught between the contradictory influences of his father who encourages reason, and the world which fosters ambition and appetite; he succumbs to the middle principle of high-spirited emulation and becomes an arrogant (ὑψηλόφρων) and ambitious man. Euripides (*Iphigenia in Aulis* 919) uses it in conjunction with θυμός in speaking of Clytemnestra's noble pride (ὑψηλόφρων) and anger at news of her husband's plan to offer their daughter as sacrifice for the expedition to rescue Helen of Troy.

[69]See above, III.A.3., pp. 119f.

[70]Note the way Dio applies the household image to his πόλις (*Oration* 48.10, and elsewhere).

[71]With Dio's οἱ προεστῶτες to refer to elected members of his city's βουλή, compare 1 Timothy's οἱ καλῶς προεστῶτες of worthy presbyters (5:17).

The future for which the Pastorals advise planning is shaped by
the two-age eschatology of early Christianity; it is a future that is at
one and the same time more concretely structured and less limited
in horizon than that of those Greek moralists and inscriptionists
who contemplate rewards for benefactions.[72] In this schema there is
one wealth that is a function of this age[73] and another that belongs
to the age to come.[74] Thus, while on the one hand the similarity
between Menander's caution not to trust wealth (*Dyskolos* 285) and 1
Timothy's injunction not to hope in it (6:17) cannot help but be
noticed, there is a dissimilarity equally—if not more acutely—to be
noted: the contrast between the historically immanent nature of
expectation in the moralists and inscriptions cited, on the one hand,
and the eschatological doctrine of hope that pervades the Pastorals,
on the other.

In these epistles the timing of the believer's expectations comes
to fullest expression at Titus 2:13 where the "blessed hope" for
which the believer is waiting stands next to the epexegetical
"appearance" (ἐπιφάνεια): it is the glorious future epiphany of the
Savior God, Jesus Christ. It is because his return will inaugurate a
new age of "life" that the Pastorals can so easily refer to "Jesus
Christ, our hope" (1 Timothy 1:1), or to ἐλπίς ζωῆς αἰώνιος: "(the)
hope of (the) life of (the) age (read: to come)," or more simply,
"hope of eternal life" (Titus 1:2; 3:7). That the two-age construction
is the framework for the Pastorals' notion of hope is also apparent at
1 Timothy 4:8-10, where having one's "hope fixed on the living
God" is the fallout of confessing the profitability of a godliness
which carries "a promise for the present life and for the life to come"
(ζωὴ τῆς νῦν καὶ τῆς μελλούσης).

The dialectic between present and future takes concrete expression in the contrasting instructions to Timothy and to the rich. Even
as he is challenged to wage a mighty struggle in anticipation of the
future "appearing" of the Lord Jesus which "will be made manifest

---

[72]In the next chapter we ask about the relationship between the Pastorals'
eschatology and that of the acknowledged Pauline letters; it is at that point that
we shall ask whether the Pastorals lack some of the vibrancy of Pauline expectation. In this chapter, however, the point of comparison is the sort of hopes cher-
ished in the Greco-Roman moralists and honorific inscriptions; regardless of
how the Pastorals fare when compared with the Pauline homologoumena, they
must be counted as robustly eschatological when set alongside the eulogistic
tradition.

[73]Cf. v. 17, οἱ πλούσιοι ἐν τῷ νῦν αἰῶνι.

[74]Cf. the progression in vv. 18-19, πλουτεῖν ἐν ἔργοις καλοῖς...ἀποθησαυ–
ρίζοντας ἑαυτοῖς θεμέλιον καλὸν εἰς τὸ μέλλον.

at the proper time," Timothy is told to "take hold of the eternal life to which you have been called" (1 Timothy 6:11-16). In some sense, so Timothy is encouraged, the life of the age to come is his to be appropriated in the present. The rich, however, once reminded of the good things God does allow them to enjoy in this age (6:17d), are told to store up for the future (literally, εἰς τὸ μέλλον) so that (in the age to come) they may[75] "take hold of that life which is life indeed" (6:19). For the former, the future stands as an extension of the life that has already begun in the midst of the present struggle on behalf of the gospel. For the latter, the future stands, first, as a reminder that what is enjoyed in this age dare not be confused with "real" life, and second, as a challenge to use this life's resources judiciously.

The importance of a hope that is tied to the anticipated epiphany of Christ is worth highlighting, not just because it stands in contrast to the sort of "immortality" thought to be earned by benefactions, but also because the one piece of information we are given about the doctrine (as opposed to the ethics) of the author's opponents in this correspondence is that they claim that the resurrection has already taken place: λέγοντες τὴν ἀνάστασιν ἤδη γεγονέναι (2 Timothy 2:18).

Despite whatever caveats must be tagged on to MacMullen's thesis about muted hopes for an afterlife in Greek and Roman religion, it is evident that the Christian hope of a new age bringing with it the resurrection from the dead, rather than a vague promise of immortality, went against the grain.[76] Nor should this be left at the general level in our discussion since the one insight we are given into the theology of the opponents is that the futurity of the resurrection is being denied (2 Timothy 2:18). For the sake of a more realized eschatology, they are challenging the notion that the believer's reward and destiny lie in the future.[77] The teaching on αὐτάρκεια

---

[75]Not to make too fine a point, the contrasting moods deserve some note. The imperative to Timothy (ἐπιλαβοῦ) has an eye to something Timothy can simply go and do in the present: "take hold." The subjunctive to the rich (ἵνα ἐπιλάβωνται) serves to cast the taking hold into a more remote, though indeed possibility-laden, future.

[76]MacMullen (*Paganism*, pp. 53-57) has argued forcefully and persuasively that ancient Greek and Roman religion was vague on hopes for the afterlife. It is with the advent of Christianity and its doctrine of resurrection that the hopes of what we have come to call "paganism" (à la A.D. Nock, *Conversion: The Old and New in Religion from Alexander the Great to Augustine of Hippo* [Oxford, at the Clarendon Press, 1933]) take a more definite and otherworldly focus.

[77]Unfortunately, the specifics of the opponents' teaching on resurrection are impenetrable. The parallels with the Corinthian situation may be instructive;

as a counter to the opponents' thinking that εὐσέβεια is a means to gain, even if it is not simply written off as a rhetorical flourish, is not generally taken as having theological, much less eschatological, roots. However, if the fundamental futurity of the believer's orientation is being abandoned, the need to remind those who are most in a position to enjoy their redemption in *this* world's terms would be a pressing one.

c. Not Earthly Friends, but Heavenly Rewards

Not only does the Pastorals' doctrine of eschatological hope move beyond the orb of Hellenistic honorific discourse, this distinctive orientation toward the future brings with it a transformation in what the Christian benefactor should expect as a return on an investment in the welfare of his or her community. Abandoned in this schema is any notion that the bestowing of benefactions on others will secure future well-being by bringing a return of conferred honors or reciprocal services.

Conspicuously absent is language of friendship. And on this point, a comparison with the attitude toward wealth adopted in the Wisdom of Jesus son of Sirach (often called Ecclesiasticus, herein referred to as Ben Sirach) can profitably be taken up, since this piece of wisdom theology is advanced in some quarters as representing an expression of Jewish ethics that has accommodated Hellenistic ethics (and which is thus "bourgeois") and which can be profitably compared with the ethics of the Pastorals.[78]

Exactly as are Menander and 1 Timothy, Ben Sirach is solicitous about the wealthy person's posterity.[79] As an antidote to the

---

see Lane, "I Tim. IV. 1-3. An Early Instance of Over-realized Eschatology?" *New Testament Studies* 11 (1964): 164-167. The Acts of Paul and Thecla offer an early understanding of an accomplished resurrection: "that it has already taken place in the children whom we have, and that we are risen again in that we have come to know the true God" (14).

[78]Spicq, *Pastorales*, pp. 218, 220-223; Schwarz, *Bürgerliches Christentum?*, pp. 108-111. Spicq not only points to the similarity of *Sitz im Leben* between the Pastorals and Ben Sirach (instructions to disciples, p. 218); he even suggests the Pastorals' approach to wealth is dependent upon Ben Sirach: "L'enseignement sur l'usage des richesses, qui est l'un des plus caracteristiques du Siracide, a inspire celui de saint Paul" (p. 221).

[79]The rich are not only susceptible to losing everything they have in this life (21:4), but will also be repaid as their conduct deserves on the day they die (21:26). That such people are Ben Sirach's principal concern is apparent from his complaint about people who take advantage of their lenders. He commiserates with the rich over people who consider loans a windfall (εὕρεμα);

vagaries to which the rich person is subject, the teacher advises liberality:

> Lose your silver for the sake of a brother or a friend, and do not let it rust under a stone and be lost. Lay up your treasure (θὲς τὸν θησαυ-ρόν σου) according to the commandments of the Most High, and it will profit you more than gold. Store up almsgiving in your treasury, and it will rescue you from all affliction; more than a mighty shield and more than a heavy spear, it will fight on your behalf against your enemy (29:10-13).

For Ben Sirach, the efficacy of alms—that which gives them redemptive power and enables them to establish one's posterity—is that such generosity will be related in the assembly (ἡ ἐκκλησία, Ben Sirach 31:11). As is the case in Menander's *Dyskolos*, wealth that is squirreled away is squandered, but wealth that is invested in friends will find its way home. For the friend is someone who can take your side in your day of trouble; thus, the friend is a sure shelter, a rare treasure, an "elixir of life" (φάρμακον τῆς ζωῆς, 6:5-16). If, as Bultmann claims, this last phrase is an allusion to a kind of immortality that can be bestowed through friendship,[80] Ben Sirach is using the same pattern of discourse employed by the Hellenistic inscriptionists and moralists. A quest for such a historically imma-nent payoff for the cultivation of friends is particularly noticeable in a Jewish tract that lacks any dimension of hope for eschatological or heavenly reward.[81] At the least, undergirding Ben Sirach's view of friendship are the same sort of reciprocal expectations we have found to be characteristic of *bürgerlich* life: "Whoever returns favors gives thought to the future; at the moment of his failing he will find support" (3:30b).

In one very important sense the gospel tradition preserved in Matthew and Luke (especially in the latter) shares Ben Sirach's ambience: the way one lays up treasure for oneself is through alms-giving, through gifts to the poor. This is especially forceful in Luke, where the means of laying up treasure is stipulated: "sell your pos-sessions and give alms" (Luke 12:33; cf. Ben Sirach 29:12). There is also a connection between the dishonest steward's sagaciously

---

over the feigned humility rich people must endure at the hands of supplicants until loans are extended; over the way sycophantism gives way to insolence when it comes time for repayment; and over the way generosity is so often rewarded with contempt instead of honor (ἀντὶ δόξης...ἀτιμίαν, 29:4-7).

[80]R. Bultmann, "ἀθανασία," TDNT 3.24.

[81]Cf. esp. 17:27-28; also worthy of special mention is 11:14-28.

"making friends" (Luke 16:1-13) and the disciples' contributing to the poor[82] that is strongly reminiscent of Ben Sirach's instructions to use alms to ensure advocates will be there in your own day of calamity. On the matter of almsgiving the Pastorals are strangely silent—here perhaps as much as anywhere else the Jewish milieu seems to have been left behind.[83]

However, the similarities we have just noted between the gospels and Ben Sirach pale beside one point of contrast between the gospel tradition and the Pastorals, on the one hand, and Ben Sirach and the Hellenistic moralists, on the other: in the gospels and in the Pastorals what counts is preparation for God's visitation, not the cultivation of an earthly clientele—rich or poor—as a hedge against the vagaries of life. Even Luke's borrowing of the language of friendship/clientele makes the point that all human resources must be marshalled to gain vindication in the one really important court, God's. If the Pastorals have exchanged language of poor-relief for that of municipal beneficence (εὐμεταδότους εἶναι, κοινωνικούς), they do so to make the same point: heavenly reward or the divine benediction, not the reciprocity of human friendship is the goal.

The language of laying up treasure is a feature Ben Sirach shares both with the Pastorals and with the gospel tradition. Yet, it is Ben Sirach who has done the most to accommodate the importance in Hellenistic culture of securing an earthly future through the cultivation of friends. While the special concern for the poor through almsgiving is a feature shared between Ben Sirach and the gospel tradition, the sort of future provision envisioned in Ben Sirach is, not to put it too epigrammatically, more *bürgerlich* than biblical. By comparison, the Pastorals' future provision is decidedly non-accommodative.

d. The Apostle as Model of Christian Beneficence

If the rich are being called to a lavish self-giving without the customary returns, they are simply being asked to follow the example of the preeminent benefactor of the Pastorals: the apostle him-

---

[82]Luke Timothy Johnson, *The Literary Function of Possessions in Luke-Acts*, Society of Biblical Literature Dissertation Series, No. 39 (Missoula, MT: Scholars Press, 1977), esp. pp. 156-158.

[83]On the basic differences between Hebrew and Greco-Roman attitudes toward the poor, Hendrik Bolkestein's *Wohltätigkeit und Armenpflege im vorchristlichen Altertum: ein Beitrag zum Problem "Moral und Gesellschaft"* (Utrecht: A. Oosthoek, Verlag A.G., 1939) remains a valuable source.

self. If, as suggested in the previous chapter,[84] the apostolic delegate is to be a model in his own person of the pursuit of that kind of wealth which really counts in this age, the apostle himself holds pride of place in such a pursuit. The Pastorals' Paul has fought a noble battle on behalf of which he now exhorts his delegate.[85] As would any of his contemporaries he looks forward to having a crown bestowed on him for his faithfulness in the charge that had been entrusted to him. But unlike the crowns his *bürgerlich* contemporaries might anticipate in return for municipal or associational services,[86] his is neither a crown to be bestowed in this life, nor is it one that comes from his beneficiaries: "henceforth there is laid up for me the crown of righteousness, which the Lord, the righteous judge, will award to me on that Day, and not only to me but also to all who have loved his appearing" (2 Timothy 4:8). The notion of *quid pro quo* stands; it is, after all a "just" reward conferred by a "just" judge.

But it is reciprocity in a new key. On the one hand, because the reward anticipated is a function of the coming of the age of resurrection, the stakes are raised to a level not seriously contemplated in Hellenistic and Roman religion. On the other hand, precisely because the rich Christian is invited to join the apostle in looking for his or her reward in that age rather than this and from the Lord's hand rather than from the hands of his or her beneficiaries, the anticipated transaction amounts to a challenge to the normal bonds of social reciprocity.

e. Honor and Status in the Church

Despite the eschatological perspective with its expectation of future reward, the author of 1 Timothy does sanction some acknowledgement of people who provide services for the community. Three times, in fact, this is done in terms of the rendering of "honor": first, genuine widows, whom the apostolic delegate and the church should τιμᾶν and ἐπαρκεῖν (5:3,16);[87] second, elders (especially teaching elders) whose excellence in governance earn them διπλῆ τιμῇ (5:17);[88] and third, (pagan?) masters of Christian slaves, whose

---

[84]See above, II.D.3.b.2), pp. 93ff.

[85]Paul tells Timothy in 2 Timothy 1:13 to follow the pattern he has seen in his mentor—cf., 2 Timothy 3:10,14.

[86]Danker's bibliography on rewards for benefactions is rich (*Benefactor*, pp. 483-484, nn. 163-175).

[87]On honoring the widows, see above, II.D.3.c., pp. 103ff.

[88]On honoring the elders, see above, II.D.3.d., pp. 106ff.

ability to defame their slaves' teaching and call into question the character of their God ought to earn for them πᾶσα τιμή (6:1).[89]

Each of these three groups focuses a matter of critical concern to the author of the Pastorals. At issue in the honoring of widows is the religious valuing of domesticity, but beyond that, of the entire economy of natural life. The use of εὐσεβεῖν (5:4) in this context is interesting. When Aristotle discusses what sort of friendships can exist between unequals, one of the relationships he takes up is that between parents and children (*Nichomachean Ethics* 1158b12ff, 1161a20ff, 1162a5ff). This can never be a completely reciprocal relationship, for parents have bestowed one benefaction upon children the latter can never repay, life itself. This must account for why the author of the Pastorals considers parental homage to be a matter of εὐσέβεια, a fundamentally religious act: in honoring parents, children acknowledge the superiority of the benefits bestowed upon them.[90] Throughout the Pastorals there is a concern—no doubt as a reaction to the opposing teachers—to affirm theologically the goodness of creation, of the natural order, of human existence as such. The bestowing of honor on the destitute mothers of the community of faith is of a piece with this concern. For the widows this is a matter of *quid pro quo*—support for support.

---

[89]πᾶσα τιμή here, clearly, would be deference or respect, rather than pay. A larger question is whether the "double yoke" refers to Christian slaves of pagan masters. The expression could be tautologous, as Kelly contends, maintaining that it is needlessly subtle to suggest that non-Christian masters are in view (*Pastoral Epistles*, p. 131). As a general reference to Christian slaves, the phrase could be a reminder that even though slaves' status in Christ is that of freedpersons, they are otherwise still in the old social order (Fee, *Timothy and Titus*, p. 96). Verner says v. 1 refers to Christian slaves in general, but then he acknowledges that since v. 2 treats slaves of Christian masters as a sub-group among slaves in the church, there must have been a considerable number of slaves in the church who had pagan masters (*Household of God*, pp. 141-142). The fact that slaves of Christian masters come under special consideration in v. 2 does seem to tip the scales in favor of viewing v. 1 as referring to the special plight of Christian slaves who have non-Christian masters. See Lock, *Pastoral Epistles*, p. 65; Hanson, *Pastoral Epistles*, p. 105; Guthrie, *Pastoral Epistles*, p. 109.

[90]See also Philo *Decalogue* 120, where he says people who neglect their parents are inferior to storks who do show εὐσέβεια towards their parents and care for them; he concludes ἀμήχανον δ' εὐσεβεῖσθαι τὸν ἀόρατον ὑπὸ τῶν εἰς τοὺς ἐμφανεῖς καὶ ἐγγὺς ὄντας ἀσεβούντων ("how can reverence be rendered to the invisible God by those who show irreverence to the gods who are near at hand and seen by the eye?"—the whole section treats parents as godlike benefactors, 111-120).

The particular stress on teaching elders coheres with the Pastorals' interest in basing community life on truth. Regardless of whether "overseer" and "elder" are synonyms,[91] the effect of isolating the teaching function of those who preside over the community from what surely were more administrative matters (e.g., serving as hosts) is to say something like: be sure that gratitude (whether financial or otherwise) is shown for those who attend to the community's ideational integrity.

Non-Christian masters of Christian slaves—upper crust outsiders—would have been in a unique position to influence public opinion toward the Christian community. This, too, is a critical concern to the author of the Pastorals. As is also the case in 1 Peter, a strong apologetic motif courses through these epistles, though unlike 1 Peter, the concern here is not so much to win adherents as it is to preclude the disqualification of the Christian community's testimony.[92]

Unfortunately, it is impossible to account for whatever historical events may have occasioned such a concern. But in a social world in which wealthy household heads have a special power to influence community judgment, it is not difficult to account for the sociological occasion for this concern. The measure of the respect which Christians in the service of the Lord Jesus accord their own masters will do much to affect the credibility of the Christian community as a whole. It does not require much of an act of the imagination to put these slaves' power to bring credit or discredit to the gospel on a par with the church's own wealthy household heads who are themselves told to keep a steady eye on their testimony before outsiders (cf., 1 Timothy 3:7).

What is happening in 1 Timothy is a subtle transformation of the benefactor ideal. The deference paid to the rich and their semi-automatic elevation to leadership that would be the normal pattern in Hellenistic associations is being forsaken. At the same time, the rich are being asked to be as liberal with their resources as though business were proceeding as usual. It is not, however, as though avenues to leadership and influence were being cut off altogether, for the officer portraits in 1 Timothy 3 and Titus 1 are couched in terms most readily understandable to them. It is simply that wealth and status are not sufficient conditions for leadership (on at least

---

[91]On this question, see above, II.D.3.d., pp. 106ff, esp. n. 228.

[92]Peter Lippert, *Leben als Zeugnis: Die werbende Kraft christlicher Lebensführung nach dem Kirchenverständnis neutestamentlicher Briefe* (Stüttgart: Verlag Katholisches Bibelwerk, 1968).

two of the possible readings of 1 Timothy 5:17-18, it is not a necessary condition either).[93] Meanwhile, the Pastorals' Paul is himself presented as a model of the kind of leader the community needs, one committed to beneficent service minus the need for the standard bestowal of community honors. And our author would have what "honors" the community does bestow go to the community's widows, teachers, and potential detractors—each representing contributions of critical concern to him: domesticity, ideational integrity, reputation in the community.

3. A Special Case: Christian Benefactors and their Slaves

We cannot leave the matter of beneficence in the Pastorals without considering the single verse in this correspondence that speaks explicitly of "beneficence" (ἡ εὐεργεσία). In 1 Timothy 6:2, Christian slaves are discouraged from inferring from the fact that their Christian masters are their "brothers" that they no longer ought to be obedient to them. Rather, they should redouble their service because: οἱ τῆς εὐεργεσίας ἀντιλαμβανόμενοι are faithful and beloved. It is worth reasserting that the slaveowners who are referred to here are people of some means:[94] they will be numbered among the "rich in this world" (1 Timothy 6:17). In fact, according to our relational understanding of class, their wealth lies as much in the fact that they have slaves to do their work for them as it does in the possessions they own.

The principal question in this verse is the rendering of the last four words: οἱ τῆς εὐεργεσίας ἀντιλαμβανόμενοι.[95] Does the phrase refer to the masters as "those who receive the benefit (of their slaves' service)"?[96] Or does it refer to the masters as "those who

---

[93]See II.D.3.d. above, pp. 107-108, readings #2 and #3.

[94]See above II.D.2.b.1) & 4), pp. 83, 86; Verner, *Household of God*, pp. 56-61.

[95]A number of other points generally receive a significant amount of discussion; on the following I find myself in substantial agreement with Verner, and refer to his discussion (*Household of God*, pp. 141-142): 1) Christian slaves appear as a subset of a larger group; 2) disrespect appears to be a problem in the community (arising out of thinking like that in the tradition behind Galatians 3:28); 3) ὅτι ἀδελφοί εἰσιν supplies the reason for καταφρονεῖν rather than for μὴ κατα–φρονεῖν; 4) it is not important whether ἀγαπητοί means loved by God or by the slaves; the point is that the author counters the slaves' use of the egalitarian "brothers" with two other common but less egalitarian Christian labels.

[96]BAGD ἀντιλαμβάνω 3, RSV, NEB, NIV; among the commentators: Spicq, Danker, Kelly, Lock, Fee, Johnson.

devote themselves to the doing of beneficence"?[97] The difference in sense for the meaning of the verse as a whole could not be greater.

The former rendering (herein referred to as the "slaves-as-benefactors" position) ennobles slaves' continued ministrations by making Christian slaves their masters' "benefactors." Says Spicq: "Το δουλευέτωσαν, St. Paul opposes εὐεργεσία and transforms the obeisance of infamous servitude into a noble beneficence."[98] Danker is reminded of Jesus' teaching in Luke 22:25 that meaningful benefi-cence derives from a service-oriented frame of mind:

> In keeping with this thought, 1 Timothy 6:2 in a dramatic language event admonishes slaves not to take advantage of Christian masters but rather to view themselves as benefactors, with the masters being recipients of their εὐεργεσία.[99]

The latter rendering (herein referred to as the "masters-as-bene-factors" position) affirms the justice of slaves' continued minis-trations due to the "benevolence" to which their masters are committed. Verner adopts this reading and says it is of a piece with two other features of the Pastorals' instructions to slaves which demonstrate our author's inability to see things from the slaves' point of view: the lack of that reciprocity which generally char-acterizes the *Haustafeln,* and the fact that slaves are simply warned against petty vices instead of being encouraged to nobility of character.[100] Brox says the phrase is further evidence of the lack of paradox and scandal in this correspondence, and thus is one more example of the governing of practical Christian existence along the lines of *bürgerlich* relationships.[101]

There are good linguistic reasons for the fact that the dispute over the meaning of this phrase is as old as the history of interpreta-tion itself.[102] For the data can be variously construed; nonetheless,

[97]BAGD ἀντιλαμβάνω 2, BDF §170(3); among the commentators: Nägeli, Dibelius and Conzelmann, Verner, Jeremias, Hendriksen ("who reciprocate in good service"), Brox, Bertram.

[98]Spicq, *Pastorales,* p. 555.

[99]Danker, *Benefactor,* p. 324; Johnson has a similar comment (*1 Timothy, 2 Timothy, Titus,* Knox Preaching Guides [Atlanta: John Knox Press, 1987], pp. 105-106).

[100]Verner, *Household of God,* pp. 140-141.

[101]Brox, *Pastoralbriefe,* p. 207.

[102]Favoring "slaves-as-benefactors": the Vulgate and the Peshitta (references in Spicq, *Pastorales,* ad loc.). Favoring "masters-as-benefactors": John Chrysos-tom, Theodoret, Pelagius, Estius.

we believe, the case for the "masters-as-benefactors" reading is the stronger. Three issues are involved: 1) the meaning of εὐεργεσία; 2) the meaning of ἀντιλαμβάνεσθαι; and 3) the demands of the context.

a. ἡ εὐεργεσία: Beneficence Up? or Down?

The normal sense of εὐεργεσία is that of an act performed by a social superior on behalf of an inferior. Danker himself marshals the evidence for the normal movement of a benefaction from the top down.[103] As Spicq observes and copiously documents: "For a Greek ear of the first century, εὐεργεσία evokes a gracious, royal, imperial, or divine gift,[104] generosities accorded by superiors,[105] or by patrons."[106] By way of illustration, he cites Sammelbuch 8444 (= OGI 669 = Danker No. 51) with reference to the concern of a Roman prefect that his subjects "enjoy...the beneficence and constant foresight (of the emperors) which are the cause of...salvation." This is a curious choice because it makes the point about the normally superior position of the bestower of benefits so well that Spicq's conclusion—"Thus the masters become debtors to the slaves"—is jolting at best. Spicq, et al., also appeal to a celebrated passage in Seneca where the direction is reversed (*On Benefits* 3.18-20). This is indeed an intriguing passage because there is some parallel between, on the one hand, Seneca's argument that it is to the extent that slaves willingly go above and beyond the call of duty that their service can be called a benefaction[107] and, on the other, 1 Timothy's

---

[103]Danker, *Benefactor*, see esp., pp. 323-324; see also Mott, "Benefactor," pp. 103-105.

[104]Spicq, *Pastorales*, p. 555, providing the following references: 2 Maccabees 6:13; Acts 4:9; Polybius 5.11.16.

[105]POsl. 127.11; P. Fam. Tebt. 15.72; PThead. 20.7.

[106]Insc. of Thasos 183.3; 192.11; 237.5; of Carie 56.8; Sammelbuch 7738.7; 8303.4.

[107]Seneca's argument is that slaves no less than anyone else possess human rights, including the capacity for virtue (3.18.2). Because the bestowing of benefits is one part of virtue, slaves must be able to bestow them (3.18.4). The fact that a slave's obedience is coerced does not preclude his acting beneficently, for: a) it is merely his body, not his mind which is owned (3.20), and b) "not the status, but the intention, of the one who bestows is what counts" (3.18.2). Thus, "there are certain acts that the law neither enjoins nor forbids; it is in these that a slave finds opportunity to perform a benefit. So long as what he supplies is only that which is ordinarily required of a slave, it is a 'service'; when he supplies more than a slave need do, it is a 'benefit'; it ceases to be called a service when it passes over into the domain of friendly affection (3.21)...

call to serve these Christian masters "all the better" (μᾶλλον) because they are Christians—i.e., in a way that transcends normal obligations. But it must be noted that the length and elegance of Seneca's discussion are directly a function of his awareness that he is using the idea of beneficence in an extraordinary way.

The εὐεργ– root appears in the New Testament three times apart from 1 Timothy 6:2, all from the pen of Luke. In two of these he refers to divine beneficence, bringing no surprises to his Hellenistic audience. When Peter encounters the lame beggar at the gate of the temple, he confesses he cannot provide the expected gift of gold or silver. However, he says with some irony, he will give what he can (Acts 3:1-10). This unexpected boon—restoration of the man's legs—Peter refers to as a divine εὐεργεσία (4:9). As he later explains to Cornelius and his household: that God himself had been present with Jesus was evident in the fact that the latter had gone about "doing good" (εὐεργετεῖν) and (epexegetical) "healing all that were oppressed by the devil" (Acts 10:38).

In the third passage, though, Luke does demonstrate an ironic stance toward the normal sense of a benefaction's moving from a social superior to an inferior. In his gospel, Luke portrays Jesus, the preeminent benefactor of humankind, as a table-waiting servant who expects his followers to emulate him. And yet, as Danker rightly observes, when the followers of Jesus are told to eschew the title of benefactor, it is not the *role* of benefactor to which he is referring, but "the interest in domination that is evidenced by many rulers who try to mask their tyranny with a flourish of public works."[108] By adopting a service-oriented frame of mind (Luke 22:26-27), they actually take up the posture of meaningful beneficence—what is more, this is in imitation of Jesus himself, who though their superior has been their servant.

If Luke's use could be presupposed as background for the Pastorals, one might be prepared for the reversal of the accepted order of things posited by Spicq et al. Since that is not, however, the tack we have taken, we have to look for such evidence of reversal in the Pastorals themselves. It could be that the attitude toward the conferring of honor within the community (not to wealthy patrons,

---

And, just as a hireling gives a benefit if he supplies more than he contracted to do, so a slave—when he exceeds the bounds of his station in goodwill toward his master, and surpasses the expectation of his master by daring some lofty deed that would be an honour even to those more happily born, a benefit is found to exist inside the household" (3.22.1, Loeb translation).

[108]Danker, *Benefactor*, p. 324.

and the enduring of persecution on the part of the church's chief benefactors—elements I have called "anti-*bürgerlich*"—set the scene for such a reversal here. It could also be that the reference to slaves' faithful service as an "adorning" of the gospel in the parallel passage in Titus (2:10) bespeaks a desire to ennoble their service. Even so, it would be the subtle reader who could be expected to get this all out of 1 Timothy 6:2.

Lock is forced to the assertion that the author of 1 Timothy assumes a position like Seneca's without discussion.[109] Unfortunately, while the passage in Seneca does demonstrate that such ideas had at least some circulation, Danker's claim that the presence of such role reversal here is "a dramatic language event" is in fact an admission of the difficulty with which Lock's assertion can be accepted. And while at least an ideology—if not the consistent practice—of social levelling does characterize some important strands of early Christian literature[110] (including sections of the Pauline homologoumena),[111] it does not fit naturally into the ambience of the Pastorals. Unless other considerations emerge, it is more natural to expect to see in ἡ εὐεργεσία at 1 Timothy 6:2 the beneficence of the masters.

b. ἀντιλαμβάνεσθαι: *Giving? or Getting?*

In Bauer's entry on ἀντιλαμβάνειν the suggestion is made that if the verb is to mean "to enjoy, benefit by" at 1 Timothy 6:2 (as in the "slaves-as-benefactors" reading: "the masters enjoy their slaves beneficence"), it is as an expansion of one of the better attested uses of the verb: that of expressing mental or sensory perception—"to perceive, notice."[112] A less than striking comparison is made with the use of the verb in the *Martyrdom of Polycarp* where it is said that those witnessing Polycarp's burning at the stake "noticed" or "perceived" the fragrance of his burning.

The term's use in such contexts does not appear to be particularly relevant to its meaning in our passage. It so happens, however, that ἀντιλαμβάνειν,–εσθαι is used with some frequency when the topic is that of giving and receiving between benefactors and beneficiaries. Moreover, the term can refer either to the act of giving or of receiving. In such contexts there appear to be four basic

109Lock, *Pastoral Epistles*, p. 66.
110E.g., The beatitudes, James.
111Galatians 3:28; 1 Corinthians 7:17-24; Philemon 16-17.
112BAGD, p. 74.

nuances: 1) to receive a benefit; 2) to receive a return on a benefit; 3) to give a return on a benefit; and 4) to give a benefit. A number of instances suggest some flexibility as to whether the voice should be active or middle, and as to whether the object should be in the accusative or the genitive case. In fact, one noticeable feature of the verb's use in certain benefactor-contexts in the Hellenistic period is its resistance to the period's preference for the middle voice with a genitive object.[113] Despite the variety of forms and meanings, the concern in these contexts is generally one of either the establishing or the fulfilling of an obligation. I offer the following illustrations of the use of ἀντιλαμβάνειν, –εσθαι in order to augment Danker's benefactor-semantic field.

1) Receive a return on a benefit

In the *Nichomachean Ethics* (1164b12), Aristotle uses the verb (active voice with accusative object) in speaking of individuals who give gifts with a view to recompense. Such donors will have recovered what is really owed them when they "have been paid" (ἀντιλαμβάνειν = "to receive back") the value of the service or the sum they themselves would have been willing to pay for it. In the *Politics* (1332b40) he uses it (active voice with accusative object) to refer to a young man who submits for the time being to being ruled by his elders. In the future he will "get back his contribution to the common fund" (ἀντιλαμβάνειν τὸν ἔρανον), i.e., in his turn he will have the opportunity to govern. Similarly, when Plutarch contemplates popular lecturers who give more style than substance he says: "It is an empty pleasure they give, and an even more empty renown they acquire in return (κενοτέραν δόξαν ἀντιλαμβάνειν, *On Listening to Lectures* 41D.10). And according to the Cynic (Pseudo-) Anacharsis:[114]

> All of us possess the whole earth. What it freely gives, we accept (λαμβάνειν). What it hides, we dismiss from our minds. We protect our cattle against wild beasts, and in return receive milk and cheese (βοσκήματα ἀπὸ θηρίων σῴζοντες, γάλα καὶ τυρὸν ἀντιλαμβάνομεν, Epistle 9, *To Croesus* 48.31-50.1).

Philo uses ἀντιλαμβάνειν,–εσθαι in this reciprocal sense four times. In the *Life of Moses* 2.7, Philo uses the verb (active voice with

---

[113]BAGD, p. 74.

[114]See the critical discussion in Malherbe, *Cynic Epistles*, pp. 6-9; the first nine letters attributed to Anacharsis are dated anywhere from the third century B.C. to the early empire.

accusative object) to refer to the way different mental faculties inter-act, "mutually receiving and repaying benefits" (τὰς ὠφελείας ἀντι–λαμβάνειν τε καὶ ἀντεκτίνειν). Though the case and voice do not agree with 1 Timothy, this is one of the few places where the verb occurs with a synonym of ἡ εὐεργεσία as its object.

In back-to-back paragraphs of his *Embassy to Gaius*, Philo pro-vides examples that could be suggestive of the nuance of the verb at 1 Timothy 6:2. In these paragraphs Philo offers the emperor Gaius Caligula's treatment of his benefactors as evidence for the baseness of his character. In 60.1 Philo recalls the fate of the unlucky Macro,[115] who had overthrown Sejanus to become commander of Tiberius' Praetorian Guard, from which position he had been influ-ential in securing Gaius' accession. As recompense for his display of such φιλοτιμία on Gaius' behalf (60.6), Macro is forced to commit suicide (and is joined by his wife, Ennia, even though she was rumored to have been Gaius' mistress at one time). Thus, muses Philo, Macro

> paid (ἀντιλαμβάνειν = "received") the extreme penalty as recom-pense[116] for his excessive zeal. This is the gratitude gained by benefits bestowed on the ungrateful. In return for (ἀντὶ...ὧν)[117] the benefits they have received, they inflict the severest penalties on their benefac-tors (οἱ εὐεργετοῦντες).

While all the above examples employ the active voice and an accusative object, the next one (*Embassy* 62.5) shows how the same idea can be conveyed in the middle voice; unfortunately, a textual problem prevents the determination of the case of the object. Here Philo furthers his case against Gaius by denouncing his treacherous dealings with his father-in-law, Silanus.[118] Even after the death of his daughter, Silanus continues to show fatherly affection toward Gaius, "thinking that by thus converting his son-in-law into a son he

---

[115]Q. Naevius Cordus Sutorius; OCD, p. 635; Pauly-Wissowa (hereafter cited as PW) 21; *Annee Epigraphique* 1957, 250.

[116]A double accusative: ἀμοιβὰς τὰς ἀνωτάτω τιμωρίας; cf. the recompense (ἀμοιβή) due parents in 1 Timothy 5:4.

[117]I have adapted the Loeb translation to bring out the sense of ἀντί with the genitive relative pronoun in this clause. The ironic juxtaposition of ἀμοιβὰς τὰς ἀνωτάτω τιμωρίας *ἀντιλαβών* in the initial clause with *ἀντὶ*...ὧν ὠφελήθησαν in this sentence sets in relief the caustic apothegm in the intervening clause: τοιοῦτόν ἐστιν ἡ εἰς τοὺς ἀχαρίστους χάρις.

[118]M. Junius Silanus (PW 174); he was put to death by Gaius in A.D. 38.

would have it reciprocated (ἧς or ἥν[119] ...ἀντιλαμβάνεσθαι = 'receive it back again') by the rule of equality." That is to say, Silanus hoped that Gaius would return the favor and treat him not so much as a (former) father-in-law, but as a father. Unfortunately, what Silanus receives in consideration of his solicitude for Gaius is his own execution.

In *Special Laws* 317.6, finally, Philo speaks of all who cast aside their physical family ties for the sake of that bond which exists among those who seek the honor of God: "those who are so minded will receive in exchange (a) kinship(s) (ἀντιλαμβάνεσθαι συγγε–νείας)[120] of greater dignity and sanctity."

The "slaves-as-benefactors" reading of 1 Timothy 6:2 assumes ἀντιλαμβάνεσθαι can refer to the act of receiving instead of the act of giving. The examples above show that this is indeed the case, and that it goes for the middle voice as well as for the active (though a genitive object is not certain in any of them). But what is expressed in the object of the verb is not a benefit that has originated with the giving party. What is expressed in the object is a return on something previously given by the party who is now doing the receiving. On the one hand, the verb's object may express that in consideration of which a return is now being made (e.g., the young person's original contribution to the common fund, or Silanus' fatherly behavior toward Gaius). On the other hand, the object may express the thing now being received (e.g., the milk and cheese, or new kinships) as a return on something previously given (e.g., preservation of the cows, or abandonment of family ties).

With respect to 1 Timothy 6:2, the former meaning would yield the following sense: in their slaves' continued and redoubled service, Christian masters get back a return on their own beneficence. The latter would yield: masters ought to be able to receive their slaves' continued and redoubled service; this service is a benefit slaves bestow upon their masters to reciprocate benefits already bestowed by their masters.

---

[119]Because the textual evidence is mixed, it is impossible to determine whether Philo intends an accusative or a genitive object.

[120]συγγένεια and its two modifiers (σεμνοτέρας καὶ ἱεροπρεπεστέρας) follow the ε,ι,ρ-rule; therefore it is impossible to distinguish genitive singular endings from accusative plural. And though the discussion begins with the plural συγγένειαι to refer to earthly ties (317.4), it moves to the singular bond between devotees to God's honor (317.7); thus the context does not make clear whether Philo intends the object to be accusative plural (recalling the earthly ties) or genitive singular (further characterizing the bond between those who honor God).

These readings differ formally, the former conforming to the "masters-as-benefactors" reading and the latter to the "slaves-as-benefactors" reading. But they both agree materially with the "masters-as-benefactors" position, because even in the latter case the grounds for the slaves' service would be to give a return on their masters' service.

2) Receive a benefit

At the same time, the expression could mean exactly what the proponents of the "slaves-as-benefactors" reading intend it to mean, because the verb can mean "receive a benefit" apart from any consideration of a prior gift on the recipient's part. Quite close to the form of 1 Timothy 6:2 is Philo's *Noah's Work as a Planter* 133.1 where the verb appears in the middle voice with a genitive object in an aside about Moses' marveling that humans have been allowed "to be recipients of even secondary privileges"—"secondary privileges" here being epexegetical of the "enjoyment (ἀπόλαυσις) and use (χρῆσις)" of God's creation in 132.2. This is a significant passage because the provision of things for dependents' "enjoyment" and "use" is a persistent theme in discourse on benefactions, appearing, interestingly, in 1 Timothy 6:17 of God "who richly supplies us all good things to enjoy" (εἰς ἀπόλαυσιν).[121] In Philo, the verb is used to express the "reception" of the benefactions God provides. This is thus a phrase directly parallel to the usual "slaves-as-benefactors" reading of 1 Timothy 6:2 because it conceives of the simple reception of a benefit apart from anything done to inspire or merit it.

A second example comes from the letter of Plotina, mother of Hadrian and patroness of the Epicurean school at Athens.[122] Having successfully appealed to her emperor son to allow the Epicureans to choose a non-citizen to succeed the present head of the school, she now writes the members of the school to inform them of the happy outcome which has come about through the generosity of their benevolent emperor, and to express her faith that "the person who receives the benefit which arises from our doctrine" (ὁ ἀντιλαβόμενος <τῆς> ὠφελίας τῆς ἐκ τῶν λόγων περιγεγενημένης αὐτῷ) will be unable to prove himself unworthy of the concessions made by the emperor (lines 15-18). Although materially this expression is not far removed from the more common use of ἀντιλαμβάνεσθαι of

[121]Danker discusses the use of the χρη– family at *Benefactor*, pp. 325ff. For ἀπόλαυσις, cf., Danker No. 51.4 (= OGI 669.4).

[122]SIG3 (= Jahreshefte 2:1899, pp. 270ff).

a cognitive act, it does offer a formal parallel to 1 Timothy 6:2, and is a striking datum in support of the simple "slaves-as-benefactors" reading for 1 Timothy 6:2.

Nonetheless, Philo's *Noah* 133.1 is the only one of these examples which envisions a person receiving a benefit from another person (i.e., from God)—and in this instance it is the social inferior (humankind) who is "receiving" the benefit.

3) Give a return on a benefit

The meaning "to give a return on a benefit"—the opposite of meaning #1 above—is a nuance for which I have as yet found but one occurrence. Though I am unable to offer it as a possibility for the sense of 1 Timothy 6:2, I believe the passage in which it is so used is worth noting. Plutarch tells a story about some Pythagoreans who hear that one of their own has been helped to a noble end and has been provided an honorable burial by an impoverished man. They send a delegate to offer money to this man and his house. With their offer they hope to make a return on great favor and friendship (πολλὴν χάριν καὶ φιλίαν ἀντιλαμβάνειν, *Moralia* 583C.6). It so happens that this household is devoted to poverty as a philosophical ideal; the household's refusal to allow this return on the hospitality they had shown brings offense, thus provoking a lively discussion on the propriety of refusing a gift (582D-585D). The sort of insult that could be felt at having a return on a gift rebuffed is nicely illustrated in the following discourse offered by the Pythagorean delegate, who responds to being introduced by one of his hosts as someone who wishes to "confirm noble doctrines by noble works" (ἔργοις καλοῖς καλὰ δόγματα βεβαιοῦν):

> Are not you (his host) preventing the noblest of these works? For if it is a noble act to benefit friends, it is no disgrace to be benefited by them; for the favor, requiring a recipient no less than a giver, needs both to be made perfect in nobility. He who refuses to accept the favor, like the man who refuses to catch a well-directed ball, disgraces it, allowing it to fall to the ground without achieving its end. For what target is so delightful to hit and so painful to miss, as a man deserving kindness at whom we aim a favor? Yet in the case of the target the man who misses has only himself to blame, as the mark is fixed; whereas with favors, the man who declines and moves aside is guilty of an offence against the favor, allowing it to fall short of its goal (582E-F).

The discussion as a whole is illustrative of the philotimic contest of giving we have come to think of as the liquid capital of ancient society. And if the relevance of the whole to the Pastorals is largely indirect, the fact that ἀντιλαμβάνειν emerges here ought not to be passed over in silence. In the question of the propriety of not allowing one to "return a benefit," two value systems collide: one seeing a point of honor in the returning of favors, another willing to offend for the sake of protecting inner freedom from material goods.

This meaning of ἀντιλαμβάνεσθαι is the most difficult for 1 Timothy 6:2. I have found but one use of the verb in this sense, occurring there in the active voice with an accusative object. If this consideration could be set aside, its appropriateness in this context would still be less than transparent. Likely, it would mean something like the following: slaves are encouraged to redouble their service to Christian masters "because faithful and beloved are the masters who give a return on (their slaves') beneficence." It shares with the second meaning of ἀντιλαμβάνεσθαι (see above, "receive a benefit") the disadvantage of presupposing an unexplained reversal of the normal sense of a benefaction flowing from a superior to an inferior. It has the further disadvantage of presupposing an even more elaborate exchange between master and slave: slaves' benevolent service prompts a return from their masters, which in turn obligates the slaves to an even greater service. This would not be an impossible meaning for the term here. Nor would it be an impossible system of reciprocities, even between slaves and masters. But the whole thing is unusual enough that the interpreter ought to ask whether the original auditors would have so understood the phrase in the absence of any qualification.

4) Give a benefit

The reader of the Septuagint will be more familiar with the use of ἀντιλαμβάνεσθαι (middle voice) with a personal (genitive) object to mean: "take (someone's) part," "help," or "come to (someone's) aid."[123] Of the 51 uses of the verb in the Septuagint some 38 bear this sense; most characteristically (23 times) the one who does the helping is God. For example:

> May the Lord answer you in the day of distress, may the name of the God of Jacob protect you. May he send you help (ἡ βοήθεια) from the sanctuary and grant you support (ἀντιλαμβάνεσθαί σου) from Zion (Psalm 19:1-2 = Eng. 20:1-2).

---

[123]In the Septuagint the verb always takes the middle voice; it takes a genitive object 46 times, no object three times, a dative object once, and an accusative object once.

sanctuary and grant you support (ἀντιλαμβάνεσθαί σου) from Zion
(Psalm 19:1-2 = Eng. 20:1-2).

This background determines the use of the verb both times it
appears in the New Testament outside our text. First, in language
dependent upon Isaiah 41:8-9,[124] Mary extols the God who helps his
child Israel (ἀντελάβετο ' Ἰσραὴλ παιδὸς αὐτοῦ) for her own child-
bearing place in his merciful plan (Luke 1:53). Then, by way of
farewell to the Ephesian elders, Luke's Paul sets before them his
own manual labor as an object lesson in the need to help the weak
(ἀντιλαμβάνεσθαι τῶν ἀσθενούντων)[125] "remembering the words
of the Lord Jesus, how he said, 'it is more blessed to give than to receive'" (μακάριόν ἐστιν μᾶλλον διδόναι ἢ λαμβάνειν,[126] Acts
20:35).

Though this is a use that is distinctive of the Greek Bible, it is not
one that is exclusive to it. It is not unknown to the dramatists and
historians.[127] And it surfaces here and there in the inscriptions and
the papyri—e.g., the Roman inscription from Egypt, on the graves of
victims of murder: ἀντιλα(β)οῦ, κύριε Σάραπι ("Lord Sarapis,
help!—OGIS 697.1).[128] Dibelius cites as illustrative of the meaning
of 1 Timothy 6:2 a mid-third century B.C. inscription from Ptolemais
in honor of a benefactor of the local Dionysic guild of artists. His
philanthropic concern for the growth of the group has been manifest
in the way he has "willingly and zealously been of assistance to each
individually and all collectively" (καὶ κατ' ἰδίαν ἑκάστου καὶ κατὰ
κοινὸν πάντων ἀντιλαμβάνεται προθύμως καὶ ἐκτενῶς, OGIS 51.9-
10).

Related—whether genetically or merely generically may be
beyond demonstration—is the use of ἀντιλαμβάνεσθαι (always in

---

[124]Even though in the Septuagint of Isaiah 41:9 ἀντιλαμβάνεσθαι refers to
God "taking" his child Jacob "to himself" from the ends of the earth, Luke
alludes to the verse as though it meant "help."

[125]Cf., Septuagint Leviticus 25:35; Ezekiel 12:14; Sirach 29:9.

[126]My emphasis highlights the fact that διδόναι is not λαμβάνειν's only
antonym in this context.

[127]Euripides *Troades* 464; Diodorus Siculus 11.13; Thucydides 7.70.

[128]See the references in Friedrich Preisigke, *Wörterbuch der griechischen
Papyrusurkunden* (hereafter cited as Preisigke), p. 135; J.H. Moulton and G.
Milligan, *The Vocabulary of the Greek New Testament Illustrated from the Papyri and
Other Non-literary Sources*, reprint ed. (Grand Rapids: Eerdmans, 1930, 1980), p.
48, and BAGD, ad loc. Papyrological examples: PPetr 2.3.b.7, σὺ δὲ ἀφιλοτίμως
μου ἀντιλαμβάνης; PPar. 27.22f, καθότι οὐ διαλείπεις ἡμῶν ἀντιλαμ-
βανόμενος.

The use is concentrated in, though not exclusive to,[129] inscriptions and papyri.[130] Since it is in the nature of the case that the honorific inscriptions use the notion with regard to the undertakings of benefactors, the sense of meeting the needs of others or of being "helpful" remains in view.[131] It so happens that this is largely the case in the surviving papyri as well. Moulton and Milligan, for instance, cite the following two oaths of office: ὀμνύω...ἀντιλήμψασθαι τῆς χρείας πιστῶς κὰι ἐπιμελῶς ("I do swear that I will undertake the office faithfully and attentively"—PLond 301.6ff); and ὀμνύω... ἀντιλήμψαισθαι (i.e., –εσθαι) τῷ προσήκοντι χρόνῳ τῆς δηλουμένης χρείας, καὶ ταύτην ἐκτελέσιν ("I swear that I will take up at the proper time the said office and will discharge it"—POxy 9.1196.12ff). The object of ἀντιλαμβάνεσθαι can specify the responsibility or undertaking,[132] or it can refer to it in a more general way—e.g., τῆς ἐγχειρισθείσης αὐτῷ χρείας ("the office that has been entrusted to him"), τῆς λειτουργίας ("the liturgy"), or simply τῆς ἐργασίας ("the task").[133]

Citing this phenomenon in the inscriptions and papyri, Nägeli and Blass-DeBrunner state their preference for a translation of "devote oneself to" for ἀντιλαμβάνεσθαι at 1 Timothy 6:2.[134] And Dibelius quotes the Menas inscription where the verb is used to describe some of this public servant's gymnasiarchal activities (OGIS 339.31-32).[135] It is curious that although Danker includes this

---

[129]Plato Laws 815B.5 re: dancing; Philo Special Laws 317.6 (if συγγένειας is genitive); Plutarch Moralia 12C re: parental responsibility.

[130]Despite a uniformity of use extending from the third century B.C. (OGIS 51) through the sixth century A.D. (OGIS 697), the evidence (chiefly papyrological) happens to be more dense for the second and third centuries A.D.

[131]See again Danker's discussion on the relationship between office-holding and need-meeting (χρη–group—Benefactor, pp. 325ff).

[132]E.g., ἀντιλαμβάνεσθαι τῶν τε λαμμάτων καὶ ἀναλωμάτων responsibility for receipts and expenses; ἀντιλαμβάνεσθαι τῆς ἐφηβείας either ephebic training itself or responsibility over the body of ephebes; ἀντιλαμβάνεσθαι τῆς ὑδροφυλακίας the office of inspector of the aqueducts; ἀντιλαμβάνεσθαι τῆς παγαρχίας the heading up of a provincial agricultural district; refs. in Preisigke, p. 135.

[133]Respectively, PFlor. 2,9;183;269; POxy 1187.19; CPR 233.9.

[134]T. Nägeli, Der Wortschatz des Apostels Paulus (Göttingen, 1905), p. 54: "ἀντιλαμβάνεσθαι τινος sich einer Sache befleissigen (1 Timothy). Auf Inschr. und Pap. beliebt." BDF §170(3), citing: Edwin Mayser, Grammatik der griechischen Papyri aus der Ptolemäerzeit, II,2,199ff; and R. Helbing, Die Kasussyntax der Verba bei den Septuagint, 123ff.

[135]Dibelius/Conzelmann, The Pastoral Epistles, p. 82. Note my discussion of this inscription above, III.A.4., pp. 121f; III.B.1.c., pp. 127ff.

(OGIS 339.31-32).[135] It is curious that although Danker includes this inscription in his collection (= Danker No. 17), he does not take up the question of what light it may shed on the meaning of ἀντιλαμ-βάνεσθαι in 1 Timothy 6:2.

Menas' first term as gymnasiarch is introduced with a précis: τῆς τε εὐταξίας τῶν ἐφήβων καὶ τῶν νέων *προενοήθη*, τῆς τε ἄλλης εὐσχημοσύνης τῆς κατὰ τὸ γυμνάσιον *ἀντελάβετο* καλῶς καὶ φιλοτίμως ("he gave careful thought to the training of the epheboi and the neoi; and in an excellent manner in his passion for honor he *devoted himself to* [or *undertook*] all other gymnastic acculturation"— lines 31-33, emphasis and translation mine).[136] Though Menas serves his city in a number of capacities, it is his willingness to undertake the responsibilities of gymnasiarch a second time—and this when war is devastating the local economy—that results in the inscription that has come down to us. The inscription summarizes this second tour of duty in language reminiscent of the first: *ἐπεμελήθη* δὲ καὶ τῆς τῶν ἐφήβων καὶ νέων παιδείας, τῆς τε λοιπῆς εὐσχημοσύνης τῆς κατὰ τὸ γυμνάσιον *προενοήθη* ("he admini-stered the education of the ephebes and the neoi, and *gave thought to* [or *made provision for*] all the rest of the gymnastic program"—lines 76-77, emphasis and translation mine).[137] Juxtaposition of the sentences brings several sets of synonyms to the surface. The education of the young men is called ἡ εὐταξία in line 31 and ἡ παιδεία in line 76. Reference to the broad scope of administrative details that come under the gymnasiarch's administration is made in nearly identical terms (differing only in the use of ἄλλη in one place and λοιπή in the other).

What is of import for us is the fact that ἀντιλαμβάνεσθαι is interchangeable with προνοεῖσθαι[138] ("to give thought to," or "to

---

[135]Dibelius/Conzelmann, *The Pastoral Epistles*, p. 82. Note my discussion of this inscription above, III.A.4., pp. 121f; III.B.1.c., pp. 127ff.

[136]There follows an enumeration of the specifics: he constructed and outfitted a bath with an adjoining building and marble statue; and he sponsored monthly sacrifices and games, including races, javelin throwing, and archery.

[137]This time the specifics of what is involved precede as well as follow; they are much like the first list, except the religious dimension of the games is stressed through the mention of the gymnasium's patron gods, Hermes and Herakles; also highlighted is his noble hospitality in sharing the sacrificial offer-ings with extra-local athletes (something like a visiting team?); finally, some of the more mundane expenditures on behalf of the gymnasium are listed: under-writing the cost of the scrapers, supplying the ointments, donating the prizes.

[138]Note the parallel use in 1 Timothy 5:8; cf. 2 Corinthians 8:21; Romans 12:17.

σθαι[139] ("to administer"). It is not simply that this is a clear example of ἀντιλαμβάνεσθαι meaning "to devote oneself to or undertake an activity or an office." More than that, the expressions "he provided for and administered the εὐταξία and the παιδεία of the young men" and "he devoted himself to and provided for all other aspects of the gymnastic program" refer to the very things that have occasioned this particular outpouring of thanks. In a word, these are highmarks in the career of one who has "devoted himself to beneficence."

Danker translates ἀντιλαμβάνεσθαι as "render...assistance in"; and his translation has the virtue of reinforcing the lines of connection between the use of ἀντιλαμβάνεσθαι with a personal object to mean "help" and its use with an impersonal object to mean "undertake a helpful activity or an office." It is unfortunate that he does not consider the possibility that this meaning is determinative of the sense of the instructions to the slaves in 1 Timothy—i.e., that slaves of wealthy Christians are being asked to see in the "benefactions" which their masters "undertake" grounds not only for the abandonment of egalitarian social aspirations, but for a renewed and yet more vigorous service as well.

In sum, it is possible that ἀντιλαμβάνεσθαι in 1 Timothy 6:2 puts Christian masters in the role of recipients (meanings #1 and #2 above). Indeed, though the commentators who adopt meaning #2 and support the "slaves-as-benefactors" position do not appeal to it, there is a passage in Philo and a line in Plotina's letter that mirror the thought in form and content. But the evidence shows that when ἀντιλαμβάνειν,–εσθαι refers to the reception of something, this something is just as, if not more, likely to be a return on a benefit the receiving party has previously given (meaning #1 above). If this is the nuance intended at 1 Timothy 6:2, the thought is supportive of the "masters-as-benefactors" position: in their slaves' willing service, masters receive a return on their own beneficent activities. However, it is more likely that the phrase, by virtue of analogy with the inscriptions and papyri that speak frequently of benefactors "giving assistance" or "giving themselves to helpful tasks or offices," conceives of masters in the role of givers or providers of benefactions (meaning #4 above). Both of the more likely readings, then, support the "masters-as-benefactors" position.

---

[139]Note the parallel use in 1 Timothy 3:5; cf. Luke 10:34-35; 15:8; Acts 27:3; and the adverbial form of the verb in the oath of office above (PLond 301.6ff).

c. Contextual Considerations

When linguistic evidence is mixed, considerations of context can be expected to play a decisive role. Contextual considerations can even overrule lexical evidence. Where, in fact, a reason is given for the "slaves-as-benefactors" reading, it is in the form of an appeal to context. Spicq, for instance, waves aside the active meaning "to give" for ἀντιλαμβάνεσθαι as being hardly possible in this situation, and opts for an extension of the verb's use with sensory perceptions.[140] Lock simply asserts that masters' "taking part in receiving" their slaves' εὐεργεσία "suits the context best," while the notion that εὐεργεσία refers to acts of kindness on the part of the masters "is scarcely implied in the context."[141] In neither case is it transparent what there is about the context that dictates the choice. One is left to wonder whether the decisive consideration is that commentators and translators would like to find the impress on this Christian writer of a sensibility that is at least as attuned to the plight of slaves as is that of the pagan Seneca. The result is "a dramatic language event" where there is in reality little evidence of any such thing.

On the other hand, if, as I have argued, one of the principal concerns of 1 Timothy is to help rich Christians understand their place in the household of God and to help the church, in turn, learn how to make room for such people, a context altogether hospitable to the "masters-as-benefactors" reading is at hand. As would be the case in a pagan club, rich believers, of whose wealth the ownership of slaves is a prime index, are expected to be patrons or benefactors of the church: they are expected to be liberal and generous with their wealth (6:18), to open their homes (3:2), and be well-disposed to those beneath them (6:17)—in short, to be engaged in the doing of good (6:2). At the same time they are warned against expecting automatically to exchange their currency in status as prosperous *Bürger* for positions at the head of this new "household" (3:6; 5:22). The title *patronus* or εὐεργέτης will not be conferred.[142] Their birthdays will not be celebrated nor will crowns be placed on their heads, at least in this life. No honorific inscriptions nor statues will

---

[140]Spicq, *Pastorales*, pp. 554-555.

[141]Lock, *Pastoral Epistles*, p. 66.

[142]The title is unknown in early Christian circles, except in disdain (Luke 22:25). I owe this observation, as well as some of the language in this paragraph about the lack of honors to early Christian patrons, to Countryman, *Rich Christian*, pp. 164-165.

perpetuate the memory of their largess. Within this context 1 Timothy 6:2 suggests: what wealthy believers who devote themselves to εὐεργεσία *can* ask for is that their Christian slaves continue to serve them well, rather than pilfer from them and talk back to them (cf., Titus 2:9-10).

As his championing of the "masters-as-benefactors" position reflects, Verner appreciates the extent to which this passage is designed to speak to masters even though it is addressed to slaves. This feature is in fact of a piece with 1 Timothy's larger purpose of speaking to the special problem of wealthy Christians and their place in the church. However, what Verner gives with one hand, he takes away with the other. For rather than exploit the insight for what it might reveal about the meaning of 1 Timothy in its social world, Verner rushes to a denunciation of the author as being incapable of identifying with the slaves' condition and as being contemptuous of them as a class. So far is the author of 1 Timothy from being able to reason from the slaves' point of view that he unconditionally extols all Christian masters as paragons of virtue, to wit, "they devote themselves to works of beneficence."[143]

As the subject of a nominal sentence the phrase actually has the effect of *limiting* the predication of "faithful and beloved" to "the ones who undertake benevolence." It should be translated: "for faithful and beloved are the ones who undertake benevolence," or perhaps, "for those are faithful and beloved who undertake benevolence." The thought is similar to that in 3:13 where those who serve nobly are said to gain excellent standing and much assurance of faith. Reference could also be made to 5:17 where double honor is commended for elders who rule nobly, especially in word and teaching. In no case is it the mere possession of office or status that makes one worthy of approbation; praise is reserved for those who use their position as a venue for service. On the surface, 1 Timothy 6:2 does indeed call upon Christian slaves to remain gladly in their place rather than demand equal standing with masters who are Christian "brothers." On a more subtle level, however, a call is also being extended to Christian masters to merit their Christian slaves' hearty service by proving themselves to be among those who are not haughty, who do not trust in their riches, but who are generous and disposed to share, who, in a word, devote themselves to works of beneficence.

---

[143]Verner, *Household of God*, pp. 144, 183.

C. SUMMARY

From this chapter it should be clear that in a way that is quite without parallel in the New Testament, the Pastorals do take up issues familiar to the social world of early imperial municipalities. What is the relationship between the doing of good and the receiving of honor? How may wealth be so invested as to win the most secure of futures? Is there a moral worth attendant upon financial worth? With its egalitarian gospel, does the household of God prize the "good and noble" person or the virtues of "generosity and liberality" differently than contemporary households, associations, or municipalities would?

No one should suggest that the Pastorals' answers are scandalously radical. Divestment is not demanded of wealthy Christians. Full play is given to a generous, voluntaristic spirit on the part of the wealthy on the one hand, and to a willingness on the part of their dependents to defer to them on the other. "The good and noble" person is as valued within the church as without.

All the same, the conclusion that the Pastorals' approach is but an uncritical accepting of contemporary *bürgerlich* or even "aristocratic" values is vacuous. The assumption that wealth is an index of moral worth is dismissed out of hand. The notion that a wealthy person's future can be secured through the shrewd cultivation of "friends"—i.e., people obligated to return favors—is not even given a hearing. In reality, the whole web of human reciprocity is dismantled if it is indeed in the next age rather than in this one and from God himself rather than from earthly friends that the wealthy can expect a return on their beneficences. And altogether disingenuous is Verner's castigating of the Pastorals' author for failing to see things from the slaves' point of view and for unconditionally extolling all Christian masters as paragons of virtue.

The fallout to all this is that there are significant limitations to Dibelius' thinking of the Pastorals as participating in a program of *Bildungschristentum*. To the extent that he would have us think of an appropriation of contemporary ideas about how good citizens (*Bürger*) should use their wealth, he takes us halfway. For *bürgerlich* does indeed provide an angle of vision on the great responsibility placed upon the rich to use their wealth for the church's advantage. But the epithet does not bring into view, and perhaps even masks, the extent to which these letters challenge assumptions about what ought to motivate and be hoped for by Christian benefactors. While there is much that is familiar in these letters' appeal to Christians who are accustomed to the role of patron, there is as much that is alien. The Pastorals repudiate the presuppositions even as they appropriate the language of the cultural ideal of the wealthy *Bürger*.

CHAPTER IV

Ethics and Eschatology in
the Pastoral Epistles:
An Unheroically Conservative Ethic?

A. FRAMING THE QUESTION

The analysis so far should alert one to seductive simplicities when it comes to the Pastoral epistles. First, we have been warned against an inference about a "middle class" from the truism that Pastoral Christians are drawn neither from the super-elites of Imperial Rome nor from its disinherited masses. So to infer would be to distort the aristocratic feel and stratified contours of this Christian community. Second, we have been cautioned against a superficial reading of the broad overlap between the language used in the Greek world to bind wealthy citizens to their communities and the language used in our epistles to outline the role of the wealthy in the household of God. The cultural ideal of the *Bürger*, or citizen of means, is challenged and transcended even as its language and thought forms are being brought into the service of the church.

What remains is a consideration of the third level of meaning in Dibelius' epithet: that these letters betray a hardening of social ethics from an ad hoc to a principled conservatism based on the loss of imminent, apocalyptic expectation. Has a willingness to put up with the status quo on a provisional basis—i.e., until the imminent end of the world—given way to an actual sanctifying of present inegalitarian conditions as being necessary to the church's survival in the world? Have Christian ethics thus come to be "stamped with a conservative bent which according to their essence they did not possess"? Have they lost their heroism?[1]

---

[1]Dibelius, *Urchristentum*, pp. 22-23. The question, of course, could be put in Conzelmann's more moderate terms: have the Pastorals opted for an ethical *via media* between the extremes of legalism and gnosticism, or, in the matter of wealth, the extremes of renunciation and opulence? In some quarters, Conzelmann's caveats to Dibelius have been judged to be persuasive. For

By way of anticipation, we contend that it is a further evasion of
the subtleties of the Pastorals to put their ethical stance on wealth
somewhere to the right of Paul on a scale of conservative to revolutionary and to make such a placement a function of a toned-down
eschatology. In the first place, the ethic of wealth in these epistles is
no more supportive nor critical of the status quo than is that in the
acknowledged letters. The way this writer approaches wealth is in
line, in fact, with the approach taken on other social ethical issues in
the homologoumena, viz., ethnicity, slavery, gender. Nor, in the
second place, is there evidence (*pace* Dibelius, et al.) of the kind of
backing away from an apocalyptic expectation which is so often
deemed to provide the occasion of a rapprochement with "the
world" and its structures of inequality.

B. SOCIAL ETHICS AND ESCHATOLOGY IN THE
ACKNOWLEDGED PAULINE LETTERS

1. *Paradigms in Paul's Social Ethics*

Within the social thought of the acknowledged Paul himself
there are both "revolutionary" and "conservative" strands.[2]

---

example, F.J. Schierse ("Eschatologische Existenz und christliche
Bürgerlichkeit," *Geist und Leben* 32 (1959): 280-291, pp. 280, 286-287) speaks of
the *Sitz im Leben* of the spread of the *Haustafeln* as being the gradual leaving
behind of the extraordinary experiences of the earliest church—a function of the
delay of the parousia—and the setting in of the realization that it is precisely in
ordinary, bourgeois relations that the absolutely new character of the faith is to
become manifest. He sees the *christliche Bürgerlichkeit* of the Pastorals as an
attempt to resolve the tension between those who would make Christianity into
an esoteric mystery religion which rejects all aspects of bourgeois life on
principle, and those who would turn Christianity into a mere preparatory
training ground for eternal bliss, "which one could earn for oneself according to
the standard of practiced virtues."

[2]To borrow terms from Ernst Troeltsch, *The Social Teaching of the Christian
Churches*, 2 vols., trans. Olive Wyon (New York: Harper and Row, Publishers,
1960). One could also profitably use the language of "culture-preserving" and
"culture-critiquing" from Dibelius' *Urchristentum*, or of "ideological" and
"utopian" from Karl Mannheim's *Ideology and Utopia: An Introduction to the
Sociology of Knowledge*, trans. Louis Wirth and Edward Shils (New York:
Harcourt, Brace & World, 1936; A Harvest Book, 1936). The point is that a

Attempts to define Paul's thought on social ethics generally take Galatians 3:26-28 as their starting point:

> You are all sons of God through faith in Christ Jesus, for all of you who were baptized into Christ have been clothed with Christ. There is neither Jew nor Greek, slave nor free, male nor female; for you are all one in Christ Jesus (NIV).[3]

Indeed, it is not uncommon for scholars attempting to give some order to Paul's thinking on social ethical matters to take the group relations suggested in these verses as paradigmatic of his concerns, and even to use the implicit egalitarianism of this text as both a banner to suspend over and a critical grid through which to run his approach to social issues.[4] As fraught with revolutionary promise as these verses appear to be, however, it is extraordinary how often Paul sidesteps their potential when it comes to concrete cases. In fact, if there is a banner to be placed over Paul's social ethics, a more likely candidate might be 1 Corinthians 7:17-24, to which Dibelius[5] appealed in describing Paul's "apocalyptic passivism":

> Only, let every one lead the life which the Lord has assigned to him, and in which God has called him. This is my rule in all the churches. Was any one at the time of his call already circumcised? Let him not seek to remove the marks of circumcision. Was any one at the time of his call uncircumcised? Let him not seek circumcision. For neither circumcision counts for anything nor uncircumcision, but keeping the commandments of God. Every one should remain in the state in which he was called. Were you a slave when called? Never mind. But if you can gain your freedom, avail yourself of the opportunity. For he who was called in the Lord as a slave is a freedman of the Lord. Likewise he who was free when called is a slave of Christ. You were

---

"conservative" social ethic will tend to support an existing social order, and a "revolutionary" one will challenge it in the name of an alternative order.

[3]There is no small discussion as to whether these verses come from Paul himself and actually reflect his sentiment, or whether, as a formula of baptism, they stem from early church tradition and therefore do not necessarily reflect his own thinking. I register my indifference to the question of their origin; whether the formulation is his or not, he embraces it. See discussions in Hans Dieter Betz, *Galatians*, ad loc, and Meeks, "Androgyne," pp. 180ff.

[4]See, for example, Krister Stendahl's *The Bible and the Role of Women*, trans. E.T. Sander (Philadelphia: Fortress Press, 1966), and Richard Longenecker's *New Testament Social Ethics for Today* (Grand Rapids: Eerdmans Publishing Co., 1984).

[5]Dibelius, *Urchristentum*, pp. 17-18; and see above, I.C.1.c., pp. 20ff.

bought with a price; do not become slaves of men. So, brethren, in whatever state each was called, there let him remain with God (RSV).

S. Scott Bartchy has recently argued for the importance of this passage in understanding Paul's social ethics, appearing as it does in the middle of a chapter in which Paul is qualifying for the Corinthian church exactly what *he* understands to be the implications of "no male and female in Christ."[6] The fact that Paul can readily illustrate his point about men and women by referring to Jews and Gentiles and slaves and free persons suggests that this "three-part pattern" is basic to his thinking.[7] In the course of his analysis, Bartchy challenges the understanding of Paul's sense of "calling" here as the absolutizing of particular social standings. Paul is not urging Christians "to 'stay as you are,' as if there were some Christian value in maintaining the status quo as such."[8] The point is not to exclude social change, but to argue its irrelevance to the believer's self-understanding; the challenge before the believer is to live out the calling to obey God's commands no matter what the venue may be. Any and every social standing can be one within which one's identity in Christ can be worked out. Paul's "theology of calling" thus has a "conservative" tendency: by virtue of the fact that one's earthly situation presents no disadvantage in fellowship with God, each person is challenged to be a Christian right where he or she is. What is "revolutionary" is Paul's insistence that all who have fellowship with God in Christ should have fellowship with one another, and that all are baptized into *one* body (1 Corinthians 12:13-33).[9]

a. Jew and Gentile

Paul most dramatically insists that the leveling logic of Galatians 3:28 be allowed to restructure social relationships when it comes to: a) Gentile freedom from Torah; and b) Jewish Christian and Gentile table fellowship—to wit, his confrontation with the Galatians over

---

[6]S. Scott Bartchy, *MAΛΛON XPHΣAI: First Century Slavery and the Interpretation of 1 Corinthians 7:21*, Society of Biblical Literature Dissertation Series, No. 11 (Missoula, MT: Scholars Press, 1973), ch. 3, esp. pp. 143-148, ch. 4, esp. pp. 162-165.

[7]Bartchy, *Slavery*, pp. 163-164, n. 562.

[8]Bartchy, *Slavery*, p. 153, and n. 529, where he is dependent upon Werner Bieder, *Die Berufung im Neuen Testament*, Abhandlungen zur Theologie des Alten und Neuen Testaments 38 (Zurich, 1961), p. 58.

[9]Bartchy, *Slavery*, p. 153, and n. 529.

their proposed circumcision (his epistle to the Galatians, in toto) and with Peter at Antioch over his withdrawal from a Gentile table out of respect for visiting Jewish-Christians from Jerusalem (Galatians 2:11-14).[10]

But there are contours to Paul's thought even with respect to the paradigm of Jew and Gentile. To be sure, his argument in Romans is that despite Israel's historical advantages (3:1-4; 9:4-5), there is no difference (οὐκ ἔστιν διαστολή) between Jew and Gentile in sinfulness (1:18-3:20) and in access to God's gracious provision of justification in Christ (3:21-5:11).[11] As driven as he is to take the gospel to the Gentile world, however, Paul never renounces the priority of Israel's claim on the gospel: "to the Jew first, then to the Greek" (1:16-17). In fact, from Romans 9-11 we are to understand that the urgency of the present Gentile mission is for the awakening of a jealous faith in Israel. God is not yet finished with Israel.[12] It has been argued that when Luke consistently portrays Paul entering a new city and offering Jews the opportunity to respond to the gospel before presenting it to Gentiles (e.g., Acts 13:46; 18:6; 28:28), he does so as theologian, not as historian.[13] But even if it could be proven that Luke's point is principally theological rather than historical,[14] it would still have to be acknowledged that the theological motif came from Paul himself. Whether Luke manufactured the itinerary or not, it made complete sense to the early church which accepted Luke's accounts as congruent with Paul's teaching. As equal as Jew and Gentile are in Christ, they do not receive identical treatment in the unfolding history of redemption.

---

[10]See the essay "The Doctrine of Justification: Its Social Function and Implications," in Nils Dahl, *Studies in Paul: Theology for the Early Christian Mission* (Minneapolis: Augsburg Publishing House, 1977), pp. 95-120, esp. p. 109.

[11]Longenecker, *Social Ethics*, p. 34.

[12]See Nils Dahl's "The Future of Israel," pp. 137-158 of *Studies in Paul.*

[13]W. Schmithals, *Paul and James* SBT 46 (London and Naperville, IL, 1965), Haenchen, *Acts*, ad loc.; A.T. Kraabel, "The Disappearance of the 'God-Fearers,'" *Numen* 28, 2 (1981): 113-126.

[14]For a defense of the Lucan scenario, I.H. Marshall, *Luke: Historian and Theologian* (Grand Rapids: Zondervan, 1970), pp. 182-187; cf., M. Hengel's comments about the plausibility of the Lucan picture of a Pauline ministry among Gentile "godfearers" (*Acts and the History of Earliest Christianity*, trans. John Bowden [Philadelphia: Fortress Press, 1979], pp. 88-91).

b. Slave and Free

Paul's thinking about slavery is no less nuanced. The person who is free is to take on the self-understanding of a slave—Christ's slave (1 Corinthians 7:22). Slaves who become Christians are free to understand themselves as no longer slaves to human masters—they are the Lord's freedpersons (1 Corinthians 7:22-23). But precisely because this identity is to be such a compelling one, it is not something which must be expressed in literal freedom.[15] The escaped slave Onesimus is returned to his owner. While Paul earnestly hopes that Philemon will not require it, and while Paul at the very least expects the new relationship between the converted slave and his master to be predicated on their now being brothers in Christ (verse 16), Onesimus may have to resume his servitude to Philemon in Colossae. Paul offers to pay damages and recalls to Philemon the latter's own spiritual indebtedness in hopes of having the slave sent back to him in Rome (verses 18-22).[16] But even if this strategy is successful, the idea would be that Onesimus would continue to minister to Paul on Philemon's behalf (verses 13-14).

c. Male and Female

The paradigm at which Paul demurs most markedly from deriving a revolutionary praxis from the slogan "there is neither...nor" is that of male and female. The Corinthians likely saw themselves carrying forward the Pauline program, especially in the area of gender relationships. The best way to interpret the freedom of Corinthian women to speak openly in the assembly, the church's questioning the need to fulfill marital contracts, and the acceptance in some quarters of the violation of consanguinity taboos and of traditional

---

[15]At the same time, as Bartchy demonstrates, it is not incompatible with the acceptance of freedom. See his discussion on the interpretation of 1 Corinthians 7:21's μᾶλλον χρῆσαι; rejecting both traditional alternatives ("rather use slavery" or "indeed take freedom"), Bartchy suggests the point is that when freedom is imposed on a slave through an owner-initiated manumission, the slave is to "live according to God's call"—i.e., according to the commands of God—in freedom no less than in slavery (pp. 155-183).

[16]See Meeks, *Writings*, pp. 102-103, for the judgment that despite Paul's reticence to pull rank and demand Onesimus' freedom, he puts Philemon in such a position as to make it all but impossible not to grant the slave his freedom. However, from vv. 13-14, it appears that the decision Paul would have Philemon make is not over manumission, rather over whether Onesimus will serve his master directly in Colossae, or indirectly back in Rome with Paul.

scruples about trafficking among prostitutes is that the dawning of the new age in Christ has made all lines between male and female an irrelevance.[17] Though these are understandable inferences from the Pauline gospel, they are not inferences that please the apostle. While he will have women participate in worship through public prayer and charismatic prophecy (1 Corinthians 11:2-16)—activity which was a departure from synagogue practice and was probably seen as fulfillment of the eschatological promise of the prophets (e.g., Joel 2:28-32)—he will not have them take part in the "judging" of the prophets (1 Corinthians 14:33b-36).[18] And in the process of reaffirming the futurity of the resurrection and the nature of the life it will bring (chapter 15), he also affirms traditional bounds of consanguinity (chapter 5) and scruples about commercial sex (6:12-20)—he is, in fact, shocked that his readers would endorse practices even pagans instinctively condemn (5:1). He does indeed commend celibacy to the unmarried who can bear "the gift" (7:7-9); but far from lauding those who would forsake their marriage partners in quest of a heightened spiritual existence, he reminds husbands and wives of their sexual responsibility to their mates (7:1-6,10-11). What the "new creation" (2 Corinthians 5:17) actually calls for—

----

[17]See Meeks, "Androgyne," pp. 202-203. My understanding of the Corinthian situation is largely shaped by James B. Hurley's "Man and Woman in 1 Corinthians: Some Exegetical Studies in Pauline Theology and Ethics" (Ph.D. dissertation, Clare College, Cambridge University, 1973) and Bartchy, *Slavery*.

[18]Hurley, "Man and Woman," pp. 71-75. For the opinion that 1 Corinthians 14:33b-36 is a textual gloss based on 1 Timothy 2:11-15, see Victor Paul Furnish, *The Moral Teaching of Paul* (Nashville: Abingdon, 1979), pp. 91-92; Conzelmann, *First Corinthians*, p. 246; and Gordon Fee, *1 Corinthians*, The New International Commentary on the New Testament (Grand Rapids: Eerdmans, 1987), pp. 699ff. Whether Fee's reading of the textual variants can be sustained, Furnish's assertion that these verses "contradict 1 Corinthians 11:2-16, where...Paul presumes not only that women may speak during public worship, but that they participate on an equal footing with men in both the prayers and the prophesying" cannot be upheld. For Hurley convincingly argues that already in 1 Corinthians 11:2-16 Paul operates with a distinction between the "economic subordination" of women to men and their "charismatic equality" with men— see his "Man and Woman," pp. 41-71. Furthermore, F.W. Danker argues that the Hellenistic ambience would be accepting of a distinction between women's freedom to exercise a "religious" and "cultic" function (as in 1 Corinthians 11:5,13) and their lack of freedom to participate in the "business" proceedings of the assembly (as in 14:33b-35—see *Benefactor*, p. 164). My point is not to resolve the question with a particular proposal for reconciling the egalitarian and inegalitarian strands of 1 Corinthians' teaching on women, as much as to argue that Paul's thinking embraces both strands.

absent the opportunity and ability to adopt Paul's celibate example—is respect for traditional, common morality.

d. Rich and Poor

While wealth does not appear to be as weighty an issue to Paul as are ethnicity, slavery, and gender, it nonetheless is one over which he labors.[19] As Allen Verhey notes: "Paul never says that 'in Christ there is neither rich nor poor,' but the pattern is nevertheless present."[20] For Paul applies to rich and poor the same logic he uses with circumcised and uncircumcised, married and unmarried, enslaved and free:

> Only, let everyone lead the life which the Lord has assigned to him, and in which God has called him. And thus I direct in all the churches.... Every one should remain with God in the state in which he was called.... The appointed time has grown very short; from now on, let those who have wives live as though they had none, and those who mourn as though they were not mourning, and those who rejoice as though they were not rejoicing, and those who buy as though they had no goods and those who deal with the world as though they had no dealing with it for the form of this world is passing away (1 Corinthians 7:17, 24, 29-31 RSV).

To be sure, living as though one had no goods and dealing with the world as though one had no dealings with it does not mean, as Dahl puts it, "dropping out" of society.[21] Paul frankly expects Christians to buy and sell, and to have dealings with the world (1 Corinthians 5:10). In fact, his ministry is predicated upon the hospitality and beneficence of his churches' wealthier members (e.g.,

---

[19]Among the secondary sources outlining Paul's view of wealth, Nils Dahl's essay "Paul and Possessions," Chapter II in his *Studies in Paul*, pp. 22-39; Hengel's *Property*, esp. pp. 35-46, 54-59; and Allen Verhey's *The Great Reversal: Ethics and the New Testament* (Grand Rapids: Eerdmans Publishing Co., 1984), pp. 118-120, are especially helpful. See also, Robert Banks, *Paul's Idea of Community: The Early House Churches in their Historical Setting* (Grand Rapids: Eerdmans Publishing Co., 1980), pp. 89-90; Johannes Weiss, *Earliest Christianity: A History of the Period A.D. 30-150*, trans. ed. Frederick C. Grant (New York: Harper & Row, 1959; reprint ed., Gloucester, MA: Peter Smith, 1970), pp. 592-594; Countryman, *Rich Christian*, pp. 69-70, 113-114, 118 n. 47, 149-150; Wolfgang Schrage, *The Ethics of the New Testament*, trans. David E. Green (Philadelphia: Fortress Press, 1988), pp. 229-232; and Keith F. Nickle, *The Collection: A Study in Paul's Strategy*, Studies in Biblical Theology, No. 48 (Naperville, IL: Alec R. Allenson, Inc., 1966).

[20]Verhey, *Reversal*, p. 119.

[21]Dahl, "Possessions," p. 25.

Corinth's Gaius and Erastus—Romans 16:23). He demands that those living in the last days manage their economic affairs with an inner integrity and in such a way as to maintain their independence—it is, in fact, to be a "point of honor" so to live (φιλοτι-μεῖσθαι, 1 Thessalonians 4:11).[22] Not only is the force of Paul's praxis not to demand that those involved in livelihoods dealing with money drop or change their occupation, maintains Dahl, "on the contrary, Christians had an obligation to continue working in the profession they practiced before becoming Christians."[23] Even Dibelius, commenting on 1 Thessalonians 4:11-12, notices this dynamic:

> The preaching of the coming Kingdom of God could have been understood as requiring the abandoning of *bürgerlich* ways of life: Paul, who surely does not attenuate the eschatological proclamation, forbids his communities to anticipate God in this way. Alongside the other ethical commands—already in the missionary paraenesis—he places the duties of work and calling. The motivation for this is expressed in 1 Corinthians 7:20: no one may arbitrarily alter the station in which he is called. From this results the recognition of earthly responsibilities.[24]

Dahl's and Dibelius' remarks require the caveat introduced by Bartchy on 1 Corinthians 7:21: the point is not that no change is allowed, but simply that any is immaterial. Dahl describes the ethic with one of the apostle's own terms, and one that had a large circulation among contemporary Greek moralists: "autarchy," an ideal that includes: a) contentment with what one has; b) economic independence; and c) avoidance of the entrapment of wealth.[25] The

---

[22]See Abraham J. Malherbe's, *Paul and the Thessalonians*, pp. 95-107, for an attractive thesis that in 1 Thessalonians 4:9-12 and 2 Thessalonians 3:6-12, Paul carefully articulates a labor ethic that would distinguish Christian self-sufficiency and brotherly love from Cynic meddlesomeness on the one hand and from Epicurean utilitarianism on the other. Though he bases his study chiefly on 1 Thessalonians, he apparently accepts the authenticity of 2 Thessalonians. Central to his interpretation of 2 Thessalonians 3:6-12 is his rejection of the traditional notion that a heightened sense of the imminence of the parousia has occasioned the idleness of some Thessalonians (see p. 106, n. 27).

[23]Dahl, "Possessions," p. 26.

[24]Dibelius, *An Thess I,II, an Phil*, p. 23.

[25]Dahl, "Possessions," p. 23, αὐτάρκεια at 2 Corinthians 9:8, and αὐτάρκης at Philippians 4:11. As he notes, the concept can be present without the word, e.g., 1 Thessalonians 4:12: "So that you may...be dependent on nobody," or: "be in need of nothing."

apostle himself has learned to live with either plenty or want (Philippians 4:11-12). He is grateful toward those who joyfully support him financially (the letter to the Philippians, in toto),[26] but also earnest about not burdening those who cannot and about maintaining independence from those whose support would come with strings attached (see 1 Corinthians 9).

> There is no doubt that Paul advocates a high moral standard concerning the use of money. However, his exhortations are down-to-earth, little more than commonplaces. Paul neither condemns wealth nor glorifies its renunciation. He does not urge the Christian to leave everything and to imitate Jesus' life of poverty. What Paul demands of the Christian is honesty, industriousness, contentment and generosity. We get the impression that he demands solid middle-class respectability. It is obvious that Paul has appropriated the best of the ethical traditions of Judaism about possessions, traditions which largely coincided with the views of the Greek moralists. There is less of anything specifically Christian.[27]

Paul's view may very well sound much like the teachings of the Cynic and Stoic philosophers with which his urban audiences would have been familiar, especially, as Dahl himself notes,[28] of Epictetus (for which, see below). Curiously, Dahl does not draw any specific parallels, though that would be easy enough to do.[29] Nor is Dahl as careful in drawing out what is distinctive about Paul's view of "honesty, industriousness, contentment and generosity" as one might have hoped—e.g., the fact that by αὐτάρ-κεια Paul does not mean so much having enough to be independent of others as much as having enough to be helpful to them (2 Corinthians 9:6-15; 1 Thessalonians 4:9-12; cf., Ephesians 4:28). In addition to having an eye to Christians' ability to affirm their community with others by contributing to their needs, Paul is careful not to credit the self for its "self"-sufficiency, but rather to

---

[26]See the analysis by J. Paul Sampley, *Pauline Partnership*, esp. chap. 4, "*Societas Christi* with the Philippians," pp. 51-77.

[27]Dahl, "Possessions," pp. 23-24.

[28]Dahl, "Possessions," p. 25 n. 12.

[29]See, for example, Aristotle, *Politics* 1326b29f; Epictetus 1.12 περὶ εὐαρε-στήσεως; 3.13 τί ἐρημία καὶ ποῖος ἔρημος, esp. 3.13.6 τὸ δύνασθαι αὐτὸν ἑαυτῷ ἀρκεῖν; also Ep. Diogenes 28.25, 46.12 (Malherbe, *Cynic Epistles*, pp. 124, 176); Antisthenes to Aristippus (Socratic letter no. 8, Malherbe, *Cynic Epistles*, p. 244); Ep. Crates 10.10 (Malherbe, *Cynic Epistles*, p. 62).

credit God who enables contentment (Philippians 4:11-13).[30] At the
same time, it must be granted that nothing as heroic as divestment
of all resources is demanded or expected of Christians, and it is in
this sense that Paul's ethic appears to Dahl to approximate "solid
middle class respectability."

2. The Eschatological Dimension

Wolfgang Schrage notes that a number of commentators have
recognized parallels between Paul's thinking at 1 Corinthians 7:29-
31 and Cynic-Stoic thought.[31] It is his opinion, however, that the
passage shares far less with Greek moralism (even if filtered
through Jewish paraenesis) than it does with Jewish apocalypticism.
For, he asserts, the eschatological world view that separates Paul
from a representative Stoic like Epictetus makes the differences
between their notions of autarchy weightier than the correspon-
dences. *Encheiridion* 16 is indicative of Epictetus' counsel:

> When you see someone weeping in sorrow, either because a child has
> gone on a journey, or because he has lost his property, beware that you
> be not carried away by the impression that the man is in the midst of
> external ills, but straightway keep before you this thought: "It is not
> what has happened that distresses this man... but his judgement about
> it."[32]

And in *Discourse* 1 (25.28) he maintains: ἑαυτοὺς θλίβομεν, ἑαυτοὺς
στενοχωροῦμεν, τοῦτ' ἔστιν τὰ δόγματα ἡμᾶς θλίβει καὶ στενο–
χωρεῖ ("We afflict ourselves, we crush ourselves, that is to say, our
own notions afflict and crush us").[33] Contrast the pathos in Paul's
defense of his apostolic sufferings: ἐν παντὶ θλιβόμενοι ἀλλ' οὐ
στενοχωρούμενοι ("We are afflicted in every way, but not
crushed"—2 Corinthians 4:8a). To Paul the hardships with which
humans must live—focused for him in mistreatment received in the

[30]Victor Paul Furnish, *II Corinthians*, pp. 442, 447-448; idem, *Theology and Ethics in Paul*, pp. 44-51, 69-72, 81-92, esp. pp. 82, 88, 91; Dieter Georgi, *Die Geschichte der Kollekte des Paulus für Jerusalem*, Theologische Forschung 38 (Hamburg-Bergstedt: H. Reich, 1965), p. 71; G. Kittel, "αὐτάρκεια, αὐτάρκης," *TDNT* 1:466-467.
[31]Wolfgang Schrage, "Die Stellung zur Welt bei Paulus, Epiktet und in der Apokalyptik: Ein Beitrag zu 1 Kor 7,29-31," *Zeitschrift für Theologie und Kirche* 61.2 (1964): 125-154.
[32]Loeb translation.
[33]My translation.

service of Christ—are not self-inflicted δόγματα but cold, hard, objective facts of existence.

> The distance from the world that comes under discussion in 1 Corinthians 7:29ff completely presupposes an attainment through Christ and a freedom made possible only from Christ and not from people themselves (cf., Philippians 4:13, etc.). The notion that one may, through differentiating between that which is "mine" and that which is "extraneous,"[34] remain undisturbed (οὐ ταραχθήσῃ, *Diss.* 2.6.8,24, etc.) is in Paul's view frankly naive.[35]

But there are deeper grounds for Paul's taking human sufferings seriously and Epictetus' inability to do so: the one views the cosmos as a transitory power in revolt against God, the other, viewing it through the lens of pantheistic monism, sees it as

> the purposeful rational world-order, a splendid universal symbiosis (τὸ σύστημα τὸ ἐξ ἀνθρώπων καὶ θεοῦ *Diss.* 1.9.4), in which humankind understands itself to fit organically as μέρος τοῦ κόσμου (*Diss.* 2.10.3). For Paul, however, God stands beyond and in juxtaposition to the world as its creator and judge; his (Paul's) two-age-doctrine has as its presupposition the notions that God and the world are to be distinguished, that there was a *creatio ex nihilo*, and that there will be an end and judgment of the world. This contrasts vigorously with the ever renewing world-process—never beginning, never ending—in which God and the world are pantheistically joined. For Epictetus belief in the end of the ancient world-age is inconceivable; Paul, quite to the contrary, never uses as an argument the shortness of human life like Epictetus (*Diss.* 1.9.16f, etc.), but does appeal to that shortness of the world-age as a whole which encroaches upon human life....

> According to Epictetus people should turn away from the world to themselves. They should return to themselves from the alien world of externals. But Paul knows that humankind's freedom from the world lies in a history that takes hold of human existence (*in einer des Menschen Existenz umgreifenden Geschichte*) and thus lies *extra nos*: in the future, which in the cross and resurrection of Jesus Christ, has already begun, and in the present Lord, who is coming while the world is passing away.[36]

---

[34]See Epictetus' distinction between τὰ ἐφ' ἡμῖν and τὰ οὐκ ἐφ' ἡμῖν (at *Encheiridion* 1.1.5, etc.) and between τὰ ἐμὰ and the ἀλλότρια (*Discourse* 2.5.4f, etc.).

[35]Schrage, "Stellung zur Welt," p. 135.

[36]Schrage, "Stellung zur Welt," pp. 135-136, 153.

Though more impressed with the Hellenistic points of contact than Schrage, Dahl likewise recognizes that if the content of Paul's ethic of wealth is not vastly different from the demands of that "solid middle-class respectability" taught by contemporary ethicists, the broader, eschatological context is:

> Paul was aware that he was living in the last days. He expected to see Jesus' return and the end of the world. He knew that the Messiah had already come and that the process which would bring the world to an end had already started. The events which guaranteed the world's end, Jesus' death and resurrection, had already occurred. Christians, who were baptized into Christ Jesus, were already delivered from "this present evil age," they had already received the Holy Spirit as a first fruit and as a guarantee of their redemption. In this situation property and money had little significance; they belonged to the age which was perishing. Paul uses phrases like "material benefits" ("carnal things": KJV) and "matters pertaining to this life." The contrast is to the spiritual good, i.e., to matters that relate to God and to his kingdom. Economic affairs are trivial. For those who already have a share in the new age, money can no longer have any real importance....
>
> Paul is not concerned with the self-sufficiency and personal integrity of the wise man, with his inner freedom and his mastery of the external conditions of his existence. Paul states the consequences of the objective situation in which Christians live at the end of the ages. What matters is their relation to their Lord in heaven. The Christians must not attach themselves to money or to other earthly concerns, attachments which would weaken their commitment to the Lord. They ought not to be anxious about anything but to please him.[37]

The same eschatological situation that has made ethnic, social/legal, and gender distinctions irrelevant has made status derived from the possession or nonpossession of the goods of this life unimportant as well. Precisely for the reason that economic inequality, like other social distinctions that are a function of "this age which is passing away," has no bearing on the believer's actual status—making him or her neither poor nor rich in the eyes of God, no more and no less secure in the coming judgment—Paul believes it to be a mistake to put a priority on securing economic justice in this age. Three issues in Corinth make the point:

Rather than belie their future role as participants in the eschatological judgment of the cosmos by taking each other to court over

---

[37]Dahl, "Possessions," pp. 24-25, 25-26.

business dealings, believers should be willing to be defrauded (1 Corinthians 6:1-11).[38]

Some Corinthian Christians appear to be from favored social and financial situations, leading them to be comfortable with the eating of meat which their poorer brothers and sisters can only associate with pagan civic festivals—such occasions being the only times when meat is available to the poor—and the pagan gods to which even marketplace meat is likely to have been dedicated.[39] Paul urges the "illuminati" not to be arrogant in their freedom, but to respect the consciences of those whose different social worlds have left them with scruples in the matter.[40] As he explains to the Christians of Rome, because the Kingdom does not consist in food and drink, judgment about them can be left to God in the eschaton (Romans 14:10-17). Note, however, that he does not broach the issue of refashioning the social lives of believers so that variant understandings of right and wrong could never be based on structural social inequities. He leaves the economic inequities alone, and expects brothers and sisters to experience their unity in the very face of them.

Perhaps no more dramatic example exists than his handling of the Lord's Supper.[41] To be sure, Paul is adamant that the kinds of social and economic distinctions that contemporary κοινωνίαι allow to shape their meetings have no place in the Christian assembly— the privileged are not to gather for their own private bash before the arrival of οἱ πολλοί (1 Corinthians 11:21a); nor is a disequilibrium in the distribution of food and drink—some getting drunk while others go hungry—to serve as a gauge of where a person stands on the social scale (verse 21b). Rather than allow the "have nots" (οἱ μὴ ἔχοντες of verse 22) to be humiliated at such a meal and the solidarity of Christ's body so to be rent, Paul relegates the regular meal to private homes (verses 22, 34) and dictates that the shared

---

[38]Erich Dinkler, "Zum Problem der Ethik bei Paulus: Rechtsnahme und Rechtsverzicht (1 Kor 6,1-11)," *Zeitschrift für Theologie und Kirche* 49 (1952): 167-200.

[39]See Theissen, *Social Setting,* pp. 121-143.

[40]Whether these "strong" Christians are as "integrated" as Theissen maintains is questioned by Schütz ("Primitive Christianity," pp. 6-7) and Meeks (*Urban Christians,* p. 70). Nor is it certain how far Theissen's comparison with second century Gnosticism can be pressed; nonetheless, his suggestion that there is within a segment of the Corinthian Christian community an elitist self-consciousness combined with considerable liberalism about interacting with the pagan world appears to be sound.

[41]See Theissen, *Social Setting,* pp. 145-174.

meal at the assembly be simply the ritual meal instituted by the Lord (verses 23-26,33). On the one hand, the effect is to banish inequality from the Lord's Table, preserving the unity of the body of Christ as it anticipates the eschatological, messianic banquet where all divisions among men and women will be leveled ("proclaiming the Lord's death until he comes," verse 26). On the other hand, however, the practice tacitly sanctions inequality in the various homes from which the believers come—Paul's idea of community does not lead him to urge that a common meal be equally shared in the assembly, even less does it compel him to address and redress the underlying social causes for there being "haves" and "have nots" in a fellowship of brothers and sisters in the first place.

In each of the social paradigms considered—Jew and Gentile, slave and free, male and female, rich and poor—an equality that will be fully realized in the eschaton is conditioned in the present by the fact that the history of redemption is still unfolding within "this age" and its differentiated social relations. What is generally referred to as Paul's "eschatological reserve" does correspond to a "social ethical reserve": acquiescence to certain dimensions of the status quo and a refusal to insist that the eschatological promise of equality be appropriated in its entirety in the here and now.

But there are two significant caveats to be offered concerning the relationship between Paul's eschatology and his ethical conservatism.

First, Paul's eschatology is not finally dependent upon the imminence but rather upon the certainty of the consummation of the ages. Paul indeed believes the consummation will be soon, but he counts only upon its eventuality. And that eventuality is assured on the basis of its realized firstfruits, the resurrection of Christ. So runs the argument in 1 Corinthians 15: inexorably, the Lord's resurrection brings in its wake the resurrection of those who are "in him." Thus, we notice the lack of difficulty with which passages in which Paul expresses his understanding that "we"[42] will be around for the consummation (1 Thessalonians 4:15ff and 1 Corinthians 15:51) stand alongside passages in which he deals forthrightly with the fact of believers' deaths prior to the parousia (1 Thessalonians 5:10; Romans 14:7-9; 8:10,11,38)—and not only with believers' deaths in general, but with the specific possibility of his own death (2

---

[42]Herman Ridderbos, *Paul: An Outline of His Theology*, trans. John Richard de Witt (Grand Rapids: Eerdmans Publishing Co., 1975), p. 491, for the point that the broader context of Paul's teachings requires a hypothetical or facultative understanding of the "we" passages.

Corinthians 4:11; 5:1ff; Philippians 1:22ff; 2:17). The death of other believers twenty years after Christ's ascension does not take him by surprise (1 Thessalonians). The need to prepare for his own death ten years later does not phase him (Philippians). Nor—and this is the point—is there any indication that his views on social matters change with the realization that history may very well continue past his ministry. In fact, the "conservative" clarification of his ethics takes place between Galatians and 1 Corinthians. And if the social ethics of 1 Thessalonians are "bourgeois" (as Dibelius asserts), it is difficult to see how those of Romans and Philippians are any less so.

Second, and not unrelated: attention to that reserve in Paul's social ideas which is a function of the "not yet" of redemption should not blind one to the strong element of fulfillment—to the "already"—that also informs his ethical conservatism. In his celebrated article "Paul and Early Catholicism," Ernst Käsemann likens the apocalyptic Paul to John the Baptist—both would-be forerunners of the end of the world, the latter looking directly and the former indirectly for Israel's repentance as the tripwire for the end of world history.[43] The comparison is not especially apt. For his part, John the Baptist is in the truest sense a prophet of doom, a harbinger of judgment. The news he brings is of an axe laid at the root, the coming of one who will baptize with fire. He looks entirely forward and speaks of judgment—his ethical injunctions are truly a means of preparing for the end (Luke 3:7-17). Paul, on the other hand, describes himself as an ambassador of a reconciliation already available, the herald of a new creation that has begun with the crucified and resurrected Christ (2 Corinthians 5:11-6:2). He betrays no interest in measuring or dating "the fullness of the Gentiles" which must come about before the consummation (Romans 11:12,25). As proclaimer of the "now" as the "acceptable day of the Lord" (2 Corinthians 6:2), the Paul of the homologoumena is rather more caught up with the motif of fulfillment—the "already"—than is often appreciated. Accordingly, as Schrage notes in a corrective to Dibelius' *Urchristentum und Kultur*, "for Paul ethics does not replace eschatology but follows from it":

> Not even at the outset was Paul a fanatic, fired with eschatological hope and refusing to take seriously the oppressive problems of this world. His urgent insistence on ethics is not an emergency measure

---

[43]Ernst Käsemann, *New Testament Questions of Today* (Philadelphia: Fortress Press, 1969), p. 241.

forced upon him by the so-called realities of continuing history. It is neither a compromise nor an accommodation to the world, but a consequence and an expression of the fact that in Christ a new world has begun and that everything is moving toward Christ's universal victory and the absolute sovereignty of God. In any case, eschatology does not evoke in Paul an apocalyptic quietism or a burning desire to flee this world. Instead of impeding action, it works as a sustained goad to action.[44]

While for Schrage the point is to emphasize the fact that "yearning for the Lord does not make life here and now irrelevant,"[45] it also must mean that the so-called "bourgeois" or conservative, "non-heroic" dimensions of Paul's ethical thinking have some positive relation to the realized dimension of his eschatology. Doing, for instance, that which is honorable in the eyes of all people (Romans 12:17b, καλός)—like showing obedience to governing authorities (13:1-7)—is not simply a function of the fact that "salvation is nearer than when we first believed" (13:11), it is also something done in view of the mercies of God already revealed (12:1-2), as exegeted by Paul in chapters 1-11.

More to the point: even though language of "enrichment" (πλουτεῖν) has played some part in the Corinthians' misappropriation of end-time promises,[46] Paul does not back away from the use of such language to refer to the "wealth" of their spiritual gifts (1 Corinthians 1:5) or to the "riches" of the salvation they have come to enjoy (2 Corinthians 8:9).[47] Moreover, in the present age, the "now" of salvation can be expressed by relatively prosperous Gentile Christians' use of their wealth to underwrite the impoverished Judean church, establishing a reciprocal relationship (Gentile benevolence for Jewish thanksgiving) which Paul can call "equality."[48] Thus, Dahl can refer, if cautiously, to the sacramental sig-

---

[44]Schrage, *Ethics*, p. 184.

[45]Schrage, *Ethics*, p. 185.

[46]1 Corinthians 4:8, (of the Corinthians) ἤδη ἐπλουτήσατε, cf. the biting tone of 2 Corinthians 6:10, (of himself) ὡς πτωχοὶ πολλοὺς δὲ πλουτίζοντες.

[47]Furnish, *II Corinthians*, p. 405, on 2 Corinthians 8:9, noting the parallel use of πλουτέω/πλοῦτος in Romans 10:12; 11:12.

[48]2 Corinthians 8:13, ἀλλ' ἐξ ἰσότητος. See the discussion in Furnish, *II Corinthians*, pp. 407-408, who sagely compares Paul's view of equality here with that in Philo (*Who Is the Heir* 145): "One essential form of equality is the proportional (ἡ διὰ ἀναλογίας), in which the few are regarded as equal to the many, and the small to the greater. This is often employed by states on special

nificance wealth can have for the apostle: voluntarily put to a right use, it can "make visible an invisible grace,"[49] in this case the eschatological unity between Gentile and Jew.[50] In the process, Corinthian wealth receives a surprisingly positive theological evaluation:

> You are enriched in every way (πλουτιζόμενοι) for the greatest generosity, which through us brings about thanksgiving to God; for the ministration of this service (the collection) not only supplies the needs of the saints but also overflows with many thanksgivings to God (2 Corinthians 9:11-12).[51]

What informs Paul's conservatism is not hopeless quietism but quiet hopefulness. Paul's eschatology leads him to a reserve about living out Christ's exaltation in this age (1 Corinthians 4:8), but it also leads him to embrace the opportunities for living in union with Christ in a way that is appropriate to this age, which is to say, as a servant.[52] To Paul, this means that one can accept an inferior status—or a superior one for that matter—not only because the eschaton *will* turn the world's injustices on their heads, but also because what Christ has *already* given is an identity that transcends the world-system. And with that identity comes the opportunity to use all of one's personal resources—including venue of service, be it as

occasions when they order each citizen to make an equal contribution from his property, not of course numerically equal, but equal in the sense that it is proportionate to the valuation of his estate...." See Paul's own calculus of the exchange of spiritual for physical goods: Galatians 6:6; 1 Corinthians 9:11,14; Romans 15:27. See also Hermas *Similitude* 2.5.7. And recall the Aristotelian notion of φιλία, *Nichomachean Ethics* 1159b12—see above, III.A.1., pp. 112ff.

[49]Dahl, "Possessions," pp. 31-32.

[50]For the eschatological implications of the Gentile collection on behalf of Judean Christianity, see Furnish, *II Corinthians*, pp. 411-413, with references to Isaiah 2:2-3; Micah 4:1-2; Isaiah 60:5-6; see also Nickle, *Collection*, pp. 130-142; Georgi, *Kollekte*, pp. 84-86.

[51]Following the translation of Furnish, *II Corinthians*, p. 440, who takes πλουτιζόμενοι as standing in place of a finite verb (BDF § 468.2).

[52]See esp., 2 Corinthians 13:4 and Philippians 2:1-11, and the repeated counsel to become imitators of Paul as he is an imitator—in servanthood—of Christ, e.g., 1 Corinthians 4:16; 11:1; Philippians 3:17; 1 Thessalonians 1:6. See also John Howard Yoder's chapter "Revolutionary Subordination," pp. 163-192, in his *The Politics of Jesus* (Grand Rapids: Eerdmans Publishing Co., 1972)—the concerns of that chapter are not directly germane to ours, since he is arguing for the essentially Pauline nature of the *Haustafeln*, but in the process he nicely highlights the motif of servanthood in Paul's ethics.

Jew or Gentile, slave or free person, man or woman, patron or dependent—to build the community of faith and to do that which is understood to be good even by outsiders.

3. *"Love-Patriarchalism" in Paul and the Pastorals*

There is a strongly community-formative thrust to this eschatologically conditioned and conservatively framed ethic. And despite persistent efforts to define the social ethics of the "real" Paul in terms of a rudimentarily structured *communitas* of equal individuals,[53] Ernst Troeltsch got it basically right when early in this century he dubbed Paul's ethic one of a mildly conservative "patriarchalism."[54] According to this view, Paul's ethic does not challenge the inequities between people, but sees in those very differences the building blocks of a new type of human community. We are reminded of Aristotle's view of community based upon φιλία between the wealthy who strive for honor and the poor who seek benefits.[55] Like Aristotle and Menander and Dio Chrysostom and the inscriptionists,[56] Paul envisions a community of social unequals who are dependent upon one another. Unlike Hellenistic theorists, however, Paul does not forge bonds made of human reciprocity. In Troeltsch's reconstruction of Paul's thought, social superiors are stewards of God's resources and are answerable to Him for using those resources in the service of their inferiors. In their turn, social inferiors are not in the first place answerable to their earthly counterparts, but rather to their heavenly Lord. It is thus for a purpose that inequities are willingly accepted, as Troeltsch puts it, "making them fruitful for the ethical values of personal relationships":

> All action is the service of God and is a responsible office, authority as well as obedience. As stewards of God the great must care for the small, and as servants of God the little ones must submit to those who bear authority; and, since in so doing both meet in the service of God, inner religious equality is affirmed and the ethical possession is enlarged by the exercise of the tender virtues of responsibility for and of trustful surrender to each other. It is undeniable that this ideal is

---

[53]V. Turner, *The Ritual Process*, pp. 94-165; Meeks, "'Since Then You Would Need to Go out of the World': Group Boundaries in Pauline Christianity," *Critical History and Biblical Faith*, pp. 4-29, esp. 12-13; *Urban Christians*, pp. 88-89, 90, 109, 157, 159, 191, 225 n. 81; "Androgyne," esp. pp. 199-204; Bassler, "Widow's Tale," p. 30; D. MacDonald, *Legend*, pp. 44-45, 112 n. 58.

[54]Troeltsch, *Social Teaching*, pp. 69-89.

[55]Aristotle *Nichomachean Ethics* 1163b1-6,12,13; see above, III.A.1., pp. 112ff.

perceived dimly by Paul, and only by means of this ideal does he desire to alter given conditions from within outwards, without touching their external aspect at all.[57]

Without using Troeltsch's language, Dahl places Paul's treatment of wealth securely within the same orb:

> The poor and the rich have the same Lord, who gives both groups a share in his bounty and who joins them in the same church: this is the strikingly new element in Paul's thought. The congregation becomes the decisive social reality for the Christian way of life, and communal life by necessity involves the use of possessions. Herein lies an important part of the reason for the difference from the ideals of the Stoic sages and Cynic preachers. Here too we find part of the explanation for the difference between what Jesus and what Paul say about money.[58]

Gerd Theissen has championed Troeltsch's characterization, renaming it "love-patriarchalism," and offering a significantly refined description of the social reality underlying Paul's congregations.[59]

---

[56]See above, III.A., pp. 111-124.

[57]Troeltsch, *Social Teaching*, p. 78.

[58]Dahl, "Possessions," p. 26.

[59]Troeltsch says Paul's faith in "the omnipotence of good-will" is a function of "the urban character of the local churches and the relative insignificance of the social differences within them" (*Social Teaching*, p. 78). This ethic, he maintains, was compatible with the artisan and lower middle class origins of the movement. In the first place, such a social philosophy does not have to be predicated upon a picture of a church with relatively insignificant social differences within it. As we saw in the two previous chapters, the Hellenistic and Roman world was vitally interested in the "willingness" of the wealthy to give, precisely where social differences were most marked. It was an age of voluntarism, and communities devised a host of strategies to win the beneficence of their elites.

Theissen's contribution has been to show that it cannot be assumed that the churches of Pauline Christianity were socially one-dimensional, and certainly not exclusively made up of people of the lower classes (see especially "Social Stratification," pp. 69-119, in *Social Setting*). By drawing upon a cross-section of the communities within which they emerged, Paul's churches necessarily reflected the cleavages within their society. Theissen's social description weans us from the homogeneous view of the Christians of Paul's churches, and points to the differences in social background as the grounds for many of the disputes within the churches.

This love-patriarchalism takes social differences for granted but ameliorates them through an obligation of respect and love, an obligation imposed upon those who are socially stronger. From the weaker are required subordination, fidelity, and esteem. Whatever the intellectual sources feeding into this ethos, with it the great part of Hellenistic primitive Christianity mastered the task of shaping social relations within a community which, on the one hand, demanded of its members a high degree of solidarity and brotherliness and, on the other, encompassed various social strata. This primitive Christian love-patriarchalism, with its moderate social conservativism, made a lasting impact on Christianity. It prevailed against Montanism and Gnosis in the second century. It produced the church's fundamental norms and fashioned lasting institutions. It solved problems of organization and prepared Christianity to receive the great masses. Its historical effectiveness is rooted not least of all in its ability to integrate members of different strata. Members of the upper classes could find a fertile field of activity, so that ancient Christianity never lacked for distinguished leadership figures—beginning with Paul. But the lower strata were also at home here. They found a fundamental equality of status before God, solidarity and help in the concrete problems of life, not least of all from those Christians who enjoyed a higher station in life. Christian brotherhood probably would have been more radically carried out within socially homogeneous groups. That is much easier, however, than realizing a measure of brotherhood within communities which are sharply stratified socially. It was here that primitive Christianity's love-patriarchalism offered a realistic solution.[60]

Now, in treating wealth the Pastorals differ from the acknowledged Pauline letters in several ways. The denunciation of an acquisitive spirit is a Pauline commonplace; however, in the homologoumena and in Colossians and Ephesians as well, it is "greed" (πλεονεξία) that is proscribed,[61] while in the Pastorals it is "love of money" (φιλαργυρία).[62] And as much as the homologoumena dwell on financial matters, they never mention money straight out;[63] even when the homologoumena lay special obligations upon the wealthy,

---

[60]Theissen, *Social Setting*, pp. 107-108.

[61]πλεονεκτεῖν, 1 Thessalonians 4:6. πλεονέκτης, 1 Corinthians 5:10,11; 6:10; Ephesians 5:5. πλεονεξία, Romans 1:29; 2 Corinthians 9:5; Ephesians 4:19; 5:3; Colossians 3:5; 1 Thessalonians 2:5.

[62]φιλαργυρία, 1 Timothy 6:10. φιλάργυρος, 2 Timothy 3:2. ἀφιλάργυρος, Titus 3:3.

[63]Nicely brought out by Dahl in "Possessions," p. 24, and illustrated in his discussion of Paul's approach to Philemon, his relationship with the Philippian church, the collection for the Jerusalem church, and the financing of his own ministry (pp. 29-36).

they do so obliquely.[64] Yet, as we have seen, the Pastorals directly condemn the love of money (1 Timothy 6:9-10). Beyond that, the Pastorals lay claim to the single instance in the entire Pauline corpus in which the rich qua rich are addressed (1 Timothy 6:17-19), evidenced by the fact that this exhortation conforms exactly to the Station Code Schema identified by Verner.[65]

Whatever considerations have to be invoked to explain these differences in style and strategy—whether they point to a different author, a different amanuensis, or simply differences in the situation out of or to which the apostle himself writes—what is even more clear is that the substance of Paul's approach is being carried over in the Pastorals.[66] It has struck some that the Pastorals are one-sided in presenting to social inferiors their obligations without a corresponding word to superiors, as happens even in the *Haustafeln* of Colossians and Ephesians. If, however, as we suggested in the previous chapter, the problems that have arisen in these churches come from wealthier household heads whose social aspirations exceed their doctrinal understanding and spiritual maturity, then more rather than less of the social ethical content of these letters—certainly of 1 Timothy—is addressed to them, specifically, the overseer and deacons lists, and the teaching on contentment and the responsibility of wealth.

The effect of our analysis of the Pastorals' approach to wealth should be to solidify the relationship between these letters and the homologoumena on social ethics. The same vision of community between social unequals based on a sense of "family" that Troeltsch and Theissen have found in Paul is present in the Pastorals. Perhaps it is the case that the "love-patriarchalism" is more pronounced here, especially since in 1 Timothy the author uses as his driving motif the image of the "household of God," and since he sets forth

---

[64]See Dahl, "Possessions," pp. 37-38, for the circumlocutions Paul uses to refer to the Jerusalem collection.

[65]See Verner, *Household*, Chart 2, p. 93, and Chart 4, pp. 96-97, and the discussion above, III.B., pp. 124ff.

[66]One way in which Theissen moves beyond Troeltsch is in working with a multi-layered Pauline corpus. For much of his analysis of the New Testament, Troeltsch depended on the work of his friend A. Deissmann (see *Social Teaching*, p. 69), who assumed a thirteen letter corpus. Yet Theissen notes that though *Liebespatriarchalismus* comes into its own in the deutero-Pauline and Pastoral epistles, its features are already evident in Paul (namely in 1 Corinthians 7:21ff; 11:3-16—*Social Setting*, p. 107). Dahl, likewise separating the Pastorals from the acknowledged letters, nonetheless affirms that the Pastorals represent Pauline catechetical traditions ("Possessions," p. 22 n. 1).

in his programmatic statement the goal of restoring a proper administration of ἀγάπη (1 Timothy 1:3-7). But even this distance between Paul and the Pastorals is diminished the more one appreciates the fact that functional inegalitarianism stands alongside principial egalitarianism as a pervasive rather than an isolated feature of Paul's social ethics.

C. THE ESCHATOLOGICAL BASE FOR THE PASTORALS' SOCIAL ETHICAL POSTURE

The more serious question is not whether the Pastorals are more conservative than is the acknowledged Paul—they are not. Rather, the question is whether their ethical posture, though similar to the apostle's, is based upon a toned down eschatology and reflects a heavy investment in a status quo with which the church anticipates having to live for an extended period of time.

1. The Critical Consensus

An imposing consensus of critical opinion supports Dibelius' judgment that in the Pastorals "the dynamic tension of the eschatological gospel of Paul is not to be found."[67] The sharing of that opinion becomes the linchpin for much of Conzelmann's theological refining of Dibelius' commentary. Conzelmann maintains, for instance, that the *Bürgerlichkeit* of these epistles is a result of the church's making "adjustments for a prolonged stay in the world in the face of the evolution of both orthodoxy and heresy within the Christian communities." While acknowledging the presence of elements of the concept of *Bürgerlichkeit* in Paul himself, Conzelmann nonetheless asserts that it is elaborated in the Pastorals without eschatological conditioning.[68] These ethics "serve to regulate the time until the parousia, which is no longer felt to be imminent."[69] There is a changed "conceptual structure," a function of "the reorientation toward a longer duration of life in the world"; and while this reorientation is consistent with a life based on faith, "doubtless the dialectic of the eschatological existence is no longer understood in its original keenness."[70] "The eschatological expec-

---

[67]Dibelius, *Die Pastoralbriefe* (1931), p. 3.
[68]Dibelius/Conzelmann, *The Pastoral Epistles*, p. 8.
[69]Dibelius/Conzelmann, *The Pastoral Epistles*, p. 40.
[70]Dibelius/Conzelmann, *The Pastoral Epistles*, p. 41.

tation, as well as the present understanding of salvation (and...especially the establishment of a basis for the paraenesis) have become independent of the *imminent* expectation of the parousia."[71]

Five factors converge to make this reading of the Pastorals' eschatology and its relation to ethics convincing to many:

First is the notion of the passing of the "period of religious ecstasy" in which charismatic gifts were operative within the church in general.[72] Käsemann, for instance, offers the Pastorals as a foil to the Pauline view of ministry. For the latter, every Christian receives the eschatological Spirit at baptism and is equipped with some χάρισμα, or gift, for service.[73] But in the former, "a dwindling of the element of primitive Christian eschatology" brings in its wake a focus on order within the church, a focus which Käsemann—not otherwise a champion of Dibelius' epithet—acknowledges to be an index of *christliche Bürgerlichkeit*.[74] Now office stands over against the rest of the community and is the real bearer of the Spirit; the primitive, Pauline view "recedes into the background and indeed, for all practical purposes, disappears."[75] Gifts and ministry reside in the offices and officers of the church (χάρισμα appears only at 1 Timothy 4:14 and 2 Timothy 1:6, and only of a church officer); and the church itself, through its discipline and supervision, has become "the pillar and bulwark of the truth" (1 Timothy 3:15). In Kümmel's judgment, "There is no longer any indication of active cooperation and responsibility on the part of the community."[76] And so,

---

[71]Dibelius/Conzelmann, *The Pastoral Epistles*, p. 89, emphasis in the original.

[72]Bultmann, *Theology*, 2:185-186.

[73]Ernst Käsemann, "Ministry and Community in the New Testament," in *Essays on New Testament Themes*, SBT 41, trans. W.J. Montague (London: SCM Press, 1960), pp. 85-87.

[74]Ernst Käsemann, "Amt und Gemeinde im Neuen Testament," in *Exegetische Versuche und Besinnungen I* (Göttingen, 1964), p. 127: *Man hat die in den Pastoralen tradierte Gemeindeordnung als Ausdruck christlicher Bürgerlichkeit verstanden. In gewisser Weise dürfte das zutreffen, wie das Schwinden der urchristlichen Eschatologie beweist.* "Ministry," p. 85, "The Church order of the Pastorals has sometimes been seen as an expression of the fact that Christians were settling down in the world. This may be true to some extent; the dwindling of the element of primitive Christian eschatology is certainly evidence for it." For his reticence to speak of the *Verbürgerlichung* of Christianity in the Pastorals, see Käsemann's *Der Ruf der Freiheit*, 5th ed. (Tübingen: J.C.B. Mohr [Paul Siebeck], 1972), pp. 169ff, and *Jesus Means Freedom*, trans. Frank Clark (Philadelphia: Fortress Press, 1970), pp. 88ff.

[75]Käsemann, "Ministry," p. 87.

[76]Kümmel, *Introduction*, p. 382.

maintains Käsemann, "We can now speak inelegantly, but with absolute accuracy, of the Spirit as the ministerial Spirit."[77]

Second, the church is consciously living with an eye to the future. Timothy is urged, maintains Kümmel, to make provision "for the time after the death of the bearers of tradition appointed by the apostolic disciples (2 Timothy 2:1f).... (A)lthough there is a maintenance of belief in a coming consummation (1 Timothy 6:14; Titus 2:13, etc.), there is no longer a living expectation of the End, as the careful preparation for coming generations shows."[78] In the prayer for a quiet and peaceable life through God's support for the civil authorities (1 Timothy 2:1-2), Bultmann finds evidence for the assumption that the world is calculated to last for a considerable time; the attributing of an educative function to grace at Titus 2:11ff betrays the same consciousness.[79] Accordingly, says Kee:

> ...(T)he community behind these documents is the early-second-century equivalent of a middle-to-upper-middle-class organization, worried about its reputation, the tightness of its hierarchy, the purity of its doctrine, and the stability of its enterprise throughout succeeding generations (2 Timothy 1:5).[80]

A third factor is a perceived theological shift away from Paul's emphasis on the essential futurity of salvation. As Bultmann puts it: "reference to the future recedes behind the consciousness of present salvation."[81] "Paul's understanding of the eschatological character of the present has greatly paled and there is no longer a trace either of the tension between the present and the future or of longing for the fulfillment."[82] The christological hymn of 1 Timothy 3:16, with its string of six aorist passive verbs, may be cited as indicative of this stress on the presence of salvation. The same is frequently claimed for the use of the Hellenistic term ἐπιφάνεια to refer not merely to the parousia of the Lord at some point in the future (as at 1 Timothy 6:14 and Titus 2:13) but also to his historical appearing in the past (2 Timothy 1:10 for the noun, and Titus 2:11, and 3:4 for the verb).[83] In

---

[77]Käsemann, "Ministry," p. 87.
[78]Kümmel, *Introduction*, pp. 382-383.
[79]Bultmann, *Theology*, 2:116.
[80]Kee, *Christian Origins*, p. 119.
[81]Bultmann, *Theology*, 2:185.
[82]Bultmann, *Theology*, 2:115-116.
[83]In one of his expansions on Dibelius' comments, Conzelmann (Dibelius/Conzelmann *The Pastoral Epistles*, p. 89—cf. Dibelius, *Die Pastoralbriefe* (1931), p. 55) notes the dual referent of ἐπιφάνεια, and suggests that it intimates the

the christological hymn of 2 Timothy 1, the note of a redemption that is "already" is so strong that the author can place God's "saving" act unambiguously in the past (verse 9, God is ὁ σώσας ἡμᾶς), without even the qualifying expression of hope in becoming heirs of eternal life offered at Titus 3:7, much less the careful caveat of hope that brackets the single statement about "salvation's" past dimension in the homologoumena.[84] In fact, according to 2 Timothy 1:10, immortality has already been revealed and death has already been "abolished."[85]

Consequently, and fourth, since the church expects to be around a long time and is focused on present salvation, the notion of the appearance of Christ in the future takes on only a very general character.[86] Gone are the characteristically Pauline, "the appointed time has grown very short," "the form of this world is passing away," and "salvation is nearer to us now than when we first believed" (1 Corinthians 7:29,31; Romans 13:11). In their place are the less charged, "in later times," "at the proper time," "in the last times," and "awaiting our blessed hope" (1 Timothy 4:1; 6:15; 2 Timothy 3:1; Titus 2:13).

The net result, fifth, is the notion that eschatology has little impact on ethics in the Pastorals. Directly linked to the general nature of the expressions of hope in these letters, in Koester's eyes, is the fact that, "(a) specifically eschatological motivation for Christian moral behavior is completely missing."[87] Houlden speaks of a nearly "autonomous" ethic in which "(n)either an urgent escha-

---

schema of the two ages that is being refined in the Pastorals' (and Luke's) generation—see Conzelmann's *The Theology of St. Luke*, trans. Geoffrey Buswell (Philadelphia: Fortress Press, 1961) for his interest in this motif. Bultmann claims that ἐπιφάνεια is an eschatological term which the author appropriates for use with a historical referent (*Theology*, 2:115). Kee, on the other hand, claims that ἐπιφάνεια is a general Hellenistic term for mystical disclosure which the author substitutes for the eschatological term παρουσία (*Christian Origins*, p. 119).

[84]Romans 8:24-25: τῇ γὰρ ἐλπίδι ἐσώθημεν· ἐλπὶς δὲ βλεπομένη οὐκ ἔστιν ἐλπίς· ὃ γὰρ βλέπει τίς ἐλπίζει; εἰ δὲ ὃ οὐ βλέπομεν ἐλπίζομεν, δι' ὑπομονῆς ἀπεκδεχόμεθα.

[85]Kee, *Christian Origins*, p. 119.

[86]Koester, *Introduction*, 2:302.

[87]Koester, *Introduction*, 2:302.

tology nor a live sense of existence centred on Christ seem to exert any pressure."[88] Perhaps most forceful is Schrage's verdict:

> Future hope is mentioned, but it has lost its critical and motivating function, and can neither hold in abeyance the enduring structures of this world nor force the Christian community to advance. ...(E)schatology has vanished as a critical and inspiring force; the provisional nature of the present world is no longer taken seriously.[89]

It is certainly a verdict with which Dibelius would have agreed, as is Verhey's:

> The eschatological situation is never quite forgotten (see 1 Timothy 4:7-8; Titus 1:1-2; 2:12-13), but the ethic of the Pastorals is settling into the world, establishing itself over against the world-denial of the heretics, whether in the form of asceticism or libertinism. The ethic is moderate, not heroic.[90]

2. *Points of Demurral*

Yet there are significant points of demurral to be offered in the face of each of these factors, points which together undermine the view of an ethic based upon a toned-down, non-apocalyptic eschatology.

a. Spirit and Office

Without assuming responsibility for answering the whole question of "early catholicism" in the Pastorals,[91] we can say that despite a surface reading, these letters do not betray a passing over into an era when "ministers minister and congregations congregate," when charisma has given over to office, and ardor to order. It is easy to be overly impressed with the spectacular manifestations of the Spirit that get so much attention in the Corinthian correspondence—the main source of data for Bultmann's "period of religious ecstasy"—

---

[88]J.L. Houlden, *Ethics and the New Testament* (New York: Oxford University Press, 1977), pp. 64-65.

[89]Schrage, *Ethics*, pp. 258, 264.

[90]Verhey, *Reversal*, p. 129.

[91]Käsemann, "Amt"; Hans Küng, "'Early Catholicism' in the New Testament as a Problem in Controversial Theology," in *The Council in Action*, pp. 159-195. Schwarz devotes a section to the topic, "Charisma und Amt in den Pastoralen," in *Bürgerliches Christentum?*, pp. 141-148—these few pages ought to change the landscape in the discussion over "early catholicism" in the Pastorals, and I am heavily dependent upon them in the following discussion.

and, in so doing, to overlook the dominance of mundane gifts of the Spirit in the more reflective letter to the Romans and the matter of fact reference to ἐπίσκοποι and διάκονοι in the letter to the Philippians (1:1). As Schwarz points out, it is not Paul who cannot hold Spirit and office together, but rather the Corinthian charismatics. When he is able to set the terms of the discussion himself, Paul speaks of the value of less spectacular, *bürgerlich* gifts (Romans 12:6-8).[92] Moreover, Donelson offers a sage caution against assuming an exact correspondence between the order the Pastorals promote and the situation that actually exists.[93]

A number of factors signal the fact that ardor continues to stand alongside order in the churches of the Pastoral epistles. Timothy's own call to the work of the ministry is said to have come "through prophecy," and his ordination presupposes at the very least the participation of his fellow congregation members.[94] The fact that officers must be tested in the first place shows that the conferring of office is not mechanical and automatic (1 Timothy 3:10); nor is there anything static about a χάρισμα of office that must be protected

---

[92]The term *bürgerlich* here is Schwarz's, and appears to mean simply "non-supernatural," "mundane," or "pedestrian"; see his *Bürgerliches Christentum?*, p. 142, where he observes that all of the extraordinary gifts of 1 Corinthians 12:28-31 are missing from the list at Romans 12:6-8. He notes also (p. 142 n. 61) that with one exception, all the χαρίσματα of Romans 12:6-8 appear materially in the Pastorals: the prophetic word (1 Timothy 1:18; 4:14); service (1 Timothy 1:12; 2 Timothy 4:5,11—also as a verb at 1 Timothy 3:10,13; 2 Timothy 1:18, etc.); teaching (1 Timothy 4:11; 6:2; 2 Timothy 2:2); admonition (1 Timothy 5:1; 6:2; 2 Timothy 4:2, etc.); giving (1 Timothy 6:18); ruling (1 Timothy 5:17)—the showing of mercy appears only as an attribute of God in the Pastorals (cf. 1 Timothy 1:13).

[93]Donelson, *Pseudepigraphy*, pp. 5, 192-193. Note especially, pp. 192-193: "...(T)he sociological information in the letters is limited. They are telling only one side of the story. In fact, although the author deals at great length with the rowdiness of heresy, he is painting an idealized picture of his church.... In fact, the bishop-elder-deacons structure, which the author advocates, with ordained officers rather than spirit-inspired people having all the teaching and preaching authority, may have very little to do with the actual state of affairs in his church. We have noted several indications that he is an abandoned leader who is promulgating an authority structure as he wishes it could be rather than as it is. Thus the portrait of the church painted here, with its carefully arranged taxis, its school-like setting, and its pursuit of the quiet, virtuous life, may be drawn more from the imagination than from reality." One is reminded of the difference between *Sein und Schein* in the view of office in the letters of Ignatius of Antioch—see William R. Schoedel, *Ignatius of Antioch: A Commentary on the Letters of Ignatius of Antioch* (Philadelphia: Fortress Press, 1985), p. 12.

[94]Schwarz, *Bürgerliches Christentum?*, p. 146.

from neglect (μὴ ἀμέλει) and be constantly actualized (μελέτα, 1 Timothy 4:11-16; and ἀναζωπυρεῖν, 2 Timothy 1:6).[95]

A further indication that the situation is not a static one, maintains Schwarz, lies in the fact that the author does not restrict proclamation in the churches to its officers.[96] If Timothy is to forbid ἑτεροδιδασκαλεῖν (1 Timothy 1:3), that does not mean he is to put down διδάσκειν in general. The prohibition against *women* teaching would be nonsensical were there already a prohibition against teaching among congregational members in general (1 Timothy 2:12); and note that in Titus 2:3 women do have a teaching responsibility among themselves. The evidence of the activity of women and false teachers forces us to assume that gifts of the Spirit are being used by people other than Timothy and Titus, that a "laity" is ministering vigorously—but that such "lay" ministry is not in and of itself the problem.

Schwarz argues, and convincingly, that what Paul means by χάρισμα, i.e., Spirit-empowered service by every believer, does indeed appear materially in the Pastorals under the rubric of καλὰ ἔργα. What, in the power of the Holy Spirit, χάρισμα is in the homologoumena, καλὰ ἔργα are in the Pastorals: "the absolute and relentless willingness to obey of the whole person in the whole of the Christian life."[97]

> Καλὰ (ἀγαθά) ἔργα are the content of the preaching of the office-bearer (1 Timothy 6:18; Titus 3:1,8, etc.). They are the fruit of faith (Titus 3:8) and cause the life of the Christian "not to be without fruit" (Titus 3:14). They are not merely pious performances of a duty, but they ought to be put into practice precisely where they are needed (Titus 3:8,14; cf. the saying on the charismatic gifts at 1 Corinthians 12:7). Not only office-bearers but also congregation members should learn the good (Titus 2:3). The congregation leader should thereby distinguish himself so he can present an example in the fulfilling of "good works" (Titus 2:7). Even the reading of Scripture is suited to making the community "prepared and equipped for every good work" (2 Timothy 3:17). Individual social stations are encouraged to good works: women (1 Timothy 2:10), widows (1 Timothy 5:10). "Καλὰ ἔργα" serves as a general expression of the fruit of Christian life. The following acts of service are characterized expressly as "good works": raising children, hospitality, footwashing, helping the needy (1 Timothy 5:10), liberality, sharing (1 Timothy 6:18); not least, even

[95]Schwarz, *Bürgerliches Christentum?*, pp. 146-147.
[96]For this paragraph, see Schwarz, *Bürgerliches Christentum?*, pp. 145-146.
[97]Schwarz, *Bürgerliches Christentum?*, p. 143, citing R. Pesch, "Christliche Bürgerlichkeit (Tit 2,11-15)," in *Am Tisch des Wortes* 14 (1966): 28-33.

competition for the office of ἐπίσκοπος is called a καλὸν ἔργον (1 Timothy 3:1)! Office is accordingly not simply imposed "from above," rather it can and should be striven after by congregation members. Even if legitimization on the part of authorized preachers is necessary, nonetheless believers are encouraged to display the "charisma" of a congregation leader.

When one brings together everything that appears in the Pastorals by way of a commendation to "good works," a view results which is quite different than that of a static community. Although conceptually the καλὰ ἔργα are to be distinguished from the Pauline gifts, *materially* they stand in close proximity to what Paul says about them.[98]

If, with Titus 2:11-14, the design of redemptive history is to produce a people eager for "good works," and if, with Titus 3:4-7, the renewing work of the Holy Spirit empowers believers—not just officers—for this life, then a door is opened to at least a broadstroke equation between Paul's doctrine of χάρισμα and the Pastorals' teaching on καλὰ ἔργα. At any rate, enough is established to lay aside the "early catholic" shibboleth about the Pastorals possessing a ministerial rather than a charismatic Spirit.

b. Provision for the Future

Second, it is difficult to see how any more provision for the future is being made in the Pastorals than had been made in the acknowledged letters. There is nothing (*pace* Bultmann) remotely suggesting an extended time frame in the prayer for civil authorities. And (again, *pace* Bultmann) the passage about the educative function of grace explicitly commends a posture of waiting for the epiphany of the Lord. Even the instruction to women about marrying and raising children (1 Timothy 2:9-15; 5:9-15) has less to do with plans for an indefinite future than it does with getting women out of behaviors the author deems inappropriate and disruptive (1 Timothy 5:13-15; Titus 1:11; 2 Timothy 3:6-7). What future plans are made in these letters are of the mundane sort familiar enough from the homologoumena ("Bring Mark with you...and the cloak and the books.... Try to come before winter.... Try to come to me at Nicopolis, for I have decided to spend the winter there.... I am writing these things to you, hoping to come to you before long; but in case I am delayed, I write so that you may know..."—2 Timothy 4:11,13,21; Titus 3:12; 1 Timothy 3:14-15). As in, for example, the letter to the Romans, the ultimate future is

---

[98]Schwarz, *Bürgerliches Christentum?*, pp. 144-145. Emphasis in the original.

certain and looked for, but plans are nonetheless made (compare Titus 3:12 with Romans 15:22-29).[99]

c. *The Presence of Salvation*

Third, despite all that can legitimately be said about an emphasis on the presence of salvation in the Pastorals, these letters actually stress the futurity of salvation over against those who want it all now. Alongside 2 Timothy's ὁ σώσας ἡμᾶς and Titus' ἔσωσεν ἡμᾶς are the several instances in which salvation is emphatically placed in the future and held out as a goal and hope—see especially 1 Timothy 2:15, of woman: σωθήσεται διὰ τῆς τεκνογονίας; 1 Timothy 4:16, of the apostolic delegate: σεαυτὸν σώσεις καὶ τοὺς ἀκούοντας; 2 Timothy 4:18, of the apostle himself: (με) σώσει εἰς τὴν βασιλείαν; and 2 Timothy 2:10, of what the apostle hopes his endurance will secure for the elect: ἵνα καὶ αὐτοὶ σωτηρίας τύχωσιν (see also 1 Timothy 2:4).

If there is represented in the Pastorals an eschatology according to which (à la Bultmann) "the future recedes behind the consciousness of present salvation," it does not belong to the author but to his opponents. It is they who proclaim a resurrection that is "already" (2 Timothy 2:18). It is he (no doubt in line with his tradition) who looks to living with Christ and reigning with him (2 Timothy 2:11b,12a; 4:6-8,18).

It is they who sever what to our author is a present solidarity between women and the primeval woman who was deceived (NB: the perfect tense in ἐν παραβάσει γέγονεν at 1 Timothy 2:14). It is our author who stubbornly maintains that salvation is a matter of the future and will come to women only on the far side of adherence to a form of σωφροσύνη apposite to the residual effects of Eve's deception: submission to male leadership in the church and the acceptance of domestic life as their primary venue of service (cf. 1 Timothy 2:11-15; 5:3-16; 2 Timothy 3:6-7; Titus 2:3-4).

It is the opponents who are alleged to be promising that attention to their version of εὐσέβεια will bring some sort of financial gain (1 Timothy 6:5). It is our author who counters that αὐτάρκεια is the gain which εὐσέβεια brings, and that furthermore what life in this age requires is patient endurance and generosity, all in hope of eschatological reward (1 Timothy 6:7-19). They offer a εὐσέβεια the promise of which is exhausted in this life. His εὐσέβεια holds a

[99]Fee, *Timothy and Titus*, p. xxxi.

promise that is good both in this life *and* the one to come (1 Timothy 4:8).

So central, in fact, are endurance, suffering, and persecution—in a word, hope deferred—to the author's vision of life in this age, that it is difficult to see where the notion that there is a loss of the longing for eschatological fulfillment ever came from. The apostle is held up as an example of one who suffers evil, enduring imprisonment as a criminal. Not only is his delegate called into direct association with him in this suffering (2 Timothy 1:8; 2:3 συγκακο– παθεῖν), but this "suffering together" is placed in the broader (and Pauline) theological context of having died with Christ in hope of living with him, and of enduring (now) in hope of reigning with him in the future (2 Timothy 2:11b-12a; cf., especially Romans 6). And while Dibelius makes much of a contrast between the heroic ethic of suffering on the part of Paul and Timothy and the unheroic, bourgeois ethic for everybody else, 2 Timothy explicitly makes the suffering of persecution constitutive of life for *all* who desire to be εὐσεβής (2 Timothy 3:12). What is strikingly at work in the Pastorals is reserve in the face of a realized eschatology.

d. *Apocalyptic Hope*

So far, in fact, are these letters from betraying the preparation for an extended stay on planet Earth, that they give rather more the appearance of expecting at any moment the anticipated cosmic cataclysm. And here is our fourth point of demurral from the critical consensus. Rather than a vague and general hope in the Lord's return, the Pastorals articulate a pointedly apocalyptic understanding of the cosmos.

Not only are exhortations presented in the light of the approaching judgment of the world and consummation of the Kingdom of God (2 Timothy 4:1), but the forces which to this writer are the tripwire to the denouement of the apocalyptic drama have already been released: the presence within the church—the very pillar and foundation of the truth!—of false teaching is evidence of the fact that the prophesied "latter days" have come (1 Timothy 4:1).[100] This verse's attribution of false teaching to the activity of deceitful spirits and of demons brings into view the early Christian schema of the last days when the Lord's return is immediately preceded by a demonically energized apostasy, endangering the fate even of the elect (Matthew

---

[100]Schwarz (*Bürgerliches Christentum?*, p. 108) makes the same point. See also Fee, *Timothy and Titus*, p. 60.

24:24-25; Mark 13:22-23; 2 Thessalonians 2:9-12; Revelation 13:11-18).[101]

Nor is it merely the proliferation of false teaching as such that is a sign that the final eschatological conflict has begun, but the rise within the church of an ethical style of life which the author characterizes as love of self, of money, and of pleasure rather than love of God (2 Timothy 3:2-4). These are the marks of the "difficult times" (καιροὶ χαλεποί) which comprise the "last days" (ἐν ἐσχάταις ἡμέραις, 2 Timothy 3:1).

If our author charges that it is precisely from among the ranks of individuals bearing these last-days-marks that the opponents have emerged, it is a telling index of just how advanced is the ticking of the cosmic clock. Because in 2 Timothy the eschatological tension is manifest in a conflict between alternative lifestyles, the language in Titus 2:11ff of "waiting" for the appearing of Christ ought to be taken with complete seriousness. For if at that point our author spurns "impiety and worldly desires," employs the Hellenistic ethical triad (σώφρων, δίκαιος, and εὐσεβής), and particularizes the triad's relevance to "the present age," he does so because he enjoys a living expectation of the end of the age.

e. Eschatology and Ethics

This leads to the fifth point at which we depart from the conventional wisdom with respect to the eschatology of these letters: what we see in the Pastorals, and pointedly in the theologically self-conscious formulation of Titus 2:11-14, is (*pace* Koester) moral behavior indeed being given a specifically eschatological motivation.[102] In the context of the Pastoral corpus as a whole, the ethical rapprochement with Greek ethics is an altogether provisional arrangement, a distinctly endtime—that is to say, apocalyptic—phenomenon. If the vices the author associates with the opponents are signs that the last days have arrived, grace empowers virtues appropriate to waiting this time out.

One of the principal merits of Donelson's study of the ethical argument of the Pastorals is his demonstration that "the expectation

---

[101]Note Luke Timothy Johnson's judgment: "The appearance and activity of the opponents is here attributed to the eschatological conflict of the last days (1 Timothy 4:1)"—*Timothy and Titus*, p. 82.

[102]Schwarz says that Titus 2:13 *muß uns ebenfalls vorsichtig werden lassen, zu leicht das Klischee des "Frühkatholizismus" an die Past heranzutragen; denn hier wird ganz ausdrücklich gesagt, daß mit einem tugendhaften Leben nicht die Preisgabe der Parusieerwartung verknüpft ist (Bürgerliches Christentum?*, pp. 143-144).

of a future judgment becomes a major warrant in the letters."[103] The author of the Pastorals offers, for instance, positive and negative paradigms of those who will face Jesus as

> judge who weighs in balance the ethical and non-ethical thrust of people's lives.... "Paul" wishes for Onesiphorus, who supported Paul in his troubles and thus represents as an illustrative paradigm the church member who aligns his allegiances correctly, "mercy on the day of the Lord" (2 Timothy 1:18). On the other side of the ethical and organizational fence, the Lord is invoked to repay for his deeds the coppersmith Alexander, who is rigorously opposed to Paul and the sound teachings (2 Timothy 4:18). Again, the opponents are relegated to the same fate as that of Jannes and Jambres (illustrative paradigms) who opposed Moses and thus opposed the truth (2 Timothy 3:8). The author obviously participates in the general apocalyptic framework of early Christianity with its inheritance of the judgmental language of Judaism.... There will be a judgment day and Jesus will be the judge. It is a major motivational force.[104]

As standards for judgment Jesus will rely on the virtues and vices, on adherence to right teaching, and on allegiance to the right teachers. Donelson notes the way the author uses the motif of a future judgment to speak to the puzzling paradox of the opponents' success (1 Timothy 5:24, 2 Timothy 3:9): "Faced with the inescapable affront that his opponents have more influence than he does, the author uses a common argument for those who possess an apocalyptic arsenal: on the day of the Lord his orthodoxy will be proven."[105] Eschatological reward does not lie ahead merely for the teacher who perseveres in the truth, but for "all who have loved his appearing" (2 Timothy 4:8). And in the cause and effect hymn of 2 Timothy 2:11-13, Donelson finds a significant articulation of the ethical and cosmological connections which lie at the heart of the author's theology: denial of Jesus or of sound (read: sanctioned) teaching will issue in exclusion from salvation, while faithfulness to Jesus and to sound (again read: sanctioned) teaching will bring the

---

[103]Donelson, *Pseudepigraphy*, p. 148.

[104]Donelson, *Pseudepigraphy*, p. 147. The following comment is worth pondering: "Only defenders of authenticity have, for the most part, admitted the connection between this second epiphany and ethics, though they, of course, read the connection in Pauline terms, as the inbreaking of the endtime. So Jeremias, *Die Briefe an Timotheus und Titus*. I know of no systematic treatment of the second epiphany as a motivational force for the ethic" (p. 148 n. 84).

[105]Donelson, *Pseudepigraphy*, p. 148.

reward of salvation.[106] The cosmological argument—eschatological reward and punishment—is essential to the author's attempt to win adherence to his teaching. And thus the author appeals to his delegate to stay the course (i.e., hold fast the received tradition) until the epiphany of the Lord Jesus (1 Timothy 6:13-16).[107]

This posture of what is called "waiting" at Titus 2:13 colors much in the ethical argument of the Pastorals:

The "man of God" is to stay the course "until the epiphany" of the Lord or until his own "course is run," looking to the eschatological reward, the crown of righteousness (1 Timothy 6:11-16; 2 Timothy 4:6-8).

All who wish to live in what our author thinks of as a godly way—which is to say, all those who love the epiphany of the Lord—can expect persecution in this world (with 2 Timothy 3:12 compare 4:8). Thus, all are called to join the author and his delegate in suffering together for the sake of the gospel (with 2 Timothy 3:12 and 4:8 compare 1:8 and 2:3).

Women are to await the final dissolution of their ethical solidarity with Eve, assuming for now, where possible, a posture of service within the traditional family structure (1 Timothy 2:9-15; 5:3-16; Titus 2:3-5).

Slaves are to forego claims to status in this age which their position in Christ suggests they ought to be given, this in the interest of adorning the gospel through redoubled efforts to serve their masters. Those with Christian masters who exercise beneficence toward the church will be returning thanks to the church's benefactors; those with nonbelieving masters will at the very least be protecting the church from slander and may in fact find their lives serving to make the gospel more attractive (cf., 1 Timothy 6:1-2 and Titus 2:9-10).

The rich are to invest themselves and their resources in a community of people who are beneath them, awaiting a return—the conferring of "real life"—at the epiphany of the Lord Jesus, rather than looking to the building up of social capital in the reciprocal bonds of patron-client relationships.

Little here approaches a giving up on the provisional nature of the church's arrangements with the social status quo. How much closer the worldviews of Paul and the Pastorals are to each other than either is to theoretical sources is brought into relief by

---

[106]Donelson, *Pseudepigraphy*, pp. 149-151.
[107]Donelson, *Pseudepigraphy*, p. 152.

Schrage's comments about the cosmic view of Epictetus' Stoicism.[108] What is curious is that Schrage[109] and others do not see an apocalypticism like Paul's undergirding the exhortation of the Pastorals as well.

If, as Dibelius maintains, the Pastorals are indeed unique within the New Testament canon in the extent to which they structure life under the banner of *christliche Bürgerlichkeit*,[110] they do so by extrapolating from the logic of the social ethics of the homologoumena, and they do it under a similarly apocalyptic umbrella.[111]

Though the language is distinctive, the vision is strikingly Pauline and as daring at that: an endtime people of social unequals displaying God's benevolence towards all. While the responsibility is a common one, its particular form is differentiated, not just according to individual gifts and abilities, but also according to location in the social nexus. In the interim before the epiphany of God's glory, this responsibility expresses itself precisely through attention to "average morality." If the Pastorals' social vision is in this respect socially conservative, it coheres at a fundamental level with the acknowledged letters. But if there is a certain heroism in the acknowledged letters' staking all on the eventuality of the consummation of the ages, there is likewise a counter-cultural thrust to the Pastorals' end-times rapprochement with the Hellenistic ideal of the wealthy *Bürger*.

---

[108]Schrage, "Stellung zur Welt," pp. 135-136, 153, and see above, IV.B.2., pp. 169f.

[109]Schrage, *Ethics*, pp. 258, 264, and see above, IV.C.1., pp. 184f.

[110]Dibelius/Conzelmann, *Die Pastoralbriefe* (1966), p. 33, and see above, I.C.1., pp. 9f.

[111]I regret that during the writing of my dissertation I did not have the advantage of the critical input of Dale Martin, who did, however, join the faculty of Duke University in time to be enlisted for my examination committee. Martin's response to my reading of the relationship between the acknowledged and the Pastoral letters was that it would have proved beneficial if I had given attention to: 1) the way Paul's apocalypticism centers on the coming reversal of the hierarchical values of the dominant culture: "strong and weak," "wisdom and foolishness," "rich and poor"; and 2) the centrality of the cross in the ethics of the acknowledged letters and absence of an "atonement theology" and accordingly an ethics grounded in the "offense" of the cross in the Pastorals. I do anticipate weighing these considerations in my future work on the Pauline movement. Certainly my discussion would have been richer and more nuanced had I included these questions in the present study, but I do not think my basic construal of the relationship between Paul and the Pastorals would have been significantly different.

CONCLUSIONS:

Celsus Versus Origen, Revisited

One of the perils of a study like this is that conclusions are not unequivocally forced upon one by the data. In the case of any social description in antiquity, the data themselves are uncomfortably soft; the difficulty is compounded when—as in the case of the Pastorals—part of what is at issue is basic historical information: authorship, date, and destination. Measuring cultural accommodation is inherently impressionistic; furthermore, I have necessarily been restricted in my reconstruction of the ideal of the wealthy *Bürger* by the limits of my present knowledge of the contemporary, extrabiblical sources. One would think that an answer to the question of the relation between ethics and eschatology in the Pastorals and in Paul would rest on a surer base; even here, however, it is difficult to account for the reasons why one scholar accepts Pauline language or thought-forms in the Pastorals at face value and another downplays them as mere accommodations to Pauline tradition.

Despite these caveats, I forward my growing sense that on the matter of "bourgeois" Christianity there is more that unites the Pastorals and Paul than there is that divides them. A return to the (again, one-way) discussion between the third century apologist Origen and the second century critic Celsus sets the issues in relief as we review the preceding chapters.

A. SOCIAL PROVENANCE (CHAPTER II)

In at least one regard, Origen's use of 1 Timothy is on the mark: the Pastorals evidence a literate, educated constituency. But it would be altogether problematic for us to think of this as a "bourgeoisie" or "middle class" in the modern sense.

E.A. Judge's work is especially helpful in inviting us to describe the social constituency of the Pastoral churches: a) in terms appropriate to the ancient rather than the modern world, and b) in terms that fit these churches' provincial municipalities rather than the elitist sensibilities of the Roman senatorial and equestrian ranks. If the social description of early Christianity is to take as normative the contours of the Roman system of orders—as appears to be the case with Celsus and his modern followers—inevitably, and unfortunately, the general conception will be one of proletarian provenance.

The Pastorals suggest a readership that does not easily conform to the romantic conception of Christianity's emergence from the poorest of the poor in the Hellenistic municipalities of the first century. At the same time, it is not likely that any Pastoral Christians come from Roman senatorial or equestrian ranks, nor is it certain that any are of curial rank. The result is that it is too easy to conceive of Pastoral Christians as coming from a "middle class" somewhere in between, especially when one finds that just such a group had already been idealized for the ancient world by Aristotle.

When the language of gradational class is employed, indications are that Rostovtzeff's "municipal bourgeoisie" are represented in the Pastorals. It is important to realize that, despite the impression Rostovtzeff himself leaves, members of early imperial "municipal bourgeoisies" did not comprise a burgeoning, western industrial "middle class," but discrete, local upper classes.

Analysis in terms of relational class structure is more helpful in understanding the way social polarities would have been perceived in ancient societies, societies in which one was either on top or at the bottom of two-term relationships. Such polarities are abundantly present in the Pastorals, and the concern is largely with helping social superiors (especially, prosperous household heads) relate to the rest of the community of faith.

Language of status allows discussion of the motives behind individual behavior in group settings, and invites attention to the place benefactor relationships had in binding wealthy Christians to their communities; and E.A. Judge's analysis helps focus the discussion of exchange relationships between benefactors and dependents within relevant, contemporary venues, viz., πολιτεία, οἰκονομία, κοινωνία.

A survey of the data of the Pastorals suggests wealthy Christians have established a commanding, if minoritarian, presence within these communities. The virtues forwarded in the Pastoral epistles and the language used to describe these virtues belong to the upper strata of the imperial municipalities. One could expect this readership to comprise the audience of a Musonius Rufus, a Dio Chrysostom, or a Plutarch, and to aspire to the honors accorded municipal and associational benefactors. Because it is difficult to dissociate from anachronistic connotations, however, language of a "bourgeoisie" is problematic. It is better to think in terms of upper class or upper strata people who are nonetheless not necessarily members of the aristocratic (curial or above) *ordines*. The letters are written in no small part to help precisely these people understand what our author thinks are the points of continuity and discontinuity between his and their social expectations about their place in the household of God.[1]

However, it is too much to claim—with Dibelius or Spicq—that these congregations are socially emergent when compared with the churches of the acknowledged Pauline letters. This is the genuine contribution of Judge et al., and the "new consensus" on the Pauline homologoumena. For it is not at all certain that Paul's language in 1 Corinthians 1:26ff should be taken at face value. Too many other indices of social status in the Corinthian correspondence point in the other direction—from the fact that one of their members is the city οἰκόνομος, to their having their own benefactors, to the lawsuits among them, to the economic differentiation that surfaces in the controversy over eating meat and at the Lord's Supper, to the expectation that their liberality on behalf of Jerusalem should exceed that of the impoverished but generous Macedonians (who, judging from their generous financial support of Paul's personal ministry, are themselves probably not all that impoverished), to Paul's frustrated "you are already filled, you have already become rich, you have become kings." If the Pastorals presuppose members of the local upper strata among their readership, they are not at far remove from the acknowledged letters in doing so.

Had we been able to speak with Origen before his response to Celsus, we would have advised him not to give so much ground. To be sure, because Celsus measures social standing by the senatorial standards that are familiar to us from the literature, he would no doubt have remained unimpressed.

B. CULTURAL ACCOMMODATION (CHAPTER III)

In Origen we meet a Christian who unabashedly asks that the faith be measured by standards of the prevailing culture. If there does exist in early Christian literature a program of Dibelius' *Bildungschristentum*—a brand of Christianity that finds in the faith "the

---

[1]I have gratefully incorporated suggestions from Dale Martin in the wording of this paragraph.

fulfillment of the educated person's intuitive expectations"[2]—
evidence for it indeed lies in Origen's *Contra Celsum*. His explicit
appeal is that if virtue is the goal and if education is the means to
the goal, Christianity is a superior teacher:

> For we, by readings of the Bible and explanations of the readings,
> encourage men to be pious towards the God of the universe and the
> virtues that share piety's throne; whereas we discourage people from
> despising the Deity and from all action contrary to right reason. Even
> philosophers would desire to gather so many to hear their words of
> exhortation to goodness (3.50).

While critical of the particulars of various philosophies and anxious
to demonstrate the superiority of Christianity, Origen establishes
common ground wherever he can.[3] The grounds upon which Christianity should be accepted are immanent to the classical tradition
(even the appeal to divine revelation has precedent in the Pythagorean school), for what makes Christianity superior is that it does
better what other philosophies aspire to do: make people more
noble and virtuous. He even makes explicit the comparison
between the virtue called for in municipal authorities and in ecclesiastical authorities (i.e., bishops), claiming that among the latter,
"broadly speaking, there is superior progress towards the virtues
surpassing the character of those who are councillors and rulers in
the cities" (3.30; cf., 6.8; 8.75).

The situation is not quite as clear in the Pastoral epistles. As
often as the similarities between the officer lists and contemporary
virtue lists are cited in the commentaries, the Pastorals themselves
never make explicit the comparison Origen does. Nonetheless, I
contend that the instructions to wealthy Christians in these epistles
do presuppose cultural notions about how the well-off should use
their resources and about the sort of relationships that should exist
between benefactors and their clientele. Principal motifs we have
found to reside in Aristotle (the relationship between wealth, beneficence, and honor), Menander (the wisdom of securing the future

---

[2]Dibelius, *Urchristentum*, p. 16, and see above, I.C.1.b., pp. 16ff, esp. pp. 19f.

[3]E.g., likening the Christian view of the coming judgment to the Stoic view of
the conflagration and the pagan sense of accountability after death, while
simultaneously rejecting the specifics of the doctrine of conflagration (3.75). See
Chadwick's discussion (*Contra Celsum*, pp. ix-xiii) of the dexterity with which
Origen moves back and forth between arguments derived from the Stoa and the
Academy, depending upon whether Celsus happens to be sounding Academic
or Stoic.

through friendships), Dio Chrysostom (the moral worth of the wealthy), and the inscriptions (the quest for lasting glory through beneficence).

If these sources and their motifs are allowed to provide the general background for a *bürgerlich* understanding of the perils, responsibilities, rewards, and perquisites of wealth in the social world to which the Pastorals are addressed, a number of both *bürgerlich* and anti-*bürgerlich* features surface. On the one hand, the Pastorals affirm cultural ideas about the wisdom of investing in others due to wealth's precariousness. On the other hand, the Pastorals warn against haughtiness about wealth (against even a presumption that wealth entitles one to lead), encourage an eschatological rather than a social expectation of a return on generosity, and divorce the bestowal of honor within the community from traditional benefactors (widows and teachers rather than generous donors are to be the recipients of honor).

Two exceptions to the last point are illuminating: a) non-Christian household heads are entitled to "all honor" from their Christian slaves, most likely because of their power within a household-based social world to pass communal judgment on the Christian congregation; and b) Christian household heads who do exert themselves on behalf of the church, though not entitled to receive the standard perquisites of their beneficence, should still receive what their Christian slaves have to offer in thanks: continued, enthusiastic service.

Although H.R. Niebuhr does not discuss Origen in his modern classic, *Christ and Culture*,[4] he does place Origen's Alexandrian mentor Clement in the camp of those Christians who, without looking for an easy road to discipleship, are nonetheless optimistic about synthesizing loyalty to Christ with loyalty to "culture."[5] Paul he places among those who, by virtue of a deeper conviction of the pervasiveness of sin, keep Christ's and "culture's" authority in tension, or set them in paradox.[6] Though I have not seen scholars who apply Dibelius' epithet to the Pastorals comment on Niebuhr's categorization, my guess is that they call these letters "bourgeois" precisely because they see in them that accommodating spirit which is so sparse in Paul but so abundant in Clement and Origen.

---

[4]H. Richard Niebuhr, *Christ and Culture,* (New York: Harper and Row, 1951; Harper Colophon Books, 1975).

[5]Niebuhr, *Christ and Culture,* pp. 123-128.

[6]Niebuhr, *Christ and Culture,* pp. 159-167.

My contention is that against the backdrop of the normal function benefactions had in cementing reciprocal relationships between
wealthy people and their dependents, the ideal held before wealthy
Christians in the Pastorals is far less culturally integrative than mere
vocabulary and reticence to demand a heroic divestment of possessions suggest. In fact, because wealthy *Bürger* are challenged to
assume a familiar *noblesse oblige* yet are simultaneously discouraged
from expecting a culturally recognizable return on their generosity,
there is as much to horrify as to attract them. In a word, cultural
notions of the role of benefactors are shared in part and repudiated
in part—the content of the ideal is transformed even as its language
is appropriated. Because in these letters language of the ideal *Bürger*
is used in such an anti-*bürgerlich* way, I would be hard pressed to
place the Pastorals among those Christian thinkers who simply add
to pagan virtues (e.g., Stoic detachment) Christian virtues (e.g.,
love). By cutting the philotimic heart out of a culturally assumed
social bond without absolving the wealthy of their responsibility for
liberality and generosity, the Pastorals accept precisely the sort of
tension between loyalty to cultural demands and loyalty to Christ
which one expects from the Pauline mind.

C. UNHEROIC CONSERVATISM (CHAPTER IV)

Celsus charges the Christian movement with dangerous sedi-
tion, with trying to upset the social order by appealing to the
illiterate rabble and turning children against their parents and
teachers (3.55), with discouraging the patriotic act of swearing
loyalty to the emperor (8.65), with not allowing men to fight in
Rome's armies or even to serve on city councils (8.73,75). Much of
Origen's defense of the faith is spent allaying Celsus' fears about
Christianity's radicalism, arguing that the gospel is the best preservative the empire has.
Christianity, Origen maintains, does indeed aim at the education
of all people, but in doing so merely aspires to the highest of
philosophical ideals and would never be found objectionable to
parents and teachers who were really interested in their children's
learning noble and sound teaching (3.58).[7] He argues that the

---

[7]Stephen Benko, *Pagan Rome and the Early Christians* (Bloomington, IN:
Indiana University Press, 1984), p. 157, suggests the weakness of this argument
may be an admission of guilt.

prayers which Christians—"a special army of piety"—send up on behalf of the emperor and his soldiers are more effective in fighting the empire's enemies than are the efforts of those soldiers themselves (8.73). And if Christians refuse to accept public office it is because they devote themselves to office in the church, and thereby offer a greater benefit to mankind (8.75). In a word, "Christians do more good to their countries than the rest of mankind, since they educate the citizens and teach them to be devoted to God, the guardian of their city" (8.74).

Despite its radical appearance, in other words, the faith properly understood supports the social order. And even if it appears that this apologist is trying to make Christian discipleship sound less heroic than it must have actually been on the eve of renewed persecution,[8] there is in Origen something of what Dibelius refers to as a social ethic that takes seriously the enduring structures of the world. But the very fact that he feels accountable to the non-Christian world—that he is compelled to demonstrate the social usefulness of the gospel—is testament to how far things have moved beyond Paul *and* beyond the Pastorals.

It was Albert Schweitzer who so forcefully thrust the issue of ethical heroism into modern scholarly discussion of the New Testament. This he did by calling attention to the motif of Jesus' heroic, eschatological faith with that hauntingly Nietzsche-like image of the would-be Messiah laying "hold of the wheel of the world to set it moving on that last revolution which is to bring all ordinary history to a close. It refuses to turn, and He throws Himself upon it..."[9] It was Schweitzer, too, who gave us the notion that the ethics of such a would-be apocalyptic Messiah could be good only for the interim. In *Christ and Culture*, Niebuhr reminds us that it was Schweitzer's distinct aim in accenting the radical nature of Jesus' eschatological hope "to depict the figure of Jesus in its overwhelming heroic greatness and to impress it upon the modern age and upon modern theology."[10] As Niebuhr explains:

> There was an extremeness in the hopefulness of Jesus that sets him apart from all other men who expect lesser glories or more frequently,

---

[8]See 3.15, and Chadwick's discussion (pp. xiv-xv) of the likelihood that the *Contra Celsus* was written immediately prior to and in expectation of the persecution under Decius (A.D. 249-250).

[9]Albert Schweitzer, *The Quest for the Historical Jesus: A Critical Study of Its Progress from Reimarus to Wrede*, trans. W. Montgomery, intro. James M. Robinson (New York: Macmillan Publishing Co., 1968), pp. 370-371.

no glory at all. Average morality presupposes complacency tempered by a little cynicism, or resignation qualified by moderate expectations of good. Intense anticipation of supernal good must result in a transformation of ethics.[11]

Radical hope, it would seem, is incompatible with the humanistic spirit; attention to "average morality" is intrinsically and inevitably unheroic. Both the Pauline homologoumena and the Pastoral epistles challenge this premise. In the social ethics of the acknowledged letters, mildly conservative (Theissen's term) positions are taken on key issues (ethnicity, servitude, gender, wealth). Dibelius himself admits that crucial aspects of the Pauline ethic are *bürgerlich* (read: mundane, quotidian—1 Thessalonians 4:11-12 and Philippians 4:8). Yet this conservatism is predicated upon the unfolding of an eschatological drama, one which is now partly realized but also partly still unfulfilled. It is an ethic in which the "already and the not yet" cast a shadow of reserve over the struggle to make visible in this age the equality that will be evident in the eschaton and urge a posture of joy at the challenge of living a life of servanthood in the here and now.

The Pastorals extrapolate from the logic of the homologoumena, maintaining both the basic Pauline social posture and the apocalyptic orientation. There is in both ends of the Pauline corpus a heroic embracing of "average morality" based on radical hope. In Galatians (e.g., 6:10) and Romans (e.g., 3:29; 12:17b,18) and in the Timothies and Titus[12] alike, an intense anticipation of "supernal good" issues in a robustly humanistic ethos.

We have come full circle to Dibelius' and Spicq's competing nuances of the Pastorals' "bourgeois" expression of the faith—the former suggesting an unheroic and the latter a humanistic version of Christianity. In reality, Dibelius appears to claim too little, Spicq too much.

---

[10]Niebuhr, *Christ and Culture*, p. 20, quoting Schweitzer's *Mystery of the Kingdom of God* (1914, p. 274).

[11]Niebuhr, *Christ and Culture*, p. 20.

[12]Among Origen's 46 citations of or allusions to the Pastorals in the *Contra Celsum* (using *Biblia Patristica*'s count), these letters are appealed to 10 times to support the claim that Christianity is a boon to the human race at large—in these 10 appeals to the Pastorals, 8 passages from the Pastorals show up (1 Timothy 1:15, at 1.63 and 4.28; 1 Timothy 2:1-2, at 7.73; 1 Timothy 2:8, at 3.60; 1 Timothy 3:2, at 3.48; 1 Timothy 3:16, at 3.31; 1 Timothy 4:10, at 3.49; 4.4; and 4.28; Titus 1:9-11, at 4.48; and Titus 3:3-6, at 1.64).

As familiar as much of the Pastorals' exhortation must have been to wealthy citizens of early imperial municipalities, too much of what is being asked defies normal expectations to allow the aura of banality which Dibelius intends the epithet *bürgerlich* to convey. And the eschatological warrant for obedience—what Donelson calls the cosmological argument—is quite alien to that milieu. Given the normal reciprocal exchange between elites and their dependents, surely it would have been at least mildly heroic for a Christian elite to invest themselves in a community of unequals through public-spirited generosity, yet to look for a return not in the "lesser glory"[13] of social honor but in the greater glory of an eschatological crown.

On the other hand, as much as the humanistic ideal of καλο–κἀγαθός does loom in the background of the ethic of wealth, there is no small overstatement in Spicq's treating as litotes the Pastorals' concern to avoid scandal (the ἵνα μή's of 1 Timothy 6:1; Titus 2:5, cf., 8,10), as though the Pastorals were prescribing the strategy by which the world was "so swiftly (to be) won to Christianity."[14] Since the posture of waiting remains central to Christian lifestyle, even the rapprochement between the Hellenistic moral ideal (to live εὐσεβῶς καὶ δικαίως καὶ σωφρονῶς) and Christian living is but an ethic for the short interim between the epiphanies of mankind's savior. Such a vision of a Christian society as Spicq attributes to the Pastorals awaits the likes of an Origen who can finally imagine the day when all humankind would be

> converted to the word of God and would be most law-abiding and mild. And all other worship would be done away and only that of the Christians would prevail. One day it will be the only one to prevail, since the word is continually gaining possession of more souls (8.68).

Meanwhile, the Pastorals share the Pauline reticence to speak of this-worldly millennial hopes. In solidarity with the acknowledged letters, the Pastorals sound no such note of cultural triumphalism, betray no broader vision of a Christian civilization, lay down no mandate for the regeneration of society at large.

---

[13]Niebuhr's term (*Christ and Culture*, p. 20, and see above, p. 199).
[14]Spicq, *Pastorales*, p. 296, and see above, I.C.2., pp. 28f.

BIBLIOGRAPHY

Aland, Kurt. "The Problem of Anonymity and Pseudonymity in Christian Literature of the First Two Centuries." *Journal of Theological Studies, N.S.* 12 (1961): 39-49.

Balch, David L. *Let Wives Be Submissive: The Domestic Code in 1 Peter.* Chico, CA: Scholars Press, 1981.

Baltzell, E. Digby. *The Protestant Establishment: Aristocracy and Caste in America.* New York: Random House, 1964; Vintage Books, 1966.

_____. *Puritan Boston and Quaker Philadelphia: Two Protestant Ethics and the Spirit of Class Authority and Leadership.* New York: MacMillan, The Free Press, 1979.

Bammel, Ernst. "πτωχός." *Theological Dictionary of the New Testament.* 6.885-915.

Banks, Robert. *Paul's Idea of Community: The Early House Churches in their Historical Setting.* Grand Rapids: Eerdmans Publishing Co., 1980.

Barrett, C.K. *The Pastoral Epistles in the New English Bible.* Oxford, at the Clarendon Press, 1963.

Bartchy, S. Scott. *ΜΑΛΛΟΝ ΧΡΗΣΑΙ: First Century Slavery and the Interpretation of 1 Corinthians 7:21.* Society of Biblical Literature Dissertation Series, No. 11. Missoula, MT: Scholars Press, 1973.

Barton, S.C., and Horsley, G.H.R. "A Hellenistic Cult Group and the New Testament Churches." *Jahrbuch für Antike und Christentum* 24 (1981): 7-41.

Bassler, Jouette M. "The Widows' Tale: A Fresh Look at 1 Timothy 5:3-16." *Journal of Biblical Literature* 103 (1984): 23-41.

Bauer, Walter. *Orthodoxy and Heresy in Earliest Christianity.* 2nd German ed. (1934) by Georg Strecker. Translated by the Philadelphia Seminar on Christian Origins. Edited by R.A. Kraft and G. Krodel. Philadelphia: Fortress Press, 1971.

206   *Wealth and Beneficence in the Pastorals*

Bauer, W., Arndt, W., and Gingrich, F. *A Greek-English Lexicon of the New Testament and Other Early Christian Literature.* 2nd ed. Revised and augmented by F. Gingrich and F. Danker. Chicago and London: The University of Chicago Press, 1957, 1979.

Bellah, Robert N. *Beyond Belief: Essays on Religion in a Post-Traditional World.* New York: Harper & Row, 1970.

_____ et al. *Habits of the Heart: Individualism and Commitment in American Life.* Berkeley and Los Angeles: University of California Press, 1985.

Benko, Stephen. *Pagan Rome and the Early Christians.* Bloomington, IN: Indiana University Press, 1984.

Benne, Robert. *The Ethic of Democratic Capitalism: A Moral Reassessment.* Philadelphia: Fortress Press, 1981.

Berger, Peter L., and Luckmann, Thomas. *The Social Construction of Reality: A Treatise in the Sociology of Knowledge.* Garden City, NY: Doubleday & Co., 1966. Anchor Books, 1967.

Bertram, Georg. "καλός." *Theological Dictionary of the New Testament.* 3.536-556.

_____. "παιδεύω." *Theological Dictionary of the New Testament.* 5.596-625.

Betz, Hans Dieter. *Der Apostel Paulus und die sokratische Tradition: Eine exegetische Untersuchung zu seiner "Apologie" 2 Korinther 10-13.* Tübingen: J.C.B. Mohr (Paul Siebeck), 1972.

_____. *Galatians: A Commentary on Paul's Letter to the Churches of Galatia.* Philadelphia: Fortress Press, 1979.

Bieder, Werner. *Die Berufung im Neuen Testament.* Abhandlungen zur Theologie des Alten und Neuen Testaments 38. Zürich, 1961.

Blass, F., and Debrunner, A. *A Greek Grammar of the New Testament and Other Early Christian Literature.* Translated and revised by Robert W. Funk. Chicago and London: The University of Chicago Press, 1961.

Bolkestein, Hendrik. *Wohltätigkeit und Armenpflege im vorchristlichen Altertum: Ein Beitrag zum Problem "Moral und Gesellschaft."* Utrecht: A. Oosthoek, Verlag A.G., 1939.

Bonner, Stanley F. *Education in Ancient Rome: From the Elder Cato to the Younger Pliny.* Berkeley and Los Angeles: University of California Press, 1977.

Bornkamm, G. "πρέσβυς." *Theological Dictionary of the New Testament.* 6.666-667.

Borret, Marcel, ed. *Origene: Contre Celse.* Sources Chretiennes, no. 132. Translated, with introduction and notes by Marcel Borret, S.J. 5 volumes. Paris: Les Editions du Cerf, 1967.

Bowersock, G.W. "Review of *The Social and Economic History of the Roman Empire* by Michael Ivanovitch Rostovtzeff." *Daedalus* (1974): 15-23.

Brinkmann, Carl. "Bourgeoisie." *Encyclopaedia of the Social Sciences.* New York: The MacMillan Co., 1930. 2.654-656.

Brown, Peter. *The Making of Late Antiquity.* Cambridge, MA: Harvard University Press, 1978.

Brox, Norbert. "Historische und theologische Probleme der Pastoralbriefe des Neuen Testaments." *Kairos* 11 (1969): 81-94.

_____. *Die Pastoralbriefe.* Regensburger Neues Testament, 7. Band, Zweiter Teil. 4th edition. Regensburg: Verlag Friedrich Pustet, 1969.

_____. "Lukas als Verfasser der Pastoralbriefe?" *JAC* 13 (1970): 62-77.

Bruce, F.F. *New Testament History.* New York: Doubleday and Co., 1971; Anchor Books, 1972.

Bruck, Eberhard F. "Ethics vs. Law: St. Paul, the Fathers of the Church and the 'Cheerful Giver' in Roman Law." *Traditio* 2 (1944): 97-121.

Brunt, P.A. "Aspects of the Social Thought of Dio Chrysostom and of the Stoics." *Proceedings of the Cambridge Philological Society.* 199 (1973): 9-34.

_____. "A Marxist View of Roman History." A review of *The Class Struggle in the Ancient Greek World from the Archaic Age to the Arab Conquests,* by G.E.M. de Ste. Croix. *Journal of Roman Studies* 72 (1982): 158-163.

Buckler, W.H. "Labour Disputes in the Province of Asia." *Anatolian Studies Presented to Sir Wm. Mitchell Ramsay,* pp. 27-50. Edited by W.H. Buckler and W.M. Calder. Manchester, at the University Press, 1923.

Bultmann, Rudolf. "ἀθανασία." *Theological Dictionary of the New Testament.* 3.22-25.

_____. *Theologie des Neuen Testaments.* 5th edition. Tübingen, 1965.

_____. *Theology of the New Testament.* 2 volumes. Translated by Kendrick Grobel. New York: Scribner's Sons, 1951, 1955.

_____. *Primitive Christianity in its Contemporary Setting.* Translated by R.H. Fuller. New York: Meridian Books, 1956. Living Age Books, 1956.

Cadoux, Cecil John. *The Early Church and the World: A History of the Christian Attitude to Pagan Society and the State down to the Time of Constantinus.* Edinburgh: T. & T. Clark, 1925.

Campenhausen, Hans von. *Ecclesiastical Authority and Spiritual Power in the Church of the First Three Centuries.* Translated by J.A. Baker. Stanford, CA: Stanford University Press, 1969.

_____. "Polykarp von Smyrna und die Pastoralbriefe." *Aus der Frühzeit des Christentums.* Tübingen: J.C.B. Mohr (Paul Siebeck), 1963, pp. 197-252.

_____. *Tradition and Life in the Church: Essays and Lectures in Church History.* Translated by A.V. Littledale. Philadelphia: Fortress Press, 1968.

Carcopino, Jerome. *Daily Life in Ancient Rome: The People and the City at the Height of the Empire.* Translated by E.O. Lorimer. Edited and annotated by H.T. Rowell. New Haven: Yale University Press, 1940.

Cartlidge, David R. *Documents for the Study of the Gospels.* Philadelphia: Fortress Press, 1980.

Chadwick, Henry, ed. *Origen: Contra Celsum.* Translated with introduction and notes by Henry Chadwick. Cambridge, at the University Press, 1953. Reprinted with corrections, 1965.

Charlesworth, M.P. "Some Observations on Ruler-Cult, Especially in Rome." *Harvard Theological Review* 28 (1935): 5-44.

Conzelmann, Hans. *A Commentary on the First Epistle to the Corinthians.* Translated by James W. Leitch. Philadelphia: Fortress Press, 1975.

_____. "Luke's Place in the Development of Early Christianity." In *Studies in Luke-Acts*, pp. 298-316. Edited by Leander E. Keck and J. Louis Martyn. Philadelphia: Fortress Press, 1980.

_____. *The Theology of St. Luke.* Translated by Geoffrey Buswell. Philadelphia: Fortress Press, 1961.

Cook, David. "The Pastoral Fragments Reconsidered." *The Journal of Theological Studies* 35 (April 1984): 120-131.

Countryman, L. William. *The Rich Christian in the Church of the Early Empire: Contradictions and Accommodations.* New York and Toronto: The Edwin Mellen Press, 1980.

Crouch, James E. *The Origin and Intention of the Colossian Haustafel.* Göttingen: Vandenhoeck and Ruprecht, 1972.

Dahl, Nils Alstrup. *Studies in Paul: Theology for the Early Christian Mission.* Assisted by Paul Donahue. Minneapolis: Augsburg Publishing House, 1977.

Danker, Frederick W. *Benefactor: Epigraphic Study of a Graeco-Roman and New Testament Semantic Field.* St. Louis: Clayton Publishing House, 1982.

_____. "Menander and the New Testament." *New Testament Studies* 10 (1964): 365-368.

Darnton, Robert. *The Great Cat Massacre and Other Episodes in French Cultural History.* New York: Basic Books, Inc., 1984.

Davis, Kingsley, and Moore, Wilbert E. "Some Principles of Stratification." *American Sociological Review* 10 (1945): 242-249.

Davis, Kingsley. "A Conceptual Analysis of Stratification." *American Sociological Review* 7 (1942): 309-321.

Deissmann, Adolf. *Light from the Ancient East: The New Testament Illustrated by Recently Discovered Texts of the Graeco-Roman World.* Translated by Lionel Strachan. London: Hodder and Stoughton, 1910.

Dibelius, Martin. *A Commentary on the Epistle of James.* Revised by Heinrich Greeven. Translated by Michael A. Williams. Edited by Helmut Koester. Philadelphia: Fortress Press, 1975.

_____. *A Fresh Approach to the New Testament and Early Christian Literature.* New York: Charles Scribner's Sons, 1936.

_____. *Der Hirt des Hermas.* Volume 4 of *Die apostolischen Väter.* Handbuch zum Neuen Testament, Ergänzungs-Band. Tübingen: J.C.B. Mohr (Paul Siebeck), 1923.

_____. *Die Pastoralbriefe.* Handbuch zum Neuen Testament, no. 13. 2nd edition. Tübingen: J.C.B. Mohr (Paul Siebeck), 1931.

_____. *An die Thessalonicher I, II, an die Philipper.* Handbuch zum Neuen Testament, no. 11. 3rd edition. Tübingen: J.C.B. Mohr (Paul Siebeck), 1937.

_____. *Urchristentum und Kultur.* Heidelberg: Carl Winters Universitäts-buchhandlung, 1928.

Dibelius, Martin, and Conzelmann, Hans. *Die Pastoralbriefe.* Handbuch zum Neuen Testament, no. 13. 4th edition. Tübingen: J.C.B. Mohr (Paul Siebeck), 1966.

_____. *The Pastoral Epistles.* Translated by Philip Buttolph and Adela Yarbro. Edited by Helmut Koester. Philadelphia: Fortress Press, 1972.

Dinkler, Erich. "Zum Problem der Ethik bei Paulus: Rechtsnahme und Rechtsverzicht (1 Kor 6,1-11)." *Zeitschrift für Theologie und Kirche* 49 (1952): 167-200.

Dodds, E.R. *Pagan and Christian in an Age of Anxiety: Some Aspects of Religious Experience from Marcus Aurelius to Constantine.* Cambridge, at the University Press, 1965; reprint ed., New York: W.W. Norton & Co., 1970.

Donelson, Lewis R. *Pseudepigraphy and Ethical Argument in the Pastoral Epistles.* Tübingen: J.C.B. Mohr (Paul Siebeck), 1986.

Downing, F. Gerald. "Philo on Wealth and the Rights of the Poor." *Journal for the Study of the Old Testament* 24 (1985): 116-118.

Duncan-Jones, Richard. *The Economy of the Roman Empire: Quantitative Studies.* 2nd edition. Cambridge, at the University Press, 1982.

Dunn, James D.G. *Unity and Diversity in the New Testament: An Inquiry Into the Character of Earliest Christianity.* Philadelphia: The Westminster Press, 1977.

Easton, Burton Scott. *The Pastoral Epistles.* New York: Charles Scribner's Sons, 1947.

Elbert, Paul. Review of *New Documents Illustrating Early Christianity, Volume 2: A Review of the Greek Inscriptions and Papyri Published in 1977,* by G.H.R. Horsley. *Novum Testamentum* 26 (1984): 88-90.

Elliott, John H. "A Catholic Gospel: Reflections on 'Early Catholicism' in the New Testament." *Catholic Biblical Quarterly* 31 (1968): 213-223.

_____. *A Home for the Homeless: A Sociological Exegesis of 1 Peter, Its Situation and Strategy.* Philadelphia: Fortress Press, 1981.

Fee, Gordon. *1 Corinthians.* The New International Commentary on the New Testament. Grand Rapids: Eerdmans, 1987.

_____. *1 and 2 Timothy, Titus.* A Good News Commentary. San Francisco: Harper and Row, Publishers, 1984.

Festugiere, Andre-Jean. *Personal Religion among the Greeks.* Berkeley and Los Angeles: University of California Press, 1954. Second printing, 1960.

Finley, Moses I. *The Ancient Economy.* 2nd edition. Berkeley and Los Angeles: University of California Press, 1985.

_____. *Ancient Slavery and Modern Ideology.* New York: Penguin Books, 1980.

_____. *Politics in the Ancient World.* Cambridge, at the University Press, 1983.

_____, ed. *Studies in Ancient Society.* London: Routledge and Kegan Paul, 1974.

Fishwick, D. Review of *Paganism in the Roman Empire*, by Ramsay MacMullen. *American Journal of Philology* 104 (Fall 1983): 306-310.

Foerster, W. "'ΕΥΣΕΒΕΙΑ in den Pastoralbriefen." *New Testament Studies* 5 (1958-9): 213-218.

_____. "σέβομαι." *Theological Dictionary of the New Testament.* 8.168-196.

Ford, J. Massingberd. "A Note on Proto-Montanism in the Pastoral Epistles." *New Testament Studies* 17 (1971): 338-346.

Furnish, Victor Paul. *Theology and Ethics in Paul.* Nashville: Abingdon Press, 1968. Fourth printing, 1978.

_____. *The Moral Teaching of Paul.* Nashville: Abingdon Press, 1979. Third printing, 1980.

_____. *II Corinthians: Translated with Introduction, Notes, and Commentary.* Anchor Bible, vol. 32A. Garden City, NY: Doubleday and Co., 1984.

Gage, Jean. *Les classes sociales dans l'empire romain.* Bibliotheque historique. Paris: Payot, 1964.

Gager, John G. *Kingdom and Community: The Social World of Early Christianity.* Englewood Cliffs, NJ: Prentice-Hall, Inc., 1975.

_____. Review of *Early Christianity and Society: Seven Studies*, by R.M. Grant; *Social Aspects of Early Christianity*, by A.J. Malherbe; and *Sociology of Early Palestinian Christianity*, by G. Theissen. *Religious Studies Review* 5 (1979): 174-180.

_____. "Shall We Marry Our Enemies?: Sociology and the New Testament." *Interpretation* 36 (1982): 256-265.

Garnsey, Peter. "Aspects of the Decline of the Urban Aristocracy in the Empire." *Aufstieg und Niedergang der römischen Welt* 2.1 (1974): 229-252.

_____. "Legal Privilege in the Roman Empire." In *Studies in Ancient Society*, pp. 141-165. Edited by Moses I. Finley. London: Routledge and Kegan Paul, 1974.

Garnsey, Peter, and Saller, Richard. *The Roman Empire: Economy, Society, and Culture.* Berkeley and Los Angeles: University of California Press, 1987.

Garzetti, Albino. *From Tiberius to the Antonines: A History of the Roman Empire, A.D. 14-192.* Translated by J.R. Foster. London: Methuen and Co., Ltd., 1974.

Gealy, F.D. *1 and 2 Timothy, Titus.* The Interpreter's Bible, 11. Nashville: Abingdon Press, 1955.

Geertz, Clifford. *The Interpretation of Cultures: Selected Essays.* New York: Basic Books, Inc., 1973.

Georgi, Dieter. *Die Geschichte der Kollekte des Paulus für Jerusalem.* Theologische Forschung, 38. Hamburg-Bergstedt: Evangelischer Verlag, 1965.

Grant, F.C., ed., *Hellenistic Religions: The Age of Syncretism.* The Library of Liberal Arts. Indianapolis, IN: Bobbs-Merrill Educational Publishing, 1953.

Grayston, K., and Herdan, G. "The Authorship of the Pastorals in the Light of Statistical Linguistics." *New Testament Studies* 6 (1959): 1-15.

Groethuysen, Bernard. *The Bourgeoisie: Catholicism vs. Capitalism in Eighteenth-Century France.* Translated by Mary Ilford. London: Barrie & Rockliff, the Cresset Press, 1927, 1968.

Guthrie, Donald. *New Testament Introduction.* 3rd ed., revised in one volume. London: Tyndale, 1970. 3rd American printing, Downers Grove, IL: InterVarsity Press, 1973.

_____. *The Pastoral Epistles.* London: The Tyndale Press, 1957; reprint ed., Grand Rapids: Eerdmans Printing Co., 1980.

_____. *The Pastoral Epistles and the Mind of Paul.* The Tyndale NT Lecture, 1955. London: The Tyndale Press, 1958.

Haenchen, Ernst. *The Acts of the Apostles: A Commentary.* Translated by Bernard Noble and Gerald Shinn. Philadelphia: The Westminster Press, 1971.

Hands, A.R. *Charities and Social Aid in Greece and Rome.* Ithaca, NY: Cornell University Press, 1968.

Hanson, A.T. *The Pastoral Epistles.* Grand Rapids: Eerdmans Publishing Co., 1982.

Harrington, Daniel J. "The 'Early Catholic' Writings of the New Testament: The Church Adjusting to World History." In *The Word in the World: Essays in Honor of Frederick Moriarty, S.J.*, pp. 97-111. Edited by R.J. Clifford and G.W. MacRae. Cambridge, MA: Weston College Press, 1973.

Harrison, P.N. *The Problem of the Pastoral Epistles*. Oxford, at the University Press, 1921.

————. *Paulines and Pastorals*. London: Villiers Publications Ltd., 1964.

Hauck, F. "πένης." *Theological Dictionary of the New Testament*. 6.37-40.

————. "πτωχός in the Greek World." *Theological Dictionary of the New Testament*. 6.886-887.

Hauck, F. and Kasch, W. "πλοῦτος." *Theological Dictionary of the New Testament*. 6.318-332.

Hendriksen, William. *Exposition of the Pastoral Epistles*. Grand Rapids: Baker Book House, 1957.

Hengel, Martin. *Acts and the History of Earliest Christianity*. Translated by John Bowden. Philadelphia: Fortress Press, 1979.

————. *Eigentum und Reichtum in der frühen Kirche: Aspekte einer frühchristlichen Sozialgeschichte*. Stuttgart: Calwer Verlag, 1973.

————. *Property and Riches in the Early Church: Aspects of a Social History of Early Christianity*. Translated by John Bowden. Philadelphia: Fortress Press, 1974.

Hennecke, Edgar. *New Testament Apocrypha*. Vol. 2: *Writings Related to the Apostles; Apocalypses and Related Subjects*. Edited by Wilhelm Schneemelcher. English translation edited by R. McL. Wilson. Philadelphia: Fortress Press, 1965.

Hitchcock, M. "Tests for the Pastorals." *Journal of Theological Studies* 1929: 276ff.

Hock, Ronald F. *The Social Context of Paul's Ministry: Tentmaking and Apostleship*. Philadelphia: Fortress Press, 1980.

Holmberg, Bengt. *Paul and Power: The Structure of Authority in the Primitive Church as Reflected in the Pauline Churches*. Philadelphia: Fortress Press, 1978.

Hopkins, Keith. "Elite Mobility in the Roman Empire." In *Studies in Ancient Society*, pp. 103-120. Edited by Moses I. Finley. London: Routledge and Kegan Paul, 1974.

_____. *Conquerors and Slaves: Sociological Studies in Roman History*, Volume 1. Cambridge, at the University Press, 1978.

Horsley, G.H.R. *New Documents Illustrating Early Christianity: A Review of the Greek Inscriptions and Papyri published in 1976.* North Ryde, Australia: The Ancient History Documentary Research Center, Macquarie University, 1981.

_____. *New Documents Illustrating Early Christianity: A Review of the Greek Inscriptions and Papyri published in 1977.* North Ryde, Australia: The Ancient History Documentary Research Center, Macquarie University, 1982.

_____. *New Documents Illustrating Early Christianity: A Review of the Greek Inscriptions and Papyri published in 1978.* North Ryde, Australia: The Ancient History Documentary Research Center, Macquarie University, 1983.

_____. *New Documents Illustrating Early Christianity: A Review of the Greek Inscriptions and Papyri published in 1979.* North Ryde, Australia: The Ancient History Documentary Research Center, Macquarie University, 1987.

Houlden, J.L. *Ethics and the New Testament.* New York: Oxford University Press, 1977.

Hunger, M. Herbert. "Φιλανθρωπία: eine griechische Wortprägung auf ihrem Wege von Aischylos bis Theodoros Metochites." *Anzeiger der österreichischen Akademie der Wissenschaften, philosophisch-historische Klasse,* 1963: 1-21.

Hurley, James B. "Man and Woman in 1 Corinthians: Some Exegetical Studies in Pauline Theology and Ethics." Ph.D. dissertation, Clare College, Cambridge University, 1973.

Jaeger, Werner. *Early Christianity and Greek Paideia.* Cambridge, MA: The Belknap Press of Harvard University Press, 1961.

Jeremias, Joachim. "Die Briefe an Timotheus und Titus." In *Das Neue Testament Deutsch,* Teilband 9, 11. Auflage. Edited by Gerhard Friedrich. Göttingen: Vandenhoeck & Ruprecht, 1975.

Johnson, Luke Timothy. *1 Timothy, 2 Timothy, Titus.* Knox Preaching Guides. Atlanta: John Knox Press, 1987.

_____. *The Literary Function of Possessions in Luke-Acts.* Society of Biblical Literature Dissertation Series, No. 39. Missoula, MT: Scholars Press, 1977.

Jones, A.H.M. *The Later Roman Empire, 284-602: A Social, Economic, and Administrative Survey.* Norman, OK: University of Oklahoma Press, 1964.

Jones, C.P. *The Roman World of Dio Chrysostom.* Cambridge, MA: Harvard University Press, 1978.

_____. "A Deed of Foundation from the Territory of Ephesos." *Journal of Roman Studies* 73 (1983): 116-125.

Judge, E.A. "The Early Christians as a Scholastic Community." *Journal of Religious History* 1 (June 1960): 4-15.

_____. "The Early Christians as a Scholastic Community, Part II." *Journal of Religious History* 1 (June 1961): 125-137.

_____. "Greek Names of Latin Origin." In *New Documents Illustrating Early Christianity: A Review of the Greek Inscriptions and Papyri published in 1977*, pp. 106-108. Edited by G.H.R. Horsley. North Ryde, Australia: Macquarie University, 1982.

_____. "Moral Terms in the Eulogistic Tradition." In *New Documents Illustrating Early Christianity: A Review of the Greek Inscriptions and Papyri published in 1977*, pp. 105-106. Edited by G.H.R. Horsley. N. Ryde, Australia: Macquarie University, 1982.

_____. "πραΰτης." In *New Documents Illustrating Early Christianity: A Review of the Greek Inscriptions and Papyri published in 1979*, pp. 169-170. Edited by G.H.R. Horsley. N. Ryde, Australia: Macquarie University, 1987.

_____. *Rank and Status in the World of the Caesars and St. Paul.* Christchurch, NZ: University of Canterbury, 1982.

_____. "St. Paul and Classical Society." *Jahrbuch für Antike und Christentum* 15 (1972): 19-36.

_____. "The Social Identity of the First Christians: A Question of Method in Religious History." *Journal of Religious History* 11 (December 1980): 201-217.

_____. *The Social Patterns of the Christian Groups in the First Century: Some Prolegomena to the Study of New Testament Ideas of Social Obligation.* London: Tyndale, 1960.

Karris, Robert J. "The Background and Significance of the Polemic of the Pastoral Epistles." *Journal of Biblical Literature* 92 (1973): 549-564.

_____. *The Pastoral Epistles.* Wilmington, DE: Michael Glazier, Inc., 1979.

Käsemann, Ernst. "Amt und Gemeinde im Neuen Testament." *Exegetische Versuche und Besinnungen I.* Göttingen: Vandenhoeck & Ruprecht, 1964, pp. 109-134.

_____. *Jesus Means Freedom.* 3rd ed., 1968. E.T., SCM Press, 1969.

_____. "Ministry and Community in the New Testament." *Essays on New Testament Themes.* Translated by W.J. Montague. SBT 41. London: SCM Press, 1960, pp. 63-94.

_____. *New Testament Questions of Today.* Translated by W.J. Montague and W.F. Bunge. SCM, 1969. Philadelphia: Fortress Press, 1969.

_____. "The Problem of a New Testament Theology." *New Testament Studies* 19 (1973): 235-245.

_____. *Der Ruf der Freiheit.* 5th edition. Tübingen: J.C.B. Mohr (Paul Siebeck), 1972.

Kautsky, Karl. *Foundations of Christianity.* Translated by Henry F. Mins. New York: S.A. Russell, 1953.

Keck, Leander E. "On the Ethos of Early Christians." *Journal of the American Academy of Religion* 42 (1974): 435-452.

Keck, Leander E., and Martyn, J. Louis. *Studies in Luke-Acts.* Philadelphia: Fortress Press, 1966, 1980.

Kee, Howard Clark. *Christian Origins in Sociological Perspective: Methods and Resources.* Philadelphia: The Westminster Press, 1980.

Kelly, J.N.D. *A Commentary on the Pastoral Epistles.* London: A & C Black, Ltd., 1963; reprint ed., Grand Rapids: Baker Book House Co., 1981.

Kennedy, G. *New Testament Interpretation through Rhetorical Criticism.* Chapel Hill, NC: The University of North Carolina Press, 1984.

Kittel, G. "αὐτάρκεια, αὐτάρκης." *Theological Dictionary of the New Testament.* 1:466-467.

Knight, George W. III. *The Faithful Sayings in the Pastoral Letters.* N.V. Kampen, the Netherlands: J.H. Kok, 1968; reprint ed., Grand Rapids: Baker Book House, Co., 1979.

Koch, K. "Pseudonymous Writing." *Interpreter's Dictionary of the Bible.* Supplemental Volume, pp. 712-714.

Koester, Helmut. *Einführung in das Neue Testament im Rahmen der Religionsgeschichte und Kulturgeschichte der hellenistischen und römischen Zeit.* Berlin and New York: Walter de Gruyter, 1980.

_____. *Introduction to the New Testament.* Vol. 1: *History, Culture, and Religion of the Hellenistic Age.* Translated by the author from *Einführung in das Neue Testament,* Chapters 1-6. Philadelphia: Fortress Press, 1982.

_____. *Introduction to the New Testament.* Vol. 2: *History and Literature of Early Christianity.* Translated by the author from *Einführung in das Neue Testament,* Chapters 7-12. Philadelphia: Fortress Press, 1982.

Kopecek, Thomas A. "The Social Class of the Cappadocian Fathers." *Church History* 42 (1973): 453-466.

_____. "The Cappadocian Fathers and Civic Patriotism." *Church History* 43 (1974): 293-303.

_____. "Curial Displacements and Flight in Late Fourth Century Cappadocia." *Historia* 23 (1974): 319-342.

Kraabel, A.T. "The Disappearance of the 'God-Fearers.'" *Numen* 28, 2 (1981): 113-126.

Kreissig, Heinz. "Zur sozialen Zusammensetzung der frühchristlichen Gemeinden im ersten Jahrhundert u.Z." *Eirene* 6 (1967): 91-100.

Kümmel, W.G. *Introduction to the New Testament.* Translated by Howard Clark Kee. New York: Abingdon Press, 1975.

_____. *The New Testament: The History of the Investigation of its Problems.* Translated by S. McLean Gilmour and Howard C. Kee. New York: Abingdon Press, 1972.

Küng, Hans. "'Early Catholicism' in the New Testament as a Problem in Controversial Theology." *The Council in Action: Theological Reflections on the Second Vatican Council,* pp. 159-195. Translated by Cecily Hastings. New York: Sheed & Ward, 1963.

Le Deaut, Roger. "ΦΙΛΑΝΘΡΩΠΙΑ dans la litterature grecque, jusqu'au NT (Tite 3:4)." *Melanges Eugene Tisserant.* Vatican: Biblioteca Apostolica Vaticana, Studi e Testi, 231.1 (1964): 255-294.

Leibeschuetz, J.H.W.G. *Continuity and Change in Roman Religion.* Oxford, at the Clarendon Press, 1979.

Lenger, Marie-Thérèse. "La notion de 'bienfait' (philanthrôpon) royal et les ordonnances des rois Lagides." In *Studi in onore di Vicenzo Arangio-Ruiz, Vol 1,* pp. 483-499. Edited by M. Laurio et al. Naples, 1953.

Liddell, H.G., Scott, R., and Jones, H.S. *A Greek-English Lexicon*. Oxford, at the Clarendon Press, 1968.

Lippert, Peter. *Leben als Zeugnis: Die werbende Kraft christlicher Lebensführung nach dem Kirchenverständnis neutestamentlicher Briefe*. Stuttgart: Verlag Katholisches Bibelwerk, 1968.

Lock, Walter. *A Critical and Exegetical Commentary on the Pastoral Epistles (I & II Timothy and Titus)*. The International Critical Commentary. Edinburgh: T. & T. Clark, 1924, 1978.

Lohse, Eduard. *Colossians and Philemon*. Translated by William R. Poehlmann and Robert J. Karris. Edited by Helmut Koester. Philadelphia: Fortress Press, 1971.

Longenecker, Richard. *New Testament Social Ethics for Today*. Grand Rapids: Eerdmans Publishing Co., 1984.

Louw, J.P. *Semantics of New Testament Greek*. Chico, CA: Scholars Press, 1982.

Luck, U. "σώφρων." *Theological Dictionary of the New Testament*. 7.1097-1104.

_____. "φιλανθρωπία." *Theological Dictionary of the New Testament*. 9.107-112.

Luckmann, Thomas. "Theories of Religion and Social Change." *The Annual Review of the Social Sciences of Religion* 1 (1977): 1-27.

Lutz, Cora E. "Musonius Rufus: 'The Roman Socrates.'" *Yale Classical Studies* 10 (1947): 3-147.

MacDonald, Dennis Ronald. *The Legend and the Apostle: The Battle for Paul in Story and Canon*. Philadelphia: The Westminster Press, 1983.

MacDonald, Margaret Y. *The Pauline Churches: A Socio-historical Study of Institutionalization in the Pauline and Deutero-Pauline Writings*. Cambridge, at the University Press, 1988.

MacMullen, Ramsay. *Christianizing the Roman Empire (A.D. 100-400)*. New Haven: Yale University Press, 1984.

_____. *Enemies of the Roman Order: Treason, Unrest, and Alienation in the Empire*. Cambridge, MA: Harvard University Press, 1966.

_____. *Paganism in the Roman Empire*. New Haven: Yale University Press, 1981.

_____. *Roman Social Relations: 50 B.C. to A.D. 284.* London: Yale University Press, 1974.

Malherbe, Abraham J. *The Cynic Epistles: A Study Edition.* Society of Biblical Literature Sources for Biblical Study, no. 12. Missoula, MT: Scholars Press, 1977.

_____. "Cynics." *Interpreter's Dictionary of the Bible,* Supplementary Volume, pp. 201-203.

_____. "Epictetus." *Interpreter's Dictionary of the Bible,* Supplementary Volume, p. 271.

_____. "'Gentle as a Nurse.' The Cynic Background to 1 Thessalonians 2." *Novum Testamentum* 12 (1970): 203-217.

_____. "In Season and out of Season: 2 Timothy 4:2." *Journal of Biblical Literature* 102-3 (1984): 235-243.

_____. *Moral Exhortation, A Greco-Roman Sourcebook.* Philadelphia: The Westminster Press, 1986.

_____. "'Not in a Corner': Early Christian Apologetic in Acts 26:26." *The Second Century* 5:4 (1985/1986): 193-210.

_____. *Paul and the Thessalonians: The Philosophic Tradition of Pastoral Care.* Philadelphia: Fortress Press, 1987.

_____. *Social Aspects of Early Christianity.* 2nd ed., enlarged. Philadelphia: Fortress Press, 1983.

Malina, Bruce J. *The New Testament World: Insights from Cultural Anthropology.* Atlanta: John Knox Press, 1981.

_____. "The Social Sciences and Biblical Interpretation." *Interpretation* 36 (1982): 229-242.

Mannheim, Karl. *Ideology and Utopia: An Introduction to the Sociology of Knowledge.* Translated by Louis Wirth and Edward Shils. New York: Harcourt, Brace & World, 1936. A Harvest Book, 1936.

Markus, R.A. *Christianity in the Roman World.* London: Thames and Hudson, 1974.

Marshall, Peter. *Enmity in Corinth: Social Conventions in Paul's Relations with the Corinthians.* Tübingen: J.C.B. Mohr (Paul Siebeck), 1987.

Mauss, Marcel. *The Gift: Forms and Functions of Exchange in Archaic Societies.* Translated by Ian Cunnison. New York: W.W. Norton & Co., 1925, 1967.

Mayser, Edwin. *Grammatik der griechischen Papyri aus der Ptolemäerzeit*. Band II.2. Berlin und Leipzig: Walter de Gruyter & Co., 1933.

McKay, A.G. *Houses, Villas and Palaces in the Roman World*. Ithaca: Cornell University Press, 1975.

Mealand, David L. "Philo of Alexandria's Attitude to Riches." *Zeitschrift für neutestamentliche Wissenschaft* 69 (1978): 258-264.

_____. "The Paradox of Philo's Views on Wealth." *Journal for the Study of the New Testament* 24 (1985): 111-115.

Meeks, Wayne A. *The First Urban Christians: The Social World of the Apostle Paul*. New Haven: Yale University Press, 1983.

_____. "The Image of the Androgyne: Some Uses of a Symbol in Earliest Christianity." *History of Religions* 13 (1974): 165-208.

_____. *The Moral World of the First Christians*. Philadelphia: The Westminster Press, 1986.

_____. "'Since Then You Would Need to Go out of the World': Group Boundaries in Pauline Christianity." *Critical History and Biblical Faith*, pp. 4-29. Villanova, PA: College Theological Society, Horizons, 1979.

_____. "The Social Context of Pauline Theology." *Interpretation* 36 (1982): 266-277.

_____. "Understanding Early Christian Ethics." *Journal of Biblical Literature* 105 (1986): 3-11.

_____. *The Writings of St. Paul*. New York: W.W. Norton & Co., 1972.

Merton, Robert K. *Social Theory and Social Structure*. 1968 Enlarged Edition. New York: The MacMillan Co., The Free Press, 1968.

Metz, Johann Baptist, ed. *Christianity and the Bourgeoisie*. New York: The Seabury Press, 1979.

Meusel, Alfred. "Middle Class." *Encyclopaedia of the Social Sciences*. New York: The MacMillan Co., 1930. 10.407-415.

Michaelis, W. *Das Ältestenamt der christlichen Gemeinde im Lichte der Heiligen Schrift*. Bern, 1953.

_____. *Pastoralbriefe und Gefangenschaftsbriefe. Zur Echtheitsfrage der Pastoralbriefe*. NF 1,6. Gütersloh: Bertelsmann, 1930.

Millar, Fergus. Review of *Continuity and Change in Roman Religion*, by J.H.W.G. Liebeschuetz. *English Historical Review* 95 (1980): 840-841.

_____. "Empire and City, Augustus to Julian: Obligations, Excuses and Status." *Journal of Roman Studies* 73 (1983): 76-96.

Moffatt, James. *The Historical New Testament*. Edinburgh: T. & T. Clark, 1901.

Mott, Stephen Charles. *Biblical Ethics and Social Change*. Oxford, at the University Press, 1982.

_____. "The Greek Benefactor and Deliverance from Moral Distress." Ph.D. dissertation, Harvard University, 1971.

_____. "The Power of Giving and Receiving: Reciprocity in Hellenistic Benevolence." In *Current Issues in Biblical and Patristic Interpretation*, pp. 60-72. Edited by G. Hawthorne. Festschrift for M. Tenney. Grand Rapids: Eerdmans, 1975.

Moule, C.F.D. *The Birth of the New Testament*. 3rd ed. New York: Harper and Row, 1982

_____. "The Problem of the Pastoral Epistles: A Reappraisal." *Bulletin of the John Rylands Library* 47 (1965): 430-452.

Moulton, J.H., and Milligan, G. *The Vocabulary of the Greek New Testament Illustrated from the Papyri and Other Non-literary Sources*. Reprint ed., Grand Rapids: Eerdmans, 1930, 1980.

Mussies, G. *Dio Chrysostom and the New Testament*. Leiden: E.J. Brill, 1972.

Nägeli, T. *Der Wortschatz des Apostels Paulus*. Göttingen, 1905.

Nickle, Keith F. *The Collection: A Study in Paul's Strategy*. Studies in Biblical Theology, no. 48. Naperville, IL: Alec R. Allenson, Inc., 1966.

Niebuhr, H. Richard. *Christ and Culture*. New York: Harper and Row, 1951; Colophon Books, 1975.

Nock, A.D. *Conversion: The Old and the New in Religion from Alexander the Great to Augustine of Hippo*. Oxford, at the Clarendon Press, 1933.

_____. "The Cult of Heroes." *Harvard Theological Review* 37 (1944): 141-174.

_____. "Deification and Julian." *Journal of Roman Studies* 47 (1957): 115-123.

_____. *Early Gentile Christianity and its Hellenistic Background*. New York: Harper and Row, 1964. Harper Torchbooks, 1964.

_____. "Notes on Ruler-Cult, I-IV." *Journal of Hellenic Studies* 48 (1928): 21-43.

_____. "Soter and Euergetes." In *The Joy of Study*, F.C. Grant Festschrift. Edited by S. Johnson. New York: Macmillan, 1951, pp. 127-148.

Osiek, Carolyn. *Rich and Poor in the "Shepherd of Hermas": An Exegetical-Social Investigation*. The Catholic Biblical Quarterly Monograph Series, No. 15. Washington, D.C.: The Catholic Biblical Association of America, 1983.

Ossowski, Stanislaw. *Class Structure in the Social Consciousness*. Translated from the Polish by Sheila Patterson. London: Routledge and Kegan Paul, 1963.

Oster, R. "Holy Days in Honour of Artemis." In *New Documents Illustrating Early Christianity: A Review of the Greek Inscriptions and Papyri published in 1979*, pp. 74-82. Edited by G.H.R. Horsley. N. Ryde, Australia: Macquarie University, 1987.

Packer, James E. "Housing and Population in Imperial Ostia and Rome." *Journal of Roman Studies* 57 (1967): 80-95.

Panagopoulos, C. "Vocabulaire et mentalite dans les *Moralia* de Plutarque." *Dialogues d'histoire ancienne* 5 (1977): 197-235.

Parsons, Talcott. *The Structure of Social Action: A Study in Social Theory with Special Reference to a Group of Recent European Writers*. 2 vols. New York: McGraw-Hill, 1937. The Free Press, 1968.

_____. *The Evolution of Societies*. Edited and with an introduction by Jackson Toby. Englewood Cliffs, NJ: Prentice-Hall, Inc., 1977.

Pascal, C. Bennett. Review of *Continuity and Change in Roman Religion*, by J.H.W.G. Liebeschuetz. *Classical Philology* 76 (1981): 249-254.

Penny, Donald N. *The Pseudo-Pauline Letters of the First Two Centuries*. Ann Arbor, MI: University Microfilms International, 1980.

Pesch, R. "'Christliche Bürgerlichkeit' (Tit 2,11-15)." *Am Tisch des Wortes* 14 (1966): 28-33.

Preisigke, Friedrich. *Wörterbuch der griechischen Papyrusurkunden*. Completed and published by Emil Kiessling. Berlin, 1914-1927.

Quinn, Jerome D. "P46—The Pauline Canon?" *Catholic Biblical Quarterly* 36 (1974): 379-385.

_____. "The Last Volume of Luke: The Relation of Luke-Acts to the Pastoral Epistles." In *Perspectives on Luke-Acts.* Edited by C.H. Talbert. Danville, VA: Association of Baptist Professors of Religion, 1978.

Ramsay, W.M. "Historical Commentary on the Epistles to Timothy: XXVII. Relation of the Two Epistles." *Expositer* 8 (1911): 262-273.

Reinhold, Meyer. "Historian of the Classic World: A Critique of Rostovtzeff." *Science and Society* 10 (1946): 361-391.

Ridderbos, Herman. *Paul: An Outline of His Theology.* Translated by John Richard de Witt. Grand Rapids: Eerdmans Publishing Co., 1975.

Robinson, John A.T. *Redating the New Testament.* Philadelphia: The Westminster Press, 1976.

Rohrbaugh, Richard L. "Methodological Considerations in the Debate over the Social Class Status of Early Christians." *Journal of the American Academy of Religion* 52 (1984): 519-546.

Rostovtzeff, M.I. *The Social and Economic History of the Roman Empire.* 2 vols. 2nd edition revised by P.M. Fraser. Oxford, at the Clarendon Press, 1957.

Sainte Croix, G.E.M. de. "Early Christian Attitudes to Property and Slavery." In *Studies in Church History*, Vol. 12, *Church, Society and Politics*, pp. 1-38. Edited by Derek Baker. Oxford: Basil Blackwood, 1975.

_____. *The Class Struggle in the Ancient Greek World from the Archaic Age to the Arab Conquests.* Ithaca, NY: Cornell University Press, 1981.

Saller, Richard P. *Personal Patronage under the Early Empire.* Cambridge, at the University Press, 1982.

Sampley, J. Paul. *Pauline Partnership in Christ: Christian Community and Commitment in Light of Roman Law.* Philadelphia: Fortress Press, 1980.

Sanders, Jack T. *Ethics in the New Testament: Change and Development.* Philadelphia: Fortress Press, 1975.

Schaeffer, Franky, ed. *Is Capitalism Christian? Toward a Christian Perspective on Economics.* Westchester, IL: Crossway Books, A Division of Good News Publishers, 1985.

Schierse, F.J. "Eschatologische Existenz und christliche Bürgerlichkeit." *Geist und Leben* 32 (1959): 280-291.

Schmidt, T. Ewald. "Hostility to Wealth in Philo of Alexandria." *Journal for the Study of the New Testament* 19 (1983): 85-97.

Schmithals, W. *Paul and James*. Studies in Biblical Theology, no. 46. London: SCM Press, LTD., 1965.

Schneider, J. "τιμή." *Theological Dictionary of the New Testament* 8.169-180.

Schoedel, William R. *A Commentary on the Letters of Ignatius of Antioch*. Edited by Helmut Koester. Philadelphia: Fortress Press, 1985.

_____. "Theological Norms and Social Perspectives in Ignatius of Antioch." In *Jewish and Christian Self-Definition: The Shaping of Christianity in the 2nd & 3rd Centuries*. Edited by E.P. Sanders, pp. 30-56. Philadelphia: Fortress Press, 1980.

Schrage, Wolfgang. *The Ethics of the New Testament*. Translated by David E. Green. Philadelphia: Fortress Press, 1988.

_____. "Die Stellung zur Welt bei Paulus, Epiktet und in der Apokalyptik: Ein Beitrag zu 1 Kor 7,29-31." *Zeitschrift für Theologie und Kirche* 61.2 (1964): 125-154.

_____. "Zur Ethik der neutestamentlichen Haustafeln." *New Testament Studies* 21 (1975): 1-22.

Schütz, John H. "Ethos of Early Christianity." *Interpreter's Dictionary of the Bible*, Supplementary Volume, pp. 289-293.

_____. "Steps Toward a Sociology of Primitive Christianity: A Critique of the Work of Gerd Theissen." Paper presented to the "Social World of Early Christianity" Group of AAR/ SBL, San Francisco, December, 1977.

Schwarz, Roland. *Bürgerliches Christentum im Neuen Testament? Eine Studie zu Ethik, Amt und Recht in den Pastoralbriefen*. Oesterreichische Biblische Studien, no. 4. Klosterneuburg: Verlag Oesterreichisches Katholisches Bibelwerk, 1983.

Schweitzer, Albert. *The Quest for the Historical Jesus: A Critical Study of Its Progress from Reimarus to Wrede*. Translated by W. Montgomery. Introduction by James M. Robinson. New York: Macmillan Publishing Co., 1968.

Scott, E.F. *The Pastoral Epistles*. New York: Harper and Brothers Publishers, 1937.

Scroggs, Robin. "The Sociological Interpretation of the New Testament: The Present State of Research." *New Testament Studies* 26 (1980): 164-179.

Selwyn, Edward Gordon. *The First Epistle of St. Peter: The Greek Text with Introduction, Notes, and Essays.* 2nd ed. London: Macmillan and Co., 1947; reprint ed., Grand Rapids: Baker Book House, 1981

Sherwin-White, A.N. *Roman Society and Roman Law in the New Testament.* Oxford, at the Clarendon Press, 1963; reprint ed., Grand Rapids: Baker Book House, 1978.

Smith, Jonathan Z. "The Social Description of Early Christianity," *Religious Studies Review* 1 (1975): 19-25.

Spicq, Ceslas. *Les Epitres Pastorales.* 2 vols. 4th revised edition. Paris: J. Gabalda, 1969.

Stählin, G. "χήρα." *Theological Dictionary of the New Testament.* 9.440-465.

Stendahl, Krister. *The Bible and the Role of Women.* Translated by Emilie T. Sander. Philadelphia: Fortress Press, 1966.

Stowers, Stanley Kent. "Social Status, Public Speaking and Private Teaching: The Circumstances of Paul's Preaching Activity." *Novum Testamentum* 26 (1984): 59-82.

Tarn, W.W. *Hellenistic Civilization.* Third edition revised by the author and G.T. Griffith, 1957; reprint ed., New York: New American Library, 1974.

Theissen, Gerd. *The Social Setting of Pauline Christianity: Essays on Corinth.* Translated by John H. Schütz. Philadelphia: Fortress Press, 1982.

_____. *Sociology of Early Palestinian Christianity.* Translated by John Bowden. Philadelphia: Fortress Press, 1978.

Thurén, Jukka. "Die Struktur der Schlußparänese 1. Tim. 6,3-21." *Theologische Zeitschrift* 26 (1970): 241-253.

Tocqueville, Alexis de. *Democracy in America.* 2 vols. Edited by Phillips Bradley. New York: Vintage Books, 1945.

Troeltsch, Ernst. *The Social Teachings of the Christian Churches.* 2 vols. Translated by Olive Wyon. New York: Harper and Row Publishers, 1960.

Turner, Jonathan H. *The Structure of Sociological Theory.* 3rd edition. Homewood, IL: The Dorsey Press, 1982.

Turner, Victor. *The Ritual Process: Structure and Anti-Structure.* Ithaca, NY: Cornell University Press; Cornell Paperbacks Edition, 1969, 1977.

Van Unnik, W.C. "Corpus Hellenisticum Novi Testamenti." *Journal of Biblical Literature* 83 (1964): 17-33.

Verhey, Allen. *The Great Reversal: Ethics and the New Testament.* Grand Rapids: Eerdmans Publishing Co., 1984.

Verner, David C. *The Household of God: The Social World of the Pastoral Epistles.* Chico, CA: Scholars Press, 1983.

Weaver, P.R.C. "Social Mobility in the Early Roman Empire: The Evidence of the Imperial Freedmen and Slaves." In *Studies in Ancient Society*, pp. 121-140. Edited by Moses I. Finley. Routledge and Kegan Paul, 1974.

Weber, Marianne. *Max Weber: A Biography.* Translated and edited by Harry Zohn. New York: John Wiley & Sons, 1975.

Weber, Max. *The Agrarian Sociology of Ancient Civilizations.* Translated by R.I. Frank. London: NLB, 1976.

_____. *Economy and Society: An Outline of Interpretive Sociology*, 2 vols. Edited by Guenther Roth and Claus Wittich. Berkeley: University of California Press, 1978.

_____. *From Max Weber: Essays in Sociology.* Translated and edited by H.H. Gerth and C. Wright Mills. Oxford, at the University Press, 1946.

_____. *The Methodology of the Social Sciences.* Translated and edited by Edward A. Shils and Henry A. Finch. New York: Macmillan Publishing Co., 1949.

_____. *The Protestant Ethic and the Spirit of Capitalism.* Translated by Talcott Parsons. New York: Charles Scribner's Sons, 1958.

Weidinger, K. *Die Haustafeln: Ein Stück urchristlicher Paränese.* Überlieferung in der Neueren Theologie 14. Leipzig, 1928.

Weiss, Bernhard. *Die Briefe Pauli an Timotheus und Titus.* Meyer Kommentar, 11. Abteilung. 7th edition, corrected. Göttingen: Vandenhoeck und Ruprecht, 1902.

Weiss, Johannes. *Earliest Christianity: A History of the Period A.D. 30-150.* Translated and edited by Frederick C. Grant. New York: Harper & Row, 1959; reprint ed., Gloucester, MA: Peter Smith, 1970.

Welles, C. Bradford. *Royal Correspondence in the Hellenistic Period: A Study in Greek Epigraphy.* London: Yale University Press, 1934; reprint ed., Chicago: Ares Publishers Inc., 1974.

White, R.E.O. *Biblical Ethics.* Atlanta: John Knox Press, 1979.

Wiedemann, Thomas. *Greek and Roman Slavery*. Baltimore: The Johns Hopkins University Press, 1981.

Wikgren, Allen, Colwell, E.C., and Marcus, Ralph. *Hellenistic Greek Texts*. Chicago and London: The University of Chicago Press, 1947.

Wilken, Robert L. "The Christians as the Romans (and Greeks) Saw Them." In *Jewish and Christian Self-Definition: The Shaping of Christianity in the 2nd & 3rd Centuries*, ed. E.P. Sanders, pp. 100-125. Philadelphia: Fortress Press, 1980.

_____. *The Christians as the Romans Saw Them*. New Haven: Yale University Press, 1984.

_____. "Collegia, Philosophical Schools, and Theology." In *Early Church History: The Roman Empire as the Setting of Primitive Christianity*, pp. 268-291. Edited by Stephen Benko and John J. O'Rourke. London: Oliphants, 1971.

_____. "Toward a Social Interpretation of Early Christian Apologists." *Church History* 39 (1970): 437-458.

Wilson, John. *Social Theory*. Englewood Cliffs, NJ: Prentice-Hall, Inc., 1983.

Wilson, Stephen G. *Luke and the Pastoral Epistles*. London: SPCK, 1979.

Woodhead, A.G. *The Study of Greek Inscriptions*. Cambridge, at the University Press, 1967.

Wuellner, Wilhelm H. "The Sociological Implications of 1 Corinthians 1:26-28 Reconsidered." *Studia Evangelica*, 4, vol. 112 of *Texte und Untersuchungen*. Berlin, 1973, pp. 666-672.

_____. "Ursprung und Verwendung der σοφος-, δυνατος-, εύγενης- Formel in 1 Kor. 1, 26." In *Donum Gentilicium: New Testament Studies in Honour of David Daube*, pp. 165-184. Edited by E. Bammel et al. Oxford, at the Clarendon Press, 1978.

Yoder, John Howard. *The Politics of Jesus*. Grand Rapids: Eerdmans Publishing Co., 1972.

Zerwick, Max, and Grosvenor, Mary. *A Grammatical Analysis of the Greek New Testament*. Rome: Biblical Institute Press, 1979.

DATE DUE

JUL 01 1996			